286257 &UCB D1758804

The

REALLY USEFUL PRIMARY DESIGN AND TECHNOLOGY BOOK

The Really Useful Primary Design and Technology Book brings together essential subject knowledge and pedagogy to support and inspire those planning to teach D&T in the primary school. Offering comprehensive coverage of the 2014 National Curriculum, as well as exciting ideas to extend beyond it, the book is packed full of everything the busy teacher needs to be able to develop children's key skills and techniques, and a range of big and small projects to put them into practice.

With crucial subject knowledge explained in detail, useful 'How To' guides at the end of each chapter reinforce the skills and technology covered with instructions for making a variety of models. Sets of lesson plans include information on the resources needed to support both more and less able children, and assessment guidance, 'Top Tips' and 'Things to Consider' provide extra help and inspiration.

Key topics covered include:

- cooking and nutrition
- textiles and the Design Cycle
- IT control and monitoring
- mechanisms
- structures
- electronic systems
- the roles and responsibilities of the D&T leader
- assessment of D&T.

The Really Useful Primary Design and Technology Book provides all the information a new teacher needs to be able to teach D&T confidently, and with valuable cross-curricular links and photocopiable templates, even experienced teachers and subject leaders will find fresh inspiration for their lessons.

Elizabeth Flinn is Lecturer in Primary Science and D&T at Middlesex University, UK.

Sarah Patel is Senior Lecturer in Primary Computing and D&T at Middlesex University, UK.

The Really Useful Series

The

REALLY USEFUL PRIMARY DESIGN AND TECHNOLOGY BOOK

Subject knowledge and lesson ideas

Elizabeth Flinn

and

Sarah Patel

Routledge
Taylor & Francis Group

LONDON AND NEW YORK

First published 2016
by Routledge
2 Park Square, Milton Park, Abingdon, Oxon OX14 4RN

and by Routledge
711 Third Avenue, New York, NY 10017

Routledge is an imprint of the Taylor & Francis Group, an informa business

© 2016 E. Flinn and S. Patel

The right of E. Flinn and S. Patel to be identified as authors of this work has been asserted by them in accordance with sections 77 and 78 of the Copyright, Designs and Patents Act 1988.

All rights reserved. The purchase of this copyright material confers the right on the purchasing institution to photocopy pages which bear the photocopy icon and copyright line at the bottom of the page. No other parts of this book may be reprinted or reproduced or utilised in any form or by any electronic, mechanical, or other means, now known or hereafter invented, including photocopying and recording, or in any information storage or retrieval system, without permission in writing from the publishers.

Trademark notice: Product or corporate names may be trademarks or registered trademarks, and are used only for identification and explanation without intent to infringe.

British Library Cataloguing in Publication Data
A catalogue record for this book is available from the British Library

Library of Congress Cataloging in Publication Data
A catalog record for this book has been requested

ISBN: 978-1-138-92781-0 (hbk)
ISBN: 978-1-138-92783-4 (pbk)
ISBN: 978-1-315-68223-5 (ebk)

Typeset in Palatino and Gill Sans
by Florence Production Ltd, Stoodleigh, Devon, UK

MIX
Paper from
responsible sources
FSC® C013604

Printed and bound by CPI Group (UK) Ltd, Croydon, CR0 4YY

Contents

UCB
286257

Acknowledgements

The authors are very grateful to the children and teachers who enthusiastically tested all the projects in this book.

We thank:

> the head teacher and children of Y1 and Y2 at Merchant Taylors' Prep;
>
> the head teacher and children of Y3 and Y6 at Durdan's Park Primary School;
>
> the head teacher and children of Y1 at Tudor Church of England Primary School; and
>
> the leaders and children of the 6th Northwood Beavers.

A particular mention for: Cleo, William, Joe, Sophia, Noah, Emily W., Matthew, Rosie, Charlie, Max, Ben, Jack, Emily S., Ziyad, Lexie, Maddy and Julia who generously did D&T for us *in the holidays*!

Illustrations by Hannah Thompson.

1 Introduction

This book is for all primary school teachers and trainee teachers who want to add new skills and ideas to their teaching repertoire. The ideas that we propose for lessons aim to be engaging, fun and practical to carry out in a primary school setting.

An overview of the Design and Technology (D&T) National Curriculum (2014) is provided along with suggestions for how it could be covered across the primary school years. It contains a chapter on each of the following D&T units: the Design Cycle, cooking and nutrition, structures, textiles, mechanisms, electronics, IT control and monitoring. Within these chapters there is a focus on the subject knowledge you will need in order to teach the unit as well as essential technical skills. A range of possible lesson ideas are provided, which are accompanied by two tried and tested half term unit plans, that follow the structure of the Design Cycle. Step by step guides of how to make various products as well as 'Top Tips' for delivering successful D&T lessons are also offered. Additional chapters include how to assess D&T, the Design Cycle and how each stage can be taught as well as a chapter providing all the information you need to be an effective D&T subject leader.

WHAT IS D&T?

D&T is the study of the production of man-made objects/systems/environments for the purpose of solving particular human needs.

D&T education involves three important elements:

1) investigating and evaluating existing products;
2) learning how things work;
3) learning to design and make functional products for particular purposes and users.

D&T lessons should provide opportunities for children to acquire and apply knowledge and understanding of materials and components, mechanisms and control systems, structures, computer control, existing products, quality and health and safety. They must also enable children to develop the skills to test, refine and develop the products they design, along with ensuring that sufficient time is given to allow children to check that their products work and improve them if they don't.

D&T is a fast moving subject, as society's needs are always changing. A correct solution today may well not be valid tomorrow. Consequently children should be encouraged to be creative and innovative in their designs as well as considering important issues such as sustainability and enterprise.

Which activities genuinely are D&T and which are not?

Modelling, drawing or using certain types of 2D or 3D materials does not instinctively make an activity a D&T activity. For example drawing a landscape would be art and design; however, using that landscape for a handmade birthday card would be design and technology. In order for the task to be deemed D&T, it must involve designing and making a product for somebody or for a particular purpose. The design must also use acceptable scientific principles, materials, technology and human resources and must be suitable for use by more than one person or be used in quantities.

D&T involves thinking about what the needs of the users are as well as the purpose and functionality of the product. In order for children to make products that move/light up/are structurally sound/taste good/are safe and healthy, they need to learn practical skills through carefully planned D&T lessons.

NATIONAL CURRICULUM (2014)

All maintained primary schools in England are required to follow the National Curriculum, which includes D&T as a compulsory subject at KS1 and KS2. The D&T programmes of study have four broad aims: *design, make, evaluate and technical knowledge* and the subject content has two main strands: *designing and making* and *cooking and nutrition*. The Design and Technology Association (DATA) recommends linking these strands wherever possible. It also provides a clear picture of the essential features of the subject, including an emphasis on:

- the user, purpose, functionality and innovation when children are designing and making;
- designing and making mock-ups at KS1 and prototypes at KS2;
- using creativity and imagination to design and make products that solve real and relevant problems;
- designing and making products using a range of materials including textiles, construction materials and food;
- creating mechanical products at KS1 and KS2 and electrical products at KS2;
- investigating and evaluating existing products and children's own ideas and products.

Key changes to the National Curriculum

Although there have been changes to the D&T National Curriculum, schools needn't panic! Rather than throwing out existing planning, this can be adapted and developed over time. As well as developing planning, teaching the new curriculum will require continuous professional development (CPD) to develop subject expertise along with new resources in areas such as cooking and nutrition, and control and monitoring.

Main changes
- using an 'iterative' process of designing and making;
- KS1 to use a design criteria and KS2 to encourage innovative design;
- using cross-sectional and exploded diagrams in KS2;
- understanding key events and individuals in D&T at KS2;
- working in a range of relevant contexts, for example: home, school, leisure, culture, enterprise, industry and the wider environment;
- understanding and applying principles of a healthy and varied diet;
- understanding where food comes from in KS1 and seasonality in KS2.

Increased technical demands at KS2, include:
- applying computing to program, monitor and control products;
- using CAD to develop and communicate ideas;
- understanding and using the concept of a 'system' when designing and making with mechanical and electrical components.

The following activities have been removed from the National Curriculum by the Department for Education (2013) but they are recommended by the Design and Technology Association (DATA) and therefore should still be considered when planning:

- IDEAs: investigating, disassembly and evaluation activities (how familiar products work and what they are supposed to do);
- FPTs: focused practical tasks (developing a range of techniques, skills, and knowledge);
- children to plan the sequence in which they make their products;
- DMAs: design and make assignments using a range of materials including:
  - KS1: food textiles and items that can be put together;
  - KS2: electrical and mechanical components, food, textiles, and stiff and flexible sheet material.

WHY TEACH D&T?

We live in a society that is dominated by ideas and products from technology, therefore our societies need people with technological qualifications at the highest level in order to enhance the UK's capacity for growth. But it's not just the job market that is the driving force behind why we teach D&T. There are many other convincing reasons:

- D&T is a multidimensional, dynamic subject that not only teaches children an assortment of skills that they can develop into exciting careers, but also allows them to put their learning from other areas of the curriculum into practice;
- D&T is often one of a child's favourite subjects; Ofsted found that primary school children enjoyed developing practical skills and made swift progress to develop knowledge and understanding about the properties of materials when they had specific problems or challenges to solve that fired their enthusiasm;
- Children are given the opportunity to solve real and relevant problems in D&T lessons, which means that they develop essential everyday skills, unlocking their ability to be the designers and innovators of tomorrow;
- D&T lessons provide opportunities for children who struggle in other subjects (where the focus is perhaps on reading and writing) to excel in practical, iterative hands-on tasks.

KEY D&T SKILLS

D&T is a subject that encourages creative ideas and allows for many cross-curricular links. It focuses on transferable skills such as:

- analytical skills – clarifying a task, analysing existing products;
- designing skills – generating and developing ideas, creating design proposals, communicating ideas, planning ideas;
- practical skills – making things, including working with materials and components, tools and processes; planning, measuring and marking out; cutting and shaping; joining and combining; finishing;
- evaluating skills – evaluating existing products as well as children's own ideas and products;
- problem-solving – finding solutions to problems such as products not working or not meeting the users' requirements.

There are also strong links to subjects such as:

- Science – predicting and fair testing, using and applying their knowledge about the properties of materials;
- Maths – measuring to an appropriate number of decimal places, drawing and interpreting tables, graphs and bar charts;
- IT – making things happen by the use of control, handling information through the use of a database or spreadsheet, use of CAD;
- Art and Design – investigating texture and colour or recording visual information.

REFERENCES

Department for Education, (2013). *National Curriculum Primary Handbook.* [online] UK Government. Available at: www.gov.uk/government/collections/national-curriculum [Accessed 3 January 2016].

2 The Design Cycle

D&T is about more than just making models. Children should be given opportunities to design products for a specific purpose. They should understand that great inventions may have gone through many changes before they were really fit for purpose. Children should learn to consider how well their own products meet the design brief and what refinements may help to improve them. During D&T lessons children should also be learning new practical skills. They should become familiar with tools and how to use them safely and they should learn about materials and their properties.

Children should experience a whole design process from first ideas to evaluation of a finished product. This process is often depicted as a cycle rather than a linear route, in order to emphasise the importance of continually evaluating and refining the product design. This is known as the Design Cycle.

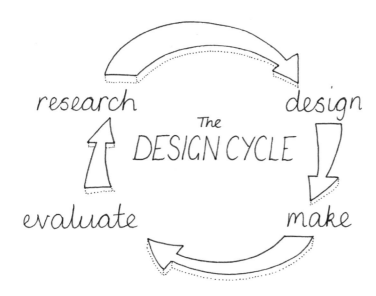

Figure 2.1

The lesson plans in this book follow the Design Cycle. It is important that during each school year, the children experience every part of the design process from research to evaluation, but at some points it may be appropriate to focus on practical skills (sawing, sewing, mechanisms) rather than on designing and making a particular product.

RESEARCH

Research can take several forms. For young children, taking apart mechanisms from toys can help to give them an understanding about the means by which the toys can be made to move. A collection of moving toys (bath toys are particularly useful) and common mechanical items which the children can unscrew and take to pieces will be a popular addition to any classroom. It is important to avoid injury, so children should be supervised and it is wise to avoid electrical items which may remain charged even after they are unplugged or the battery removed. The knowledge children gain from this type of research can help them when they come to design their own products, because they should have some idea about the shapes and arrangement of components.

Research also covers use of the Internet and reference books to gather information. As children may not be designing an innovative product, they can use research to give them ideas about style, decoration and size. This research will also teach the children about the inflated costs of products. It is educational to see that while, for example, leading pet shops sell expensive plastic dens for rabbits and guinea pigs, pets are just as happy in something made from an old cardboard box that has cost nothing and can be made bespoke to suit the needs of a particular animal.

As the children reach upper KS2 they should be starting to consider the needs of the consumer. They should talk to potential users, discuss their particular requirements and then use this information to inform their design. This market research can help the children to focus their designs on the actual needs, rather than the assumed needs, of the user. To help the children to formulate appropriate questions, teachers can set the scene when introducing the project, so that children understand the reasons for the design project. This could involve the teacher choosing an appropriate scenario and perhaps preparing some background information in advance (e.g. making a tool to be used by astronauts) or using a real-life situation where the potential users can be interviewed (e.g. planning a meal for the class picnic taking allergies and food preferences into account).

Having surveyed the available products and thought about the needs of the user, and perhaps already drawn out a preliminary design, children should make some decisions about the materials they will use in the construction of the product or the ingredients they will use to make a particular dish. Research here could cover the properties and manufacture of various materials and perhaps their cost. The seasonality and locality of ingredients can be researched too, as well as various recipe ideas.

In all situations, the children should be expected to build a research portfolio of ideas and information. The portfolio might include:

- photos or diagrams of mechanisms
- information about products available already
- pictures or samples of products or raw materials
- records of interviews
- results of surveys
- preliminary design ideas based on research

This portfolio may well be added to or annotated as children discover that they need further information or ideas. This is an example of the iterative nature of the design process because moving from the research stage to the design stage does not prevent the designer from returning to do more research if the need arises.

In many cases, research can be linked to the other curriculum areas. For example, the properties of common materials are covered in the science curriculum; geographical skills can be used to consider food miles when investigating ingredients; following the development of a particular product over time fits neatly into the history syllabus.

DESIGN

Design is perhaps the hardest process within D&T. While children may have many ideas, they do not always find it easy to convert these ideas into workable designs. Encourage the children to come up with several different designs including a very simple one. If they meet insurmountable problems with their chosen (and usually ambitious) design, then they will have a fall-back position available.

A design is more than just a drawing and should include information about:

- the materials chosen
- the processes to be used
- the equipment required
- how the product will be finished

There should be detailed drawings of structures and/or mechanisms within the product. These may be shown best as cross-sectional drawings (Figure 2.2) or as an exploded view picture (Figure 2.3).

Drawing 3D representations of structures can be made easier with the use of isometric paper (Figure 2.4) which allows the children to accurately draw the angles required for a 3D solid shape, such as a cube.

If the structures are to be made from a folded net, then a diagram to show the net should be included. A supply of nets for different shapes is an invaluable resource as many children, and some adults, find it hard to visualise the net for a particular shape.

Children should be encouraged to produce a story board, in words or pictures, with details of the practical steps towards the finished product (Figure 2.5). As children become more experienced, they will gain a good understanding of the best order in which to do things. Thus, while a KS1 child might assume that decorating the product is the final step in the process, by the end of KS2, children should have realised that it is sometimes easier to add decoration *before* the product is assembled.

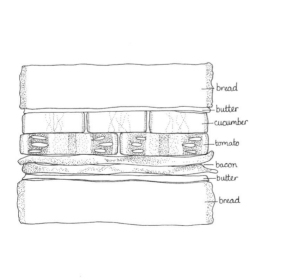

Figure 2.2 A cross-sectional drawing

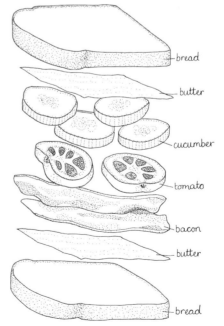

Figure 2.3 An exploded view drawing

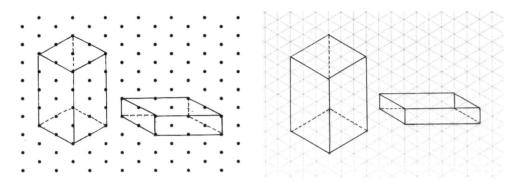

Figure 2.4

Figure 2.5 A story board showing the steps in producing a sandwich

The National Curriculum states that the design process should be iterative. In simple terms, this means a continuous cycle of thinking and doing. Thus, an original idea may look good until the child comes to consider the materials to be used. The properties of the materials chosen may not lend themselves to the structure of the product, leading to a re-think about shapes. Once the shape has been modified to suit the materials, there may be problems with the mechanism, which perhaps no longer fits inside the structure. The children will have to consider alternative arrangements and so on. As the product is manufactured, the children may see ways to improve on an already successful design. The end product should have gone through many stages of thought and action before it is finished. The iterative process can be seen at work when a child plays with a construction kit. They often make a vehicle which, after a bit of thought and play, they will alter. They might change the shape of the vehicle, add a place for a passenger to sit, add weapons or rocket launchers, find a propeller that they would like to incorporate and so on. In this way, the original car eventually becomes something more exciting. As young children will continually re-make a model in this way, encourage them to draw or photograph the model at each stage. This way, they will have a record of the changes they made.

An iterative process of design does not lend itself to neatness, as things will be crossed out, annotated or added to continually. A good design, therefore, may be rather confused. While this is to be expected and encouraged, it will sometimes be helpful for a neat copy of the finished design to be produced for construction purposes.

In most D&T lessons, children will probably be working in groups. Group work in D&T, as in all subjects helps children to learn the skills of discussion and compromise. They should also realise that, as everyone one has different skills, working as a team means that a higher quality product can be produced. During the design process the children should learn to listen to and consider the other team members' ideas and start to combine the good parts of each idea to produce a whole plan. This process may need to be modelled by the teacher several times before the children use it successfully.

MAKE

The majority of the chapters in this book are concerned with the making part of the Design Cycle. Each chapter contains subject knowledge to help teachers and children to understand the theory behind the various processes. The chapters also include various ideas for making small models, toys and gadgets. These projects offer a way for the children to learn skills which they can then use in their own designs. For example, it is no use asking children to design a moving machine before they have learned what the various mechanisms can do. By making a small cam card or a moving picture using levers and linkages, they start to understand the mechanisms and see how they produce movement. This knowledge then can be transferred to their own designs later on. These focused practical tasks (FPTs) formed part of the QCA scheme of work for the pre-2014 D&T curriculum. Although they are not included in the 2014 curriculum, there is no harm in continuing to use FPTs in D&T lessons. In addition, some D&T lessons may be entirely concerned with learning and practising various techniques such as sewing or sawing. Once again, children cannot be expected to make a decent product using fabric or wood if they do not know how to cut and join it. In these cases, it is also possible for the practice to lead to the production of a small article or toy, but not necessarily one that the children have previously designed.

Another step to the understanding of the techniques involved in the making process is to make a mock-up or prototype. A mock-up is a model of the product which can be made from any material but which doesn't function. Commercial mock-ups are often decorated to show how the final product will look but not how it will work. Mock-ups are used at KS1 when the children might build a model of their product with a construction kit to show the shape and size of their design. The prototype is introduced at KS2 and is a properly working model, although it may not be full size. A prototype is used to test the functionality of the product with the expectation that problems will be found which can be fixed before the final product is manufactured. For example, during a textiles session, KS2 children can use newspaper to make a prototype of their garment design to check that it fits the user and that the pattern pieces fit together effectively. The prototype can then be disassembled and the pieces used to adjust the pattern if necessary.

As with all practical activities, children will work at different speeds and with different levels of success. It is important for the children to realise that he who finishes first has not necessarily made the best possible product, but also that taking days to carefully cut one component may result in the rest of the process being rushed and unsatisfactory. Spending one D&T session on FPTs can help the teacher to identify those children who are confident and able to cope with the task and those who may need extra assistance. When it comes to making the designed product, resources and assistance can be deployed accordingly. Children who finish quickly generally find that, on testing, their product doesn't work as effectively as they'd hoped, so they are then able to use the extra time to refine and fix any problems. Children who are struggling with the early stages of manufacture may need to be encouraged to simplify their designs in order to produce a finished article within the allotted time. While it may be disappointing to have to do this, it is more disheartening to fail to make anything at all during the sessions.

The nature of D&T work can mean that the classroom is noisy and dusty. It is helpful to have the room zoned so that all the noisy or messy processes (sawing, gluing, blending) are kept in one area. Some tables need to be available for delicate work and there should also be space for the children to be able to lay out their designs and the various components they will be using. A named tray or box for each group can help to provide some organisation in the chaos. For cookery activities, the tables and work surfaces must be clean. There should be nothing on them but the ingredients and equipment which are required for the task. This is obvious for a food-handling situation, but there is no harm in introducing it as the way all D&T projects should be carried out. During practical sessions children may work best standing up; it allows more room for the children to work and makes access round tables easier for teachers.

Resources for D&T are expensive so it important to consider how to make the most of the resources and not waste them unnecessarily. Here are a few tried and tested suggestions:

- Put small components into labelled containers to prevent spillage and loss.
- Provide each table or group with a kit of useful items such as pens, pencils, scrap paper, scissors and glue sticks to reduce the need to be looking for them during the lesson.
- Where possible, cut A3 size card and paper down to A5 size. Felt and other fabrics can also be cut to a suitable size before the lesson. This can help to avoid the irritation of a child taking a huge piece of card or fabric and cutting out a tiny circle *from the middle*!
- Give expensive consumables directly to the pupils; make sure they put their names on them immediately. Use a permanent marker to write on motors and plastics.
- Keep back a supply of the essential but common components so that when something is unaccountably lost, you can replace it quickly.
- Having resources set out for each table can be a great time saver in a lesson; however, if the children are going to struggle not to fiddle it may be best to hand them out when they are required.

EVALUATE

When evaluating their product, children should not only be considering whether the product does what it was designed to do and whether it is aesthetically pleasing, but also be recording the changes they made to the design during manufacture and the reasons for these changes. By doing this, the children begin to gain an understanding of design as an iterative process, rather than a process which follows strict and non-flexible conditions. This can be demonstrated by considering the development of mobile phones when, as soon as a new version is released, another, better one is already being designed. The rapid advances in microprocessor technology, programming and materials mean that each phone, while still allowing the user to make a call, should be better than the previous models. Software designers often take note of feedback from users to design updates for their products. Giving the children some criteria to measure their product against can lead to more effective evaluation than simply asking them to decide what went well and what could be improved.

At KS1, evaluation can be kept simple. The children can consider how well they have met the design brief by discussing what they set out to do and thinking about how pleased they are with the end result. It is important to consider whether they had to make changes to their original ideas and what they might do differently next time. Recording the children's initial discussions on a flip chart or digital equivalent can help to remind the children of what they discussed several weeks earlier. For KS1 the 'Two Stars and a Wish' evaluation process can be sufficient. The children decide on two things they like about their product or design and one thing they would change or do better if they were to do it again. Seeing the other finished products can help with the Wish part of the process, as the children may be impressed by someone else's design ideas. The children can compare their original drawings and ideas with the finished product and try to highlight places where they have deviated from the original design. They should be encouraged to explain why they did so.

At KS2, evaluation should become a more rigorous process. If a product has been designed for a specific purpose, the children must decide whether it has met the design criteria. This might be done by asking someone else to use/try their product. The feedback from these trials can be used as part of the evaluation. So, if all goes well and the machine works as expected in a novice's hands, or if the food is eaten with enjoyment, then the children can consider that their design has met some of the criteria. The next step is to confirm that the product is doing what it should. This might involve a trial run or some analysis of the product. For example, a fruit salad may taste delicious but not offer a properly seasonal selection of fruit. The children should refer back to the design brief and check that all parts of the brief have been met. It might help to break the design brief down into various different questions. So, a brief to *Design a moving toy which can be operated by a small child using his/her foot* can be broken down into four questions:

- Does it move?
- Can it be operated with a foot?
- Could a small child operate it?
- Is this something a small child would enjoy using?

Additional questions can then be asked for each step. For the example above, the children could consider the strength of construction, the ease of use, the attractiveness of the product and the novelty of the toy (was it an original idea or was it copied from a moving toy they had seen before?)

These questions can be answered with a simple yes/no response or, as the children become more experienced in their evaluations, they could design a sliding scale of success from one (poor) to five (excellent). Anything not reaching the top level can be considered as having potential for improvement or redesign.

Asking children to design their own evaluation tool will help them to consider the design brief in detail. They could design the evaluation tool at the start of the design process to help them to focus on the important points, or they could wait until the product has been made and design an evaluation tool which takes into account some of the problems they encountered. These tools can be used by the children to inform their designs and plans for their next D&T project too. So, if they consider that their product worked well but was messily constructed, then they have a target ready-made for the next project, whether it is food or textiles or an electrical system.

3 Cooking and nutrition

Cooking and nutrition involves learning how to prepare food using the principles of nutrition and healthy eating. Practical food preparation, cooking skills and aesthetics of food are key aspects of children's work when designing and making food products.

WHY COOK IN SCHOOLS?

OK, so the 2014 National Curriculum (Department for Education, 2013) states that we should, but there are several other convincing reasons:

- City University conducted a study in Liverpool which found that cooking classes had a positive impact on both children and adults and increased the amount of fruit and vegetables eaten.
- The School Food Trust found that more than half (58 per cent) of those involved in the 'Let's Get Cooking' programme eat a healthier diet as a result of learning to cook and almost all people (92 per cent) use their new skills at home.
- Evidence shows that participating in the Food for Life Partnership increases fruit and vegetable consumption by children at school and at home (National Foundation for Educational Research, 2007).
- The British Nutrition Foundation (BNF) carried out a survey involving 27,500 five to sixteen-year-olds which highlighted huge gaps in children's understanding about where food comes from. The findings revealed that almost a third of UK primary children think that cheese is made from plants and a quarter think that fish fingers come from chicken or pigs.

Food education can make a real difference to the quality of people's lives. As teachers, we have a responsibility to ensure that we equip children with the knowledge and skills that they need to make informed decisions about food choices.

Food presents people with daily decisions to make and problems to solve, so learning about food should be as practical as possible. D&T lessons should aim to prepare children to be informed citizens who can consider health and life skills in relation to food.

Instilling a love of cooking in children will also open a door to one of the great expressions of human creativity. Learning how to cook is a crucial life skill that enables children to feed themselves well and affordably (Department for Education, 2013).

INNOVATORS AND KEY EVENTS

Children in KS2 should to be taught about how key events and individuals in D&T have helped shape the world (Department for Education, 2013).

Some key events

The Royal Society, the UK's national academy of science (2012), claims that the most important invention in the history of food is the refrigerator, with pasteurisation and the canning of food following closely behind.

The refrigerator

Preserving food has not always been easy; centuries ago people had to gather ice from streams and ponds and store it in icehouses and cellars. Even with ice, people were often limited to eating locally grown foods that had to be purchased fresh and used daily. The 19th century saw the introduction of the icebox – a wooden box lined with tin or zinc, filled with sawdust, seaweed and other materials to keep the ice from melting. Drip pans caught the water that melted and had to be emptied daily. Fred W. Wolf of Fort Wayne invented the early fridge, which consisted of a small unit mounted on top of one of these iceboxes and required external plumbing. In 1925, homeowners could purchase the stand-alone refrigerator. This changed the way we eat, allowing food to be kept fresher for longer and allowing diets and recipes to be broadened.

Pasteurisation

In 1864, the French scientist Louis Pasteur invented the pasteurisation process. Pasteur discovered that heating beer and wine was enough to kill most of the bacteria that caused spoilage, preventing these beverages from going off. This was accomplished by eradicating pathogenic microbes (microbes which can cause disease) and lowering microbial numbers to prolong the quality of the beverage. The process of pasteurisation is still used widely today in the dairy and food industries for microbial control and preservation of the food consumed.

Figure 3.1
Louis Pasteur

Canning

Decades before the discovery of pasteurisation, the French inventor Nicolas Appert invented the process of canning in 1809. This method of preserving food involves storing food in airtight containers that are then sterilised by heat. Canning provides a shelf life typically ranging from one to five years, although under specific circumstances it can be much longer. For example, a freeze-dried canned product, such as canned dried lentils, could remain edible for as long as 30 years.

Key individuals

Frank Epperson – the ice lolly

Ice lollies (also known as ice pops and popsicles) are made by freezing flavoured liquid (such as fruit juice) in a container around a stick. Once the liquid freezes solid the stick can be used as a handle to hold the ice pop. They were first created by Frank Epperson in 1905 at the age of 11 when he accidentally left a glass of powdered soda and water with a mixing stick in it on his porch during a cold night. The concept of 'frozen ice on a stick' was patented in 1923.

George Crum – the crisp

In 1853, an American chef called George Crum invented the crisp. It is said that one customer complained that Crum's french fries were too thick. Crum decided to take his revenge by producing fries too thin and crisp to skewer with a fork. However, his plan backfired, the customer loved the browned, paper-thin potatoes, and other diners began requesting Crum's potato chips.

Doctor John Pemberton – Coca Cola

Coca Cola was invented in 1886 by Doctor John Pemberton, an American pharmacist. His creation began with a flavoured syrup that was mixed with carbonated water. It was deemed 'excellent' by those who sampled it and quickly become the popular drink it still is today.

SUBJECT KNOWLEDGE

Children in KS1 should be taught to understand the basic principles of a healthy and varied diet, and children in KS2 should be taught to understand and apply the principles of a healthy and varied diet (Department for Education, 2013).

Energy

We all need energy and nutrients in order for our bodies to function properly but children need lots of energy as they are still growing. The amount of energy that food contains is measured in kilojoules (kJ) and kilocalories (kcal), which are commonly referred to as calories.

Table 3.1 The average intake of energy for children aged 7–10 years old

Age	Boys	Girls
7 yrs	6900 kJ/1649 kcal	6400 kJ/1530 kcal
8 yrs	7300 kJ/1745 kcal	6800 kJ/1625 kcal
9 yrs	7700 kJ/1840 kcal	7200 kJ/1721 kcal
10 yrs	8500 kJ/2032 kcal	8100 kJ/1936 kcal

However, these figures are only a guide and children may need more or less depending on factors such as how physically active they are. While the amount of energy intake is important, we also need a balanced, healthy eating plan.

Following government guidelines, the eatwell plate was produced to provide a pictorial representation of the proportions and types of foods children (above the age of five) and adults should eat (Figure 3.2).

Together these food groups provide our bodies with enough nutrition to provide essential processes such as: growing and building, repairing and healing, reproducing, and resisting illnesses and infections. Eating a variety of foods can also reduce the risk of conditions such as heart disease, stroke, some cancers, diabetes and osteoporosis.

Let's take a closer look at the food groups.

Food groups

Fruit and vegetables

These can include all forms such as fresh, frozen, juiced, dried or tinned (but be aware these may contain added sugar). All fruits and vegetables count except for potatoes, because they are starchy so they belong in the starchy food group. Fruit and vegetables should make up two-thirds (or more) of your plate as they provide us with vital vitamins, minerals and fibre (that helps food move through the digestive system). NHS guidelines recommend that five portions (80g/handful) of fruit and vegetables are eaten daily, and that this should include a variety as some are higher in particular vitamins and minerals than others.

The eatwell plate

Use the eatwell plate to help you get the balance right. It shows how
much of what you eat should come from each food group.

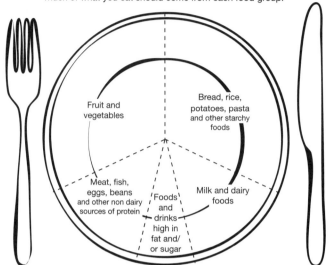

Figure 3.2 The eatwell plate

Figure 3.3   **Figure 3.4**

Fruit and vegetables also contain substances known as antioxidants, which help
protect against diseases, such as cancer and heart disease.

Starchy foods

These can be found in foods such as bread, rice, potatoes and pasta and should make
up a third of the food we eat. They are our main source of carbohydrate and therefore
their primary job is to provide us with energy. Whole-
meal and wholegrain varieties should be included as
they contain more fibre (often referred to as 'roughage'),
which keeps the gut healthy.

Dairy

Dairy includes foods such as milk, cheese and yoghurt,
which are good sources of protein, vitamins and
calcium. Calcium is the most common mineral in your
body and is necessary to keep your bones and teeth
healthy as well as helping your blood to clot. These
foods should be eaten in moderate amounts every day
i.e. 2–3 portions a day.

Figure 3.5

Meat, fish, eggs, beans and nuts

These contain protein which enables the body to repair cells and make new ones, allowing for growth and development. These foods also provide minerals such as iron, zinc and magnesium and B vitamins. These foods should be eaten in moderate amounts every day i.e. 2–3 portions a day (one portion is an egg or a serving of meat/fish the size of a deck of cards).

Figure 3.6

Fats and sugar

Fat is responsible for transporting the fat-soluble vitamins A, D, E and K around the body as well as protecting internal organs through 'cushioning'. There are two types of fat: saturated (found in foods such as cheese, sausages, butter, cakes, biscuits and pies) and unsaturated (found in oily fish, nuts and seeds, avocados, olive oils and vegetable oils). Saturated fat can raise our cholesterol, putting us at increased risk

Figure 3.7

of heart disease, whereas unsaturated fats can help to lower cholesterol and provide us with the essential fatty acids, such as omega-3 – 'essential' because the body can't make them itself.

Sugar and fats are both sources of energy; however, it is important that we only consume small amounts of these, as any energy we do not burn will be converted into fat. Too much fat can lead to obesity, which increases the risk of developing type-2 diabetes, certain cancers, heart disease and stroke.

BE AWARE: The eatwell plate classifies food by how it is produced; however, many foods belong to several groups. For example, meat contains lots of protein but also fats and minerals; milk contains carbohydrate, protein and some fat as well as several vitamins, minerals and water. Consequently, food can be grouped in a variety of ways; for example, foods may be organised by:

- main nutrient content (e.g. fatty foods, starchy foods, protein foods)
- role of the food type in human nutrition (e.g. energy foods, protective foods, body-building foods)
- individual nutrients (e.g. carbohydrates, fats, vitamins, protein)
- commercial value (e.g. cereals, roots and tubers, nuts and seeds, fruits, leafy vegetables)

While it is possible to classify some foods according to major nutrients, most foods fall into several categories.

Drinks

Two-thirds of a healthy human body is actually made up of water. This water has a vital role: it helps our blood carry nutrients and waste around the body and helps the chemical reactions that occur in our cells. To ensure that our bodies perform these functions effectively we must

Figure 3.8

Table 3.2 Summary table of food groups

Food group	Examples	Main nutritional benefits	Daily portion
Fruit and vegetables	• all fruit and vegetables, including fresh, frozen, dried, tinned etc. and fruit juice • peas, beans, sweet corn, carrots, parsnips, courgettes, peppers, onions etc. • banana, pineapples, apples, pears, strawberries, blueberries, etc.	• fibre • vitamins and minerals (especially vitamins A, C and E)	five portions
Starchy foods	• all bread e.g. white, brown, granary, wholemeal, soda bread, etc. • rice • pasta, noodles, cous cous • potatoes • breakfast cereals • grains e.g. barley, buckwheat, millet, etc.	• energy • fibre • B vitamins • iron (from some breakfast cereals)	a third of everything we eat
Dairy	• milk • cheese • yoghurt	• calcium • protein • vitamin B12	two to three portions (one portion is a small pot of yoghurt or glass of milk)

Table 3.2 Summary table of food groups *continued*

Food group	Examples	Main nutritional benefits	Daily portion
Meat, fish, eggs, beans and nuts	• meat: beef, pork, lamb • fish: cod, sea bass, prawns etc. • meat and fish can be fresh, frozen and canned • eggs • poultry: duck, chicken and turkey • pulses e.g. beans, peas, lentils • nuts • quorn	• iron • B vitamins • zinc	two to three portions (one portion is an egg or a serving of meat/fish the size of a deck of cards)
Fats and sugar	• butter, margarine, low fat spread, cooking oils, lard, etc. • mayonnaise, salad cream, oily dressings • creamy sauces and fatty gravies • sweets, chocolate, cakes, buns, biscuits • cream • crisps, corn snacks • chips • sugar, jam, honey • sugary drinks (non-diet fizzy drinks and squashes etc.) • nuts	• energy • vitamins A and D • essential fatty acids	one portion (two biscuits or a small chocolate bar)

keep hydrated. We should aim to drink 6–8 glasses (1.2 litres) of fluid per day. Water is the best drink to choose as it does not contain sugar.

See www.foodafactoflife.org.uk/Sheet.aspx?siteId=20&sectionId=118&contentId=718 for further subject knowledge, lesson ideas and resources.

WHERE FOOD COMES FROM

Key Stage 1

Children should be taught to understand where food comes from (Department for Education, 2013).

Food comes from two main sources: plants and animals.

Plants

Plants provide us with many sources of food, such as fruits, vegetables, cereals, grain as well as the spices that we use in cooking. We eat various parts of plants, such as:

- roots (radish, carrot, parsnip)
- stems (asparagus, ginger, sugarcane)
- leaves (spinach, lettuce, celery)
- flowers (artichoke, broccoli, cauliflower)
- seeds (rice, peas, peanuts)
- fruits (apple, cucumber and tomatoes)

The majority of oils like palm oil, sunflower oil and coconut oil are made from parts of plants and are used for cooking and other purposes. We get sugar from sugarcane and sugar beet plants. Plants also give us nuts like walnuts, cashew nuts and almonds.

Animals

Some of the foods we eat come from animals, including beef, veal, lamb, pork, fish and chicken.

Some foods are produced from the flesh or internal organs of animals, such as:

- pigs (pork such as bacon, sausages, chops and ribs)
- cows (beef such as ribs, steak, burger, fillet and minced beef)
- poultry such as chicken, geese and turkey (wings, nuggets, legs, breast)
- sheep (lamb which is from an animal less than a year old, or mutton, which is from an animal older than a year and come in forms such as steak, burger, mince and chops)
- fish (we eat many varieties such as cod, sea bass shrimp, squid, mussels, clams and crab)

We also eat food that animals make, for example chickens produce eggs, cows give milk and bees produce honey. Animal foods are used to make other foods such as butter, cream and yoghurt.

Many processed foods use a combination of foods from animal and plant sources to make other foods, such as cakes which use flour (made from plants) and butter, eggs and milk (sourced from animals).

Key Stage 2

Children should be taught to understand seasonality and know where and how a variety of ingredients [are] grown, reared, caught and processed (Department for Education, 2013).

Seasonality

Before reaching supermarket shelves, much of our fruit and vegetables have travelled thousands of miles, resulting in a significant reduction of vital nutrients. Buying fruit and vegetables in season not only increases the nutrients you take in, but they also taste better, are cheaper and are better for the planet. Growing fruit and vegetables is a great way for children to learn about where food comes from as well as seasonality. If you are new to growing your own fruit and vegetables start with easy-to-grow crops such as strawberries, lettuce, tomatoes and courgettes. Wellington boots, buckets and containers can be used to grow crops such as carrots, tomatoes, courgettes and potatoes, which can be handy if your school lacks space.

Children could use computers to find out when particular fruit and vegetables are in season and create graphs and calendars to represent this information. They could then use this information to find seasonal recipes.

Table 3.3 When fruits and vegetables are in season in the UK

Autumn	Winter	Spring	Summer
• apple	• apple	• apple	• apple
• blackberry	• Brussels sprouts	• asparagus	• basil
• butternut squash	• cabbage	• Brussels sprouts	• beans (runner and French)
• Brussels sprouts	• carrot	• cabbage	
• cabbage	• cauliflower	• carrot	• beetroot
• carrot	• leek	• cauliflower	• broccoli
• cauliflower	• onion	• cucumber	• carrot
• celery	• parsnip	• lettuce	• cauliflower
• kale	• pear	• onion	• celery
• leek	• potato	• parsley	• courgette
• onion	• pumpkin	• potato	• cucumber
• parsnip	• purple sprouting broccoli	• purple sprouting broccoli	• fennel
• pear			• lettuce
• potato	• rhubarb	• radish	• onion
• pumpkin	• swede	• red onion	• potato
• purple sprouting broccoli	• turnip	• rhubarb	• radish
			• raspberry
• spinach			• red onion
• turnip			• rocket
			• rhubarb
			• strawberry

Farming

In the past, farming in Britain used to employ large numbers of people but with the advancement in machinery, only a few people are now needed to run a vast farm. Organic farming (farming without artificial chemicals which can harm the environment and human health) is becoming more popular.

There are different types of farming:

- arable: growing of crops and cereals
- pastoral: rearing and production of animals including pigs, chickens, sheep, beef and dairy cattle
- mixed farming: combination of arable and pastoral
- horticulture: production of flowers, fruit, vegetables or ornamental plants
- market gardening: small-scale production of fruits, vegetables and flowers
- viticulture: grapes

Main crops

- wheat (the most widely grown arable crop in the UK)
- sugar beet (the UK is the fifth largest producer of sugar beet)
- barley
- oats
- potatoes
- vegetables
- oil seed rape
- fruits

Livestock produce

- sheep
- cattle
- poultry
- milk
- meat
- eggs
- wool

The type of farming found in different regions of Britain will depend on factors such as: relief, climate and soil type. Upland areas generally lend themselves to sheep farming whereas flat areas lend themselves to crop production and wet/warm areas to milk and beef production.

Farmers tend to keep cattle and sheep in North West England, Wales and Scotland as they can survive cold winters on the hills and moors. Dairy cattle tend to be kept in South West England where the grass is rich. Crops such as grain, potatoes and sugar beet are grown in the South East and the lowlands of Scotland while in the east of England (East Anglia), wheat, barley and vegetables grow in enormous fields.

Arable farming

In the late autumn to early winter, fields are ploughed and seeds are sown. The plough digs the soil so that the seeds can be planted and it is pulled by a tractor. In the spring, the seeds begin to grow into plants which are sprayed with fertiliser to help them grow. Sometimes they are sprayed to get rid of weeds and pests as well. Plants need light

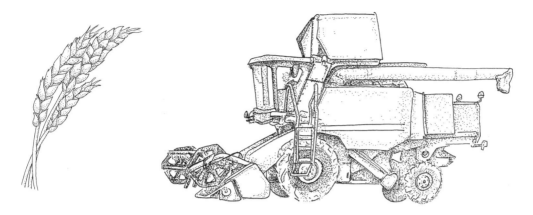

Figure 3.9 Wheat   **Figure 3.10**

from the sun, water from the rain and nutrients from the soil to grow and stay healthy. In the late summer the wheat is harvested. A combine harvester (Figure 3.10) is used to cut the wheat and separate the grain, the straw and the chaff (what is left when the grain has been separated from the ear).

The grain is stored before it goes to be milled to make flour which we can then be used to make lots of different foods, such as breakfast cereals, bread, pasta, cakes and biscuits.

Sugar beet

Sugar beet is sown from early March onwards and the operation is normally completed by early April. The seeds are sown in rows, fertiliser is applied to suit soil and crop requirements and herbicides are used to control weeds during the early stages of the plant's growth. The harvesting period, known as the 'campaign' among farmers, takes place between September and December when the amount of sugar in the beet is at its highest. Harvesters cut off the top leaves of the sugar beet which are used as animal feed for cattle and sheep or are ploughed back into the land as a natural fertiliser. The root is then cleaned to remove any soil attached to it before it is transported. Roots awaiting delivery to the factory from December to February are stored in protected storage to maintain the highest possible quality and sugar content.

Figure 3.11 Sugar beet

Pastoral farming

Cattle

For most of the year cattle live outside and eat grass. However, in the winter the fields get muddy and the grass does not grow so well, so farmers keep them in a shed and they are fed straw and silage (hay and grass). Farmers give each cattle an ear stamp so that they can be easily identified.

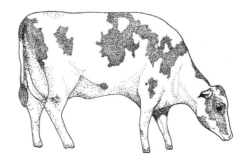

Figure 3.12

Pigs

When a mother pig has piglets they are kept in a farrowing crate for a few weeks so that she does not accidentally lie on their piglets and squash them. The piglets can lean through the bars to feed.

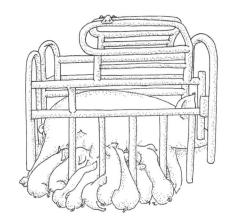

Figure 3.13 Farrowing crate

Chickens

Farmers keep chickens in a chicken house which is heated so that they keep warm. As they get older, farmers slowly cool the house. The chickens are fed and watered through pipes and feeders. Farmers put perches in the house for the chickens to sit on when they get bigger.

Most of these animals are raised until they reach a target weight, then they are slaughtered (killed) and butchered (cut up) for us to buy, cook and eat.

Figure 3.14 The feeder

Fish

Fish such as salmon and trout are farmed from freshwater (rivers or lakes) whereas fish such as crab, mussels, cod, haddock, mackerel and sardines are farmed from seawater. Nets are used to catch the fish. These are dropped from the boat and are pulled along. The holes in the nets are a special size so that small, young fish can escape. Once the fish have been caught they are kept in sea water or ice to keep them fresh. Crabs and lobsters walk along the sea bed so they are caught using crab or lobster pots which are dropped onto the sea bed. Some fish such as salmon, trout and mussels are bred in special tanks on land or in pens in the sea.

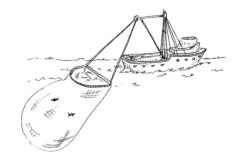

Figure 3.15

COOKING SKILLS

Children in KS1 should be able to name, use and explain the function of a basic range of cooking equipment and develop a range of basic cooking skills to prepare dishes using the basic principles of a healthy and varied diet (Department for Education, 2013).

Table 3.4 The cooking equipment required for KS1 and the cooking skills children in KS1 should be learning

Cooking equipment	Cooking skills
• bowl	• mix (with increasing thoroughness)
• knife	• spread (soft ingredients)
• grater	• grate (soft foods like cheese)
• squeezer	• juice
• cookie cutters	• cut out with cutters (biscuits)
• spoon	• spoon ingredients (into different containers)
• fork	• mash (soft foods, e.g. banana)
• cocktail stick	• thread (soft foods onto a cocktail stick, e.g. satsuma)
• rolling pin	• roll out (biscuit dough, pastry)
• sieve	• sift (flour into a bowl)
• weighing scales	• weigh ingredients

Children in KS2 should be able to name, use and explain the functions of a range of cooking equipment and develop a range of cooking skills to prepare and cook a variety of predominantly savoury dishes applying the principles of a healthy and varied diet (Department for Education, 2013).

Cooking equipment

The majority of the cooking equipment you will need can be found in most well stocked kitchens; however, you may want to invest in some child-friendly knives. There is a range of child-friendly knives (available from various suppliers) which have easy-grip handles and rounded teeth, allowing children to cut the same ingredients as adults, minus the cut fingers!

Health and safety

- A letter should be sent home to check whether any children in the class have food allergies, special dietary requirements, religious or cultural beliefs that prevent them handling or tasting certain foods.
- Classroom furniture should be in a safe, practical arrangement.
- Cooking surfaces should be wiped with antibacterial spray (and covered with plastic cloths if available).
- Equipment should be clean and ready for use (count all knives and sharp tools when distributing and collecting in equipment).
- Children must be shown by teacher demonstration how to use the equipment safely.
- All jewellery must be removed.

- Nail varnish must be removed.
- Long hair needs to be tied back.
- Hands must be washed with soap or hand wash.
- Aprons should be worn.
- Children need to know that they must remove their apron if they go to the toilet.
- Children need to know that they must wash their hands again if they blow their nose, cough or sneeze into their hands, touch hair, cuts or spots.

Table 3.4 The cooking equipment required for KS2 and the cooking skills children in KS2 should be learning

Cooking equipment	Cooking skills
• peeler	• peel
• measuring spoons, jug, scales	• measure
• garlic press	• press
• cake tin	• baking
• mixing spoon	• mix (thoroughly)
• palette knife	• spread (evenly over food)
• vegetable knife	• chop, slice
• whisk	• crack an egg and whisk
• kitchen scissors	• snip
• blender	• blend
• pastry brush	• brush
• grater	• grate (firmer foods like carrots)
• cookie cutters	• cut out with cutters (positioning carefully to avoiding wasting ingredients)
• spoon	• spoon ingredients (using two spoons)
• kebab stick	• thread (medium resistance foods, e.g. mushrooms, courgettes)
• icing bag/pipe	• decorate using icing

THINGS TO CONSIDER

- Is there a cooker available?
- Do you need to book it?
- Do any of your children have allergies?
- Are any of your children vegetarians or vegans?
- Do any of your children have religious considerations?
- Group size: needs to be small enough to allow all children to have a 'hands-on' learning experience and large enough for each group to have their own equipment and ingredients.

IDEAS FOR PROJECTS

DRINKS	<ul><li>fruit smoothies</li><li>fresh fruit juice</li></ul>
SNACKS	<ul><li>granola bar</li><li>fruit salad</li><li>quesadilla</li><li>hummus</li><li>sandwich</li><li>bread</li></ul>
MEALS	<ul><li>packed lunch</li><li>burrito</li><li>vegetable burger</li><li>pizza</li><li>soup</li><li>falafel wrap</li></ul>

© 2016, *The Really Useful Primary Design and Technology Book*, E. Flinn and S. Patel, Routledge

CROSS-CURRICULAR LINKS

LITERACY	• create an advertisement to sell your food creation • create a podcast • instructions explaining how to make . . .
NUMERACY	• change the recipe quantities (conversions, fractions) • use equipment to measure ingredients accurately • calculate the cost of the dish • calculate how much you would have to sell it for to make a profit • produce a survey and graph to find out the most popular dish
SCIENCE	• investigate how long different types of bread take to go mouldy • investigate how much sugar is in drinks • understand the importance of a balanced diet • investigate what plants need to grow
GEOGRAPHY	• use maps to plot where different food comes from • investigate how seasons affect when food is available • investigate food miles
HISTORY	• compare food available now to in the past • compare our celebration meals to celebration meals in particular eras, e.g. Tudor, Victorian • compare what was considered a healthy eating plan in the past and the present • make a recipe from the past, e.g. wartime cake
RS/RE	• compare food from different religious celebrations
MUSIC	• create music to go with food advertisements • create music to mimic the experience of tasting the dish
PSHEC	• healthy living day: prepare a balanced meal and exercise plan
PE	• design an exercise programme to keep healthy • understand the dietary needs of athletes

© 2016, *The Really Useful Primary Design and Technology Book*, E. Flinn and S. Patel, Routledge

LESSON PLANS

For each lesson you may want children to do the cooking in small groups. When modelling you could do this yourself or show clips from celebrity chefs.

KS1

Making biscuits and fruit cocktail sticks

KS2

Making Irish soda bread and Victoria sponge cake

COOKING AND NUTRITION: KS1 LESSON PLAN

Session	D&T skills	Lesson outline	Resources	Differentiation
1	Research	**Introduction** Where does food come from? Explain that food either comes from animals or plants. Choose some key examples and go through these using a PowerPoint or video clips. **Task** Children to match food to the correct animal or plant. **Plenary** Check children's understanding by playing food bingo. First play plant bingo–children write/draw four chosen vegetables and teacher shows a picture of a plant, children tick it off if they have the matching vegetable. Repeat for fruits and animals.	• Pictures of food, or food and pictures of their matching animal/plant • Whiteboards for bingo • PPT/video clip showing plants and animals and the food they provide	<u>Support:</u> children to match common fruits, vegetables and meat such as: apples, carrots, onions, chicken, sausages). <u>Extend:</u> children to match less common food (this will depend on children's culture and prior experience but may include kiwis, turnip, okra, muscles, squid).
2	Research, design, make and evaluate	**Introduction** Ensure that children wash their hands and discuss the importance of this with them. Provide children with a range of smoothies to try. Ask children to describe the drinks in terms of appearance, texture and taste. Which do they like/dislike? Why? Which combinations do they like/dislike? Model how to design a fruit/vegetable smoothie. Draw your design on the IWB and label. Model how to write/draw a simple step by step guide. **Task** Ask children to design their own smoothie. Ensure children wash their hands, wear aprons and surfaces are clean. Model how to make a smoothie, demonstrating the skills: slicing and weighing. Children to make their smoothie. **Plenary** Allow children to drink their smoothie. Can they describe the taste/texture/appearance? Do they like their smoothie? Why? Ask children if they think their smoothie is healthy? Whose is the healthiest? Why? What ingredients would go into a healthy smoothie? How would you improve your smoothie?	• Selection of smoothies • Ingredients • Aprons • Blender • Plastic table cloth • Chopping board • Knives	<u>Support:</u> children to draw a step by step guide. Encourage children to choose soft fruit such as bananas to slice. <u>Extend:</u> children to write a step by step guide. Encourage children to slice the fruit/vegetable a similar size.

© 2016, *The Really Useful Primary Design and Technology Book*, E. Flinn and S. Patel, Routledge

Session	D&T skills	Lesson outline	Resources	Differentiation
3	Research, design and evaluate	**Introduction** Discuss what makes a healthy diet. Show pictures of meals on the IWB and get children to say which ones are healthy and why. Tell the children that they are going to design and make a healthy snack (e.g. sandwich, wrap, crudités and tzatziki dip, salad – choose one for the class or have groups make different dishes and have a class picnic). Provide children with different foods to try (ensure that children wash their hands and discuss the importance of this with them). Children to describe the texture and taste as well as discover which foods complement each other. Show children what ingredients they will have available to them. Model how to design a chosen dish; this could be drawn or if you are making a sandwich or wrap you can make it with paper. Then model how to create a simple plan (e.g. story board) to show the main steps they will have to carry out to make their dish. **Task** Children to design their dish and create a story board of how to make their dish. **Plenary** Choose some designs to show. As a class, evaluate the designs. Which dishes do they think will be the tastiest? Why? Which dish is the healthiest? Why? What cooking equipment do they think they will need?	• Dishes to try (will depend on what you choose to make) • Pictures of meals	<u>Support</u>: children to include the main steps of the recipe. <u>Extend</u>: encourage children to include all the steps of the recipe.
4	Make and evaluate	**Introduction** Explain to the class that they will be working safely and hygienically to make the dish they designed last lesson. Ask children what they need to do first before handling food? (wash hands, apron, hair back, etc.). Model how to make the dish using your design from last lesson. Highlight the cooking equipment you use and make sure children can name this equipment. Can they suggest the most appropriate equipment to use for each stage? Model any skills they will need. **Task** Children to make their dishes. You might decide to do this in small groups and have one group 'cooking' at a time so that each group has adult support. **Plenary** Children to eat their dish and describe the flavour/texture/appearance/smell to their group or class. Do they like their dishes? Could their dish be improved? How?	• Aprons • Blender • Plastic table cloth • Chopping board • Knives • Ingredients • Children's step by step guides and designs from last lesson	<u>Support</u>: help children choose their cooking equipment and guide them to follow each step correctly <u>Extend</u>: encourage children to choose their cooking equipment and use their step by step guide independently

© 2016, *The Really Useful Primary Design and Technology Book*, E. Flinn and S. Patel, Routledge

COOKING AND NUTRITION: KS1 LESSON PLAN *continued*

Session	D&T skills	Lesson outline	Resources	Differentiation
5	Research, design, make and evaluate	<u>Introduction</u> Tell the children that they are going to make a healthy sweet snack, e.g. you could choose a fruit kebab with a dip or a fruit salad. Show the class the range of fruits they can make their snack from. Allow children to try the fruit and decide which ones they like and which ones complement each other. Model how to design a fruit salad/kebab. <u>Task</u> Children to design their fruit salad/kebab. Model how to make a fruit salad/kebab. If making a fruit kebab – explain that children need to be careful when using the kebab sticks because they are sharp. <u>Task</u> Children to make their dish. <u>Plenary</u> Children to compare their dish to their design – is it similar/different? Children to eat their dish. Did they like it? Is it a healthy snack? Why? Can they name other healthy snacks? Which fruits did they use? Which fruits were difficult to put on the kebab stick? Why?	• Aprons • Plastic table cloth • Chopping board • Knives • Ingredients • Kebab sticks	<u>Support</u>: provide fruit already cut into pieces. <u>Extend</u>: children to slice fruit and if time make a yoghurt dip.

© 2016, *The Really Useful Primary Design and Technology Book*, E. Flinn and S. Patel, Routledge

Session	D&T skills	Lesson outline	Resources	Differentiation
6	Make and evaluate	**Introduction** Tell the children that they are going to make a sweet dish. Explain to the class that treats are ok in moderation. What do they think this means? What happens if we eat too many treats? Show children some ingredients. What do they think we could make with these ingredients? Choose a non-bake sweet dish to make, such as chocolate covered frozen bananas, peppermint creams, rocky road, fruit jellies or fridge cake. **Task 1** If you choose either chocolate covered frozen bananas, peppermint creams or fruit jellies children can design theirs as they will be able to make theirs look individual by decorating it with sprinkles or fruit, or by choosing a shape using a cookie cutter or a jelly holder. Model how to make the dish. **Task 2** Children to make the dish. **Plenary** Children to try their treat. Can they describe the taste and texture? What have they learned to make in this unit of work? Which dishes were healthy? What makes a healthy dish? Where does food come from? What cooking skills have they learned?	• Aprons • Plastic table cloth • Mixing bowl • Mixing spoon • Cake tin • Rolling pin • Cookie cutters • Ingredients	<u>Support</u>: help children choose their cooking equipment and guide them to follow each step correctly. <u>Extend</u>: encourage children to choose their cooking equipment and make the dish independently.

© 2016, *The Really Useful Primary Design and Technology Book*, E. Flinn and S. Patel, Routledge

COOKING AND NUTRITION: KS2 LESSON PLAN

Session	D&T skills	Lesson outline	Resources	Differentiation
1	Research	**Introduction** Tell the children that they are going to be designing and making a range of dishes. Before they do this they need to research what makes a healthy diet. Look at the eatwell plate together. Discuss the different groups of food (examples of each and their nutritional benefits). You may want to link this to Science and spend an extra lesson where children: sort foods in different ways, research nutritional information, investigate amount of sugar/fat/salt, etc., create graphs, tables, fact files, etc. **Task** Children to research which foods are available in which seasons. Create a table to show this information. Using this information provide each table with a season, children to create an eatwell plate for this season. **Plenary** Each table to present their eatwell plate for their season. Which foods will help growth and repair/energy/calcium/vitamins, etc? Which seasons were hardest to plan for? Discuss which foods are available all year around. Why is it important to eat foods seasonally? Why are foods out of season more expensive? What are food miles and how do they affect the environment?	• Eatwell plate • Computers • Pictures/real food • Eatwell plate outline • Blank table for seasons	<u>Support:</u> adult support or specific websites provided and blank table to fill in the foods available in each season. <u>More able:</u> research food miles and their effect on the environment. Make a TV advert/poster to persuade consumers to eat seasonally.
2/3	Design, make and evaluate (two lessons/ whole morning)	**Introduction** Tell the class that they are going to be designing and making today's lunch which will be bread and soup. Show different types of bread (e.g. soda bread, white/brown, multigrain, focaccia, etc.) and allow children to taste these (ensure that children wash their hands and discuss the importance of this with them). Can they explain the appearance, texture, aroma, flavour? They could fill in a table for each type of bread and record this information. Which do they think is the healthiest? Why? Is bread good for you? Look at the food labels of the bread. What do they tell us? Children to design different types of bread and then choose a type of bread to make (different groups could make different types of bread). Show a clip of how to make bread. Discuss the importance of yeast.	• Cooking equipment: loaf tin, mixing bowl, mixing spoon, chopping boards, knives, peelers, saucepan, garlic crusher, weighing scales. • Ingredients • Aprons • Plastic table cloths if available • Variety of breads • Clip of making bread	<u>Support:</u> plan and make a soup. <u>Extend:</u> plan and make a soup and bread.

© 2016, *The Really Useful Primary Design and Technology Book*, E. Flinn and S. Patel, Routledge

Session	D&T skills	Lesson outline	Resources	Differentiation
	If you are able to you may want to split the class in half so that fewer children are cooking at one time.	Show the recipe for the bread that children will be making and the cooking equipment that they will be using. Model the key skills: weigh ingredients, mix ingredients, knead dough. Task Ask children what they need to do first before handling food (wash hands, apron, hair back, etc.). Start to make the bread in groups with adult support. Ensure that you model how to knead the bread, measure and mix the ingredients. Leave the bread to rise. While the bread is rising, tell the children that as a class they are going to use the information from the last lesson to design and make a seasonal soup. Show children the ingredients available. In groups, children to come up with different types of soups. As a class, choose a soup to make. If your recipe requires it, knead the bread for a second time and leave to rise. Model the key skills: weigh ingredients, chop and slice vegetables, blend, crush garlic. Task Make the soup as a class. Children can peel and chop the vegetables. Bake the bread. Plenary Eat the soup and bread. Do they like the bread and soup? Can they describe the flavours/textures/appearance/aroma? How could they improve their dishes? How could they extend their skills? As a class, evaluate their product against the design criteria.		

© 2016, *The Really Useful Primary Design and Technology Book*, E. Flinn and S. Patel, Routledge

COOKING AND NUTRITION: KS2 LESSON PLAN *continued*

Session	D&T skills	Lesson outline	Resources	Differentiation
4	Design, make and evaluate	**Introduction** Tell the children that they are going to design, make and evaluate a falafel wrap (show a picture of this). Tell the children that they will be making coleslaw, salsa, salad and falafel. Show children a recipe/clip of how to make a falafel wrap. Model how to design a falafel wrap. **Task** Children to design what their falafel will look like. Encourage them to be original. Model the key skills: estimate, weigh ingredients, slice and chop vegetables, mix ingredients, crush garlic. In groups make: falafel, coleslaw, salsa and salad, or each group could make one of these. Provide recipes which the children have to follow. Encourage children to estimate before weighing the ingredients. You may want to fry the falafels yourself. **Plenary** Children to compare their dish to their design. Is it the same/different? Why? Children to eat their dish. How would they describe the taste to someone who has never eaten falafel before? How could they improve their dish? Is it healthy? Why?	• Cooking equipment: chopping boards, knives, weighing scales, mixing bowl, mixing spoon, fork/masher • Ingredients • Aprons • Plastic table cloths if available • Recipe books	<u>Support</u>: adult support with key skills. <u>Extend</u>: encourage children to create a step by step guide of how to make a falafel wrap.
5	Design, make and evaluate	**Introduction** Tell the children that they are going to design and make biscuits (decide on savoury, sweet or both). Show children the recipe/watch clip for basic biscuits. Tell the children that they will be designing their own unique biscuit. Show them the ingredients which will be available to them (e.g. sweet: icing sugar, jam, chocolate spread, sprinkles, etc.; savoury: poppy seeds, variety of cheeses, marmite, etc.). Model how to draw and design a unique biscuit.	• Cooking equipment: weighing scales, mixing bowl, mixing spoon, sieve, whisk, rolling pin, cookie cutters, icing bag • Ingredients • Aprons • Plastic table cloths (if available) • Recipe books/computers	<u>Support</u>: adult support with key skills. <u>Extend</u>: encourage children to design and make biscuits with intricate designs. E.g. they could use icing in a piping bag.

© 2016, *The Really Useful Primary Design and Technology Book*, E. Flinn and S. Patel, Routledge

Session	D&T skills	Lesson outline	Resources	Differentiation
		Task In groups, children to draw the design of their biscuits. Provide recipe books or computers for inspiration. Either allow each group to make their biscuits or vote on the best design for all to make. Model the key skills: weigh ingredients, crack egg, whisk egg, roll out the dough and use cookie cutters (position carefully to avoid wasting ingredients). Children to make the biscuits. **Plenary** Children to evaluate their biscuit against the design criteria. Do they like the biscuits? Could they be improved? Can they describe the flavour, appearance, aroma and texture?		
6	Research, design, make and evaluate	**Introduction** Tell the children that for the last lesson they are going to play 'Ready, Steady, Cook'. Show them a clip of this cookery show. Explain that they are going to use all of the skills they have learned to plan and make a healthy dish in one hour! Show them the ingredients and the rules for what they are allowed to choose (you can make these up and change according to ability, e.g. they can only choose one carbohydrate, one protein and two vegetables). They will only be able to make a dish which does not need cooking (e.g. sandwich, wrap, salad, fruit salad, cold soup). In groups, allow them 15 minutes to plan what they are going to make and to sketch their design. You could provide recipe books and computers for inspiration. Allow children 20 minutes to make their dish. **Plenary** Groups to present their dishes. You could ask members of staff to be judges or each group could score/judge another group. Get the judges to describe and evaluate the dish to the rest of the class. Children to compare their dish to their design. Is it the same/different? Why? How could they improve their dish? Is it healthy? Why? If there is time you could do a blind tasting. In groups, children have to guess the food they are eating.	• Cooking equipment • Ingredients • Aprons • Plastic table cloths (if available) • Recipe books/computers	<u>Support</u>: allow greater freedom in choosing their ingredients. <u>Extend</u>: provide more constricting rules on choosing their ingredients.

© 2016, *The Really Useful Primary Design and Technology Book*, E. Flinn and S. Patel, Routledge

RECIPES

ALL IN ONE SPONGE

Ingredients

175 g self raising flour
175 g softened unsalted butter
175 g caster sugar
3 large eggs
2–3 drops of vanilla essence
1 teaspoon of baking powder

1 Preheat the oven 180°C/fan 170°C/gas mark 4. Grease two 20 cm (8 in) sandwich tins.

2 Measure the butter and sugar and cream together until light and fluffy and drops off the spoon easily.

3 Add the eggs one at a time, beating after each addition.

4 Stir in the drops of vanilla essence.

5 Sieve the flour into the mixture and fold in so that you keep the air in the mixture.

6 Divide the mixture evenly between two tins and level out.

7 Place in the middle of the oven and bake for about 25 minutes or until well risen, golden brown and the cakes spring back when lightly pressed.

8 Leave to cool for a few minutes then turn out and leave to cool on wire racks.

9 When completely cool, choose your filling and topping.

VICTORIA SPONGE

Spread a thin layer of jam onto one of the cakes and sandwich together. Sprinkle with icing sugar or sugar to serve.

CHOCOLATE SPONGE

Omit the vanilla essence and add two tablespoons of cocoa to the basic ingredients.

ORANGE OR LEMON SPONGE

Omit the vanilla essence and add the grated rind of a medium orange or lemon, plus one tablespoon of the juice to the basic ingredients.

© 2016, *The Really Useful Primary Design and Technology Book*, E. Flinn and S. Patel, Routledge

ICING IDEAS

BUTTER ICING

50 g softened unsalted butter
100 g icing sugar

1 Measure the softened butter and place in a mixing bowl.
2 Sift the icing sugar over the top and whisk together.

CHOCOLATE FUDGE ICING

120 g unsalted butter
8 g cocoa powder
150 ml milk
250 g icing sugar

1 Melt the butter in a saucepan and add the cocoa powder, cook for one minute.
2 Add the milk and beat until smooth.
3 Add the sifted icing sugar until you get a thick but fluid mixture.

LEMON/ORANGE DRIZZLE TOPPINGS

1 orange or lemon
60 g granulated sugar

1 Grate the rind of the orange or lemon and leave to one side.
2 Squeeze the juice into a small saucepan. Add 40 g of the sugar, heat gently and stir occasionally.
3 When the sugar has dissolved simmer gently for a few minutes until syrupy.
4 With a cocktail stick or skewer prick the cake all over.
5 Sprinkle the orange or lemon zest and left-over sugar over the cake.
6 Drizzle the syrup over the cake while it is still in the tin.

© 2016, *The Really Useful Primary Design and Technology Book*, E. Flinn and S. Patel, Routledge

BISCUITS

Ingredients

240 g unsalted butter, softened
140 g caster sugar
1 egg yolk
3–4 drops of vanilla essence
300 g plain flour

1 Preheat the oven 180°C/fan 170°C/gas mark 4. Grease a baking tray.
2 Beat the butter and sugar and cream together until light and fluffy and drops off the spoon easily.
3 Add the egg yolk and vanilla essence and briefly beat to combine.
4 Sieve the flour into the mixture and stir until the mixture is well combined – you might need to get your hands in at the end to give everything a really good mix and press the dough together.
5 Roll out and use cookie cutters to cut out the biscuits. Space well apart and place on the baking tray.
6 Bake for 12–15 mins, then transfer to a cooling rack.

CHOCOLATE CHIP BISCUITS

50 g cocoa powder
85 g white chocolate drops
85 g milk chocolate drops

Follow recipe above. At step 4 substitute 50 g cocoa powder for 50 g plain flour, add the white chocolate drops and the milk chocolate crops and mix well. Continue to follow the receipt above.

CHOCOLATE BISCUITS

50 g dark chocolate

Follow the recipe above. At step 4 melt the chocolate and knead into the cookie dough. Continue to follow the recipe above.

LEMON BISCUITS

1 lemon

Follow the recipe above. At step 3 add the grated rind of a lemon to the sugar and butter mixture. Continue to follow the recipe above.

BISCUIT SANDWICHES

Chocolate spread or jam

Sandwich two biscuits together and fill with a chocolate spread or jam.

© 2016, *The Really Useful Primary Design and Technology Book*, E. Flinn and S. Patel, Routledge

BREAD

IRISH SODA BREAD

This type of bread doesn't require yeast so you don't have to wait for it to rise, making it a quick, easy but also tasty option.

Ingredients

450 g strong white flour
1 teaspoon of bicarbonate of soda
1 teaspoon of salt
300 ml buttermilk (or 150 ml milk and 150 ml natural yoghurt mixed)
about 5–7 tablespoons of warm water

1 Preheat the oven to 200°C/fan 180°C/gas mark 6. Lightly grease a baking tray.

2 Measure the dry ingredients and mix together in a large bowl. Add the buttermilk or milk and yoghurt mixture. Add enough of the warm water to form a soft dough. Mix quickly with a table knife.

3 Turn out onto a floured surface and shape it into a flat, round loaf measuring 18 cm (7 in) in diameter.

4 Put the loaf on the baking sheet and score a deep cross in the top. (Traditionally, this lets the fairies out, but it also helps the bread to cook through.)

5 Bake for 30–35 minutes until the bottom of the loaf sounds hollow when tapped. If it isn't ready after this time, turn it upside down on the baking sheet and bake for a few minutes more.

6 Cool on a wire rack.

© 2016, *The Really Useful Primary Design and Technology Book*, E. Flinn and S. Patel, Routledge

GRANARY LOAF OR ROLLS

Ingredients

225 g strong white flour
225 g malted granary bread flour
1 tsp salt
1 tsp caster sugar
7 g sachet easy-blend yeast
150 ml warm milk
2 eggs, beaten
1 tbsp olive oil
100–150 ml warm water
Poppy or sesame seeds (optional)

1 Measure the flours and mix together in a large bowl. Add the salt, sugar and yeast. Mix.

2 Make a well in the centre of the flour, pour in the warm milk, one beaten egg, olive oil and stir. Add enough of the water to form a soft, wet dough.

3 On a lightly floured surface, knead dough for 10 mins until smooth. Put the dough in a lightly oiled bowl, cover with oiled cling film. Leave to rise in a warm place until doubled in size.

4 *To make 12 rolls*: divide the dough into 12 pieces and shape into rolls. Lightly flour 3 baking sheets. Place the rolls onto the sheets and cover loosely with oiled cling film. Set aside in a warm place for 30 mins or until they have doubled in size. Heat oven to 200°C/fan 180°C/gas mark 6. Brush the bread with beaten egg and sprinkle with sesame and poppy seeds. Bake for 15–20 mins until deep golden brown and well risen.

5 *To make a loaf:* oil the loaf tin and put the dough in the tin, pressing it in evenly. Put in a large plastic food bag and leave to rise for 1 hr or until the dough has risen to fill the tin and it no longer springs back when you press it with your finger. Heat oven to 200°C/fan 180°C/gas mark 6. Make several slashes across the top of the loaf with a sharp knife. Bake for 30–35 minutes until the bottom of the loaf sounds hollow when tapped. If it isn't ready after this time, turn it upside down on the baking sheet and bake for a few minutes more.

6 Cool on a wire rack.

© 2016, *The Really Useful Primary Design and Technology Book*, E. Flinn and S. Patel, Routledge

DIPS

HUMMUS

Ingredients

200 g/7 oz canned chickpeas
2 tablespoons of lemon juice or more
2 garlic cloves, crushed
1 teaspoon of ground cumin
Pinch of salt
100 ml/3$\frac{1}{2}$ fl oz tahini (sesame seed paste) optional
4 tablespoons of water
2 tablespoons of extra virgin olive oil
1 teaspoon of paprika

1 Drain the chickpeas and rinse. Reserve a few whole chickpeas for serving.

2 Combine the chickpeas, lemon juice, garlic, cumin, salt, tahini and water in a food processor and blend to a creamy purée.

3 Slowly pour in the olive oil as it mixes.

4 Add more lemon juice, garlic, cumin or salt to taste.

5 Serve in a bowl with the reserved chickpeas and sprinkle with paprika.

TZATZIKI

Ingredients

150 g Greek yoghurt
$\frac{1}{2}$ cucumber
2 crushed garlic cloves
1 tablespoon olive oil
1 tablespoon lemon juice (or white wine vinegar)
1 teaspoon chopped or dried mint (or dill)
$\frac{1}{2}$ teaspoon salt
Pepper or paprika to taste

1 Peel, de-seed and grate the cucumber.

2 Put the grated cucumber into a sieve suspended over a bowl, sprinkle with the salt and mix. Place a plate on top of cucumber and leave the cucumber to drain for approximately 1 hour, or until water stops dripping.

3 Combine the yoghurt, cucumber, lemon juice, crushed garlic and mix thoroughly.

4 Serve in a bowl, add a dash of olive oil and sprinkle with chopped mint and add paprika or pepper.

© 2016, *The Really Useful Primary Design and Technology Book*, E. Flinn and S. Patel, Routledge

CLASSIC TOMATO SALSA

Ingredients

4–6 medium tomatoes
half a small red onion
1 lime
1 small green chilli
salt and pepper to taste

1 Finely chop the tomatoes and green chilli and dice the onion. Place together in a bowl.

2 Cut the lime in half and squeeze over the onion, tomatoes and chilli.

3 Add salt and pepper to taste.

Options to serve with:

- warmed pita bread cut into strips
- crudités – raw vegetables thinly sliced
- breadsticks
- tortilla chips

© 2016, *The Really Useful Primary Design and Technology Book*, E. Flinn and S. Patel, Routledge

REFERENCES

National Foundation for Educational Research (2007). 'The Further Evaluation of the School Fruit and Vegetables Scheme', *NFER* Leeds University.

Reynolds, F. (2000). Managing depression through needlecraft creative activities: A qualitative study. *Arts Psychotherapy, 27*(2): 107–44.

4 Structures

A structure is defined as a framework or set of interconnecting parts of a complex building. Structures can be assembled from nets, or an open framework of rods. Structures may be free-standing or supported; they can be made from one material or a composite of materials, each adding a particular property to the finished article.

WHY TEACH ABOUT STRUCTURES?

- Learning about how to produce rigid and stable structures can help children to understand the basic principles of architecture.
- On a smaller scale, products today are sold in attractive packaging. Knowledge of how to produce such packaging could be a useful skill for a career in marketing or design.
- Children learn to measure and cut accurately and develop their fine motor skills as they construct ever more complex structures.
- This topic gives children an opportunity to see maths in action as they use measuring, scale models and nets to make their products.

INNOVATORS AND KEY EVENTS

Children in KS2 should to be taught about how key events and individuals in D&T have helped shape the world (Department for Education, 2013).

Some key events

1849 – Reinforcing concrete

Concrete is a mixture of cement, aggregate (small pebbles) and water, used widely in building. The Romans used concrete as long ago as 1400 BC for their bridges, roads and dams. A major improvement to concrete occurred in 1849 when Joseph Monier made the first reinforced concrete by embedding steel rods within the concrete. Reinforced concrete allowed the construction of tall buildings and opened the way for the development of the skyscraper.

1930s – The age of plastic

Plastics were first manufactured in 1860 by Alexander Parkes, who treated wood fibres with nitric acid to produce Parkesine. However, the real age of plastic began around 1930 when ways to make synthetic polymers from oil led to the production of PVC, neoprene, polystyrene and nylon for the first time. Polypropylene was developed in 1954. It is a tough plastic used widely in many products such as plastic storage boxes, washing-up bowls, chairs and laboratory equipment.

1950s – Carbon fibre created

Carbon fibre is a very strong, extremely lightweight material. It is five times as strong as steel and twice as stiff, yet weighs two-thirds less. Carbon fibre is very thin strands of carbon twisted together, like yarn. The fibres can be used to strengthen structures without adding to the weight and are used in aircraft and racing cars as well as tennis racquets and other sporting equipment.

Some key individuals

Abraham Darby (1678–1717)

In 1709 Abraham Darby smelted pig iron using coke rather than charcoal and made a cast iron which had fewer impurities in it and had increased strength. In 1781, the Iron Bridge, crossing the River Severn in Shropshire, was opened. Built by Abraham Darby III, it was the first arch bridge in the world to be made of cast iron. Today cast iron is used in many products, including cookware, drainpipes and mechanisms such as gears.

Isambard Kingdom Brunel (1806–1859)

Brunel was an English engineer. He designed the Clifton Suspension Bridge over the Avon Gorge in Bristol. He was responsible for the construction of the Great Western Railway running from London to Cornwall, including the building of the viaducts, bridges and tunnels. Brunel was also a ship builder, and built three great ships: the Great Britain, the Great Western and the Great Eastern.

Renzo Piano (1937–)

Renzo Piano is an architect who, in 1971 and working with Richard Rogers, designed the Georges Pompidou Centre in Paris. In the 1990s, he designed the Kansai International Airport terminal building in Japan. The terminal was built in an earthquake zone. When Japan was struck by the Kobe earthquake, the airport was undamaged, mostly due to Piano's use of sliding joints. In 2000, Renzo Piano drew the first designs for The Shard, in London, which was eventually completed in 2012. Standing 309.6 m high, on its completion The Shard was the tallest building in the EU.

SUBJECT KNOWLEDGE

- At KS1 children should be taught to build structures, exploring how they can be made stronger, stiffer and more stable.
- At KS2 children should be taught to apply their understanding of how to strengthen, stiffen and reinforce more complex structures.

Building with junk

Children love to make models and a floor covered with empty boxes, tubes, plastic cartons and scrap paper is a fertile starting point for imaginative building. After the model is finished, ask the child to draw a picture of the construction, labelling the various parts and explaining their function. (Figure 4.1)

The children in Figure 4.1 used a variety of plastic containers to make boats. It is interesting to note that, although these structures look like a pile of empty bottles taped together, to the children, each bottle had a place and a role in the model – they saw beyond the bottles to a fully functional boat with captain and passengers.

Large cardboard boxes used for the delivery of many school equipment orders can be converted into cosy dens for pets (Figure 4.2). Children can think about the animals' needs and convert the boxes accordingly.

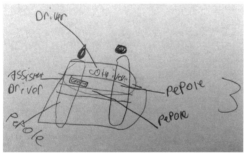
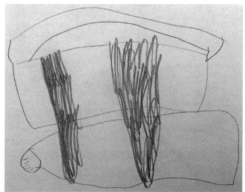

Figure 4.1

Figure 4.2

Storing junk can be a problem if space is limited. However, given a week's notice, most families can provide a good selection of junk, from cereal boxes to drinks bottles. Storing cardboard boxes can be made more efficient if they are flattened first. If the boxes are opened out fully, this can also provide the children with some lessons about the nets of 3D shapes. When reassembling the boxes, fold them inside out so that the printed side ends up inside the box. A quick dab of glue from a glue gun on each joint is sufficient to hold the box together, and the un-finished, blank inside (now on the outside) offers a much more convenient surface for decoration.

THINGS TO CONSIDER

1   Is the junk clean and safe for the children to use? Food containers need to be washed out thoroughly and anything which has held raw meat or fish should be discarded. Be aware of potential food allergies.

2   How will the models be held together? Mixed materials like this may need different glues. Check which ones are safe for children to use.

3   Junk models can get very large; is there room to store them safely between D&T sessions?

Building with cardboard

Cardboard is an ideal model-making material. It comes in a variety of thicknesses and colours and can be easily cut and folded. Although there is attractive coloured card to buy, the great thing about cardboard is that there will be a virtually unlimited supply available because it is one of the most common packaging materials. Cardboard is recyclable too, so teachers in schools with a strong eco ethos will find that reusing cardboard in D&T will give the children an opportunity to see recycling in action. Many of the models used to illustrate the chapters of this book were made from cereal and washing powder boxes.

Cutting

Use scissors to cut cardboard. Ordinary school scissors will cut through cardboard which is fairly thin. However, thicker card may need larger shears. Ask children to mark what they want to cut and then cut it for them or supervise the use of large scissors carefully. Craft knives should only be used, under strict supervision, by children in Year 5 or Year 6. When using knives, keep fingers behind the knife and always cut away from the hand holding the card (Figure 4.3). When making straight cuts, cut along a metal ruler with an M-shaped cross-section or one with a finger guard. The fingers of the hand holding the ruler are safer as they are protected by the ruler. Two or three gentle cuts along the same line are safer and more effective than one cut with the knife pressed very hard into the card.

There are rotary and ceramic cutters available which claim to be almost completely safe to use. Check them carefully to make sure that the blade is as safe as the claims. Check also to see what they can cut, as many can't cut anything thicker than regular printer paper.

Very thick corrugated card can be cut with a hacksaw if necessary.

Scoring cardboard

Scoring cardboard helps to make folds sharp and accurate. Ideally use a craft knife and a metal ruler. A ball point pen works well – use one which has run out of ink and press into the card as if drawing a line. If the card has been scored with a knife, the fold should have the cut on the outside edge. If the card has been scored with a pen, the score should be on the inside of the fold.

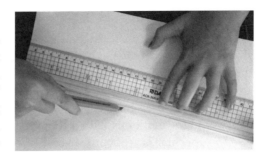

Figure 4.3

Joining

Glue guns, PVA and paper glue can be used to stick card. Sometimes it is necessary to hold the joints together while the glue sets. Masking tape, pegs or bulldog clips can be useful to hold joints firmly in place.

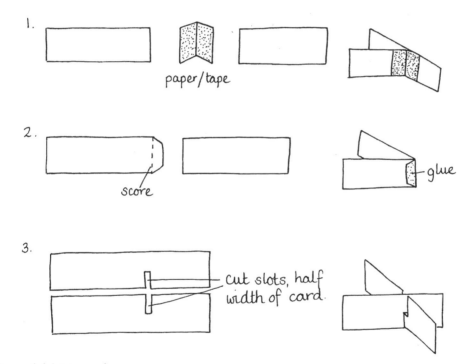

Figure 4.4 Joining card

Figure 4.5
Once children can cut, score, fold and join card, they can start to construct their own boxes

Strengthening card

The thicker the cardboard is, the stronger it is and the more successfully it will hold its shape. On some occasions, it may be necessary to use thinner, weaker cardboard and then some strengthening may be required (Figure 4.6).

Simply gluing two or three layers of card together will make the card stiffer.

In general, triangular shapes are stronger than rectangular ones. Where possible, support edges and joints with a triangle.

To support 2D cardboard structures, tape or glue a lolly stick or skewer to the back, or sandwich it between two layers of card.

To make really strong card, glue layers of corrugated cardboard together. Each layer should have the corrugations travelling at 90° to the layer below.

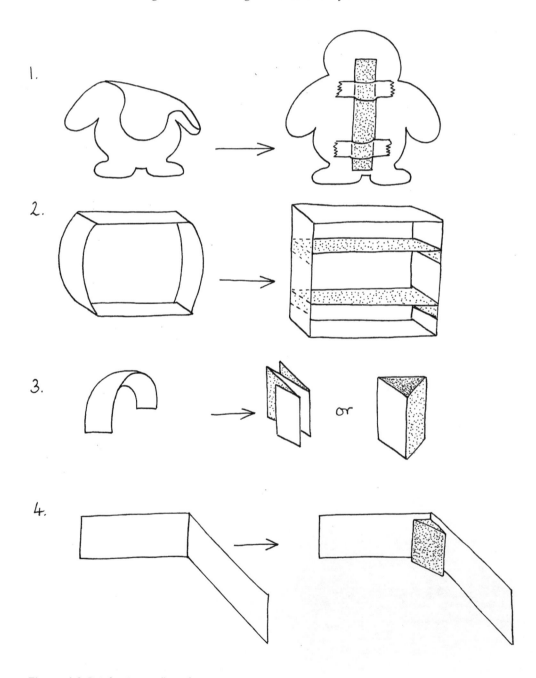

Figure 4.6 Reinforcing cardboard structures

Nets

Working with cardboard packaging can help the children to learn about 3D shapes and their nets. Have a series of different nets available to show the children. Particularly interesting ones are ready-made sandwich boxes, tea bag boxes and non-rectangular boxes (Figure 4.7). With practice, children should be able to design their own nets to produce boxes of the desired shape and size.

Figure 4.7

Figure 4.8

Nets can also be used to fold card into other useful shapes, such as furniture (Figure 4.8). Encourage children to design their own nets. Challenge them to add arms to the chair or make an L-shaped table.

THINGS TO CONSIDER

1 Storing cardboard can be difficult if cupboard space is at a premium. Flattening boxes will help reduce the volume. Aim to use junk rather than new cardboard. Ask parents for help in providing resources a few weeks before the project commences and recycle the unused cardboard at the end of the topic.

2 When reusing cardboard boxes, check whether the food or product it originally contained will cause any allergic reactions. Take care with boxes which contained dusty products like washing power.

3 Laminate opened out cardboard food packaging to produce a library of useful nets.

Building with wood

Nothing beats woodwork for sheer excitement at KS1! The thought of using tools like saws and hammers is enough for most children to feel grown-up. With care and support, there is no reason why children cannot build successfully and safely with wood, but most require considerable adult help at the start.

Woodworking tools

For cutting wood, use a junior hacksaw (Figure 4.9). The saw is small enough for a little hand, yet cuts effectively through wood with minimum effort. A pistol grip (as shown in the photo) helps children to hold the saw vertical and to saw straight (Figure 4.10).

Where possible a bench hook should be used (Figure 4.9). These are small wooden or plastic structures which hook onto the side of a table and provide a good base for cutting (Figure 4.10). Many have guide slots where the children can insert the saw and use it to help them to cut straight.

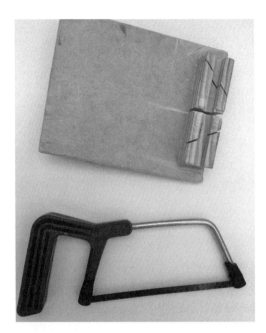

Figure 4.9
A junior hacksaw and a child-sized bench hook
(note the saw guides at the top)

Figure 4.10

Figure 4.11   **Figure 4.12**

Holding the wood in place when cutting can be difficult, especially if the wood has a round or small cross section. Use G clamps to hold both the bench hook and the wood firmly in place (Figure 4.11).

Cam bench hooks are also available from some D&T suppliers. The cam is used to hold the wood firmly in place against the saw guide.

Sandpaper is required for smoothing off rough edges to give the wood a safe and pleasant finish. Tape sheets of sandpaper to a table and encourage the children to drag the ends of sawn wood across it as if they were drawing a line with a pencil (Figure 4.12). They should rotate the wood so that each side gets sanded. For more delicate operations, small pieces of sandpaper can be used, but it requires good fine motor skills to work effectively with sandpaper.

Pine stripwood, available at most DIY superstores, is a cheap and convenient source of wood. The stripwood comes in various-sized cross-sections, some square and some flatter. The wood is easy to cut with a saw and can be marked effectively with a biro. It will also take felt pen markings without too much spreading. Although stripwood comes in a variety of sizes and shapes, much of it has a 1 cm width. This can be an advantage when children are designing, as they can use 1 cm squared paper (from maths books) to draw a pattern. The pattern can then be cut out and stuck on the wood to help with cutting the pieces.

Sawing safely

- Measure and mark the wood to show where the cut is to be made. A biro works well on wood: it doesn't soak in and spread out like felt tip, or get rubbed off easily like pencil.
- Locate the bench hook over the edge of the table. It is wise to organise children to saw opposite one another, so that the table doesn't get pushed across the floor by several children all sawing energetically on one side.

- Line up the cutting mark with the vertical saw guide. Push the wood firmly against the guide and hold in place. Try to keep fingers well away from the saw by pushing the wood against the guide with the heel of the hand.
- Drop the saw into the guide slot and start sawing by pulling the saw slowly towards the body. It is easier to pull a saw than to push it, so children may need to make several pulling strokes before they can saw easily to and fro.
- Continue to saw until the cut reaches about halfway through the wood, and then relocate the wood so that the cut hangs over the side of the bench hook.
- Saw gently until the saw passes though the wood and the cut section drops off.

Pressing down hard when sawing will result in a curved or sloped end to the wood. Hacksaws are sharp so there is no need to press down at all!

Note: If the wood isn't moved to the side of the bench hook part way through, then the bench hook will be damaged. The children won't notice when they have cut through their piece of wood and will continue to saw through the bench hook.

Although sawing is fun and satisfying, it is good to have an end product in view. A wooden name tag or key fob is an attractive starting point (Figure 4.13). Handmade wooden tags could replace the conventional lolly sticks used by many teachers for picking children's names randomly.

Joining

Wood can be joined using glue, nails, staples or a combination of these. Joints can be simple lap joints where one edge is fastened to the next, or more complicated mitre joints (Figure 4.14). The bench hook should have a 45° saw guide for mitred joints, but it is fiddly to use so stick to lap joints until the children can saw proficiently.

Wood can be glued using a glue gun but PVA glue is equally effective. Advantages of glue gun gluing are that the glue sets rapidly and the nozzle of the gun allows the glue to be placed accurately. PVA glue takes longer to dry and this means that models must be set aside safely for several hours. However, the longer drying time means that things can be adjusted should the joints be knocked out of alignment.

Nails and tacks can be used to join wood. Care should be taken that the nail is the correct size; too thick a nail will split the wood and too long a nail will cause problems as the sharp point will stick out.

Figure 4.13

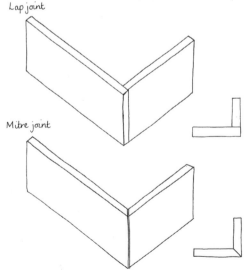

Figure 4.14 Simple wood joints

Wooden frameworks

A simple rectangular frame can be used as the basis for building anything from a model chair to a motorised model fairground ride or a vehicle chassis. Using lap joints to make a rectangular frame can cause problems if the children don't cut the wood absolutely straight. The joints will then be at an angle and the whole structure will look 'wonky' and not be as strong as it could be. To avoid this problem use Jinks' corners (Figure 4.15). A Jinks' corner is a small piece of thin card cut into a right-angled triangle shape. They can be bought from educational suppliers, but are very easy to make from scrap card in the classroom too.

Figure 4.15

A Jinks' corner is glued over each joint and the two pieces of wood are then held firmly at right angles to each other. Usually the joint is sandwiched between two Jinks' corners so the joint is solid and any faults in the sawing are hidden from view!

Figure 4.16 shows a series of rectangular frames made by Y1 children of varying abilities. Different sized Jinks' corners were provided to allow for different levels of fine motor skills. Before the glue had set, the children were able to adjust any joints which had slid out of alignment. Note that one child had great difficulty orientating the triangles correctly. Some adults also find this hard. However, with one exception, the joints have been held together effectively even so. Trim off overhanging edges after the glue has set.

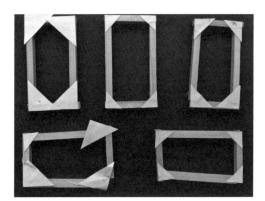

Figure 4.16

Jinks' corners are also useful in making more complicated joints; for example, legs can be added to the frame to form the basis of a table or chair (Figure 4.17)

Joining two rectangular frames will create a box (Figure 4.18). This is the basis for many 3D models, including buildings (Figure 4.19).

To hold the legs or uprights in place, use a large Jinks' corner. Fold it and glue it around the corner of the frame to form a brace (Figure 4.20). Glue the upright into the corner, being generous with the glue so that it is held firmly on both sides and the bottom.

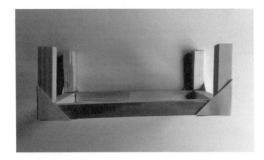

Figure 4.17

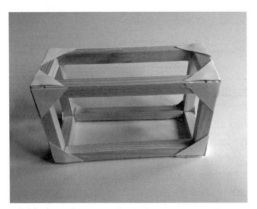

Figure 4.18

Figure 4.19

Figure 4.20

Gluing with Jinks' corners and PVA glue can get very messy. Tape an opened out bin bag or plastic table cloth over the table and leave the frames in place on it to set firmly before peeling them off. Trying to peel models off a rigid surface is almost impossible. If the table is required for lessons, then slide a tray or card under the plastic and you can lift off the plastic and models without disturbing the joints.

Drilling

As models become more sophisticated, children may need to drill holes to insert moving parts. Drilling should be very closely supervised. A hand drill and a selection of wood drill bits (Figure 4.21) are all that is required. There should also be some means of holding the wood to be drilled firmly in place. Ideally, use a drill stand, as these normally incorporate some sort of drilling guide to ensure the hole is positioned accurately. Failing this, use a couple of G clamps or a table-mounted vice. Make sure the children don't drill through onto the table or bench by hanging the portion to be drilled off the side. If this isn't possible, then arrange to drill through into a piece of scrap wood which is thick enough to prevent the bit reaching the table top. Add a tape tag to the bit to indicate how far the bit should enter the wood. This helps children to avoid drilling further than necessary (Figure 4.22).

When clamping wood with G clamps or a vice avoid damage to the item by placing a piece of scrap wood between the item and the clamp.

To make small holes, a bradawl can be used, but once again, care needs to be taken to ensure that the end of the bradawl doesn't continue through the wood into a table top or worse, a hand.

Figure 4.21   **Figure 4.22**

Hammering

Avoid hammers if possible. Hammering a nail into pine stripwood will cause the wood to split. If it is essential to use a hammer, stick to small pin hammers (Figure 4.23) and thin tacks. To hold nails or tacks safely in place use a peg or pliers in order to keep fingers away from the head of the hammer. For thin tacks, a comb makes a useful holder (Figure 4.24).

Figure 4.23
A claw hammer (L) and a pin hammer (R)

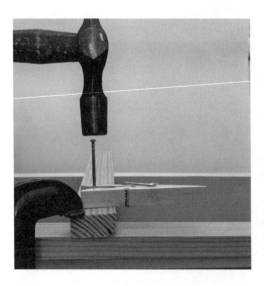

Figure 4.24

THINGS TO CONSIDER

1 Little hands tire easily and sometimes two hands are needed on the saw. You may need to hold the wood for the children.

2 Bench hooks slide along the table. This can be prevented by using a rubbery underlay – this is sold to line drawers to stop cutlery etc. sliding about. Alternatively, clamp the bench hook in place with a G clamp.

3 One adult can only safely supervise four children with saws at one time. Plan the session carefully.

4 Woodwork is messy and noisy. Don't be put off; the benefits and pleasure for the children far outweigh the disadvantages. If you can, use an outside area for sawing so the dust and noise inside can be kept to a minimum.

5 Off-cuts which are too small to be built into structures will rapidly build up. These can be used to stick in the corners of boxes etc. to strengthen the structure. With the aid of double-sided tape, fabric scraps and pens, they can also be made into little people to add play value to any playground or fairground scenes! The ones in Figure 4.25 were made to add interest to a model castle.

Figure 4.25

Plastics

Bright and colourful acrylic can be cut with a bench saw and, if heated, can be bent into interesting curves. It is expensive and requires a solvent-based glue to stick it, but if finances allow, it can be used to produce attractive and modern-looking products.

Construction kits

It would be unusual for a primary classroom to be without a construction kit. Whatever one is available, it can provide children with plenty of opportunities to build structures and to investigate various

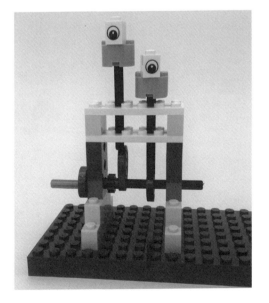

Figure 4.26
A prototype for a cam model built using a construction kit

designs. Many of the items illustrating this book were built as prototypes/mock-ups using construction kits (Figure 4.26) or were designed and built as a result of an idea formed when playing with the kits.

Building frameworks

A framework is a supporting structure used in many construction projects to provide a base on which to build. A framework is usually based on a number of long rods or poles joined together to form a 3D structure. Shorter pieces are used to give the structure strength and support. During D&T lessons, frameworks can be built using easily available items such as lolly sticks, skewers and bamboo canes (Figure 4.27).

The key to a successful framework is to ensure that the structure is well supported and strengthened. Without strengthening, sides will wobble and joints will come loose and the framework will collapse. A triangular shape is much more rigid than a square, so start off frame building by making triangles.

As structures become more complicated, the basic triangle may be hard to use as a building block. In order to keep structures as rigid as possible, use the triangle shape to strengthen and support the corners of squares and rectangles. There are various different ways to do this (Figure 4.28). Most are variations on a Jinks' corner and will strengthen and support a right-angled joint in the structure.

Once children understand the principle of strengthening and supporting joints, they can easily assemble interesting and complex structures (Figure 4.29).

Frameworks can be strengthened further if an outer cover is added. A thin cardboard coat wrapped around a framework will both support and decorate the model.

Fabrics can also be used as a covering (Figure 4.30). Some fabrics such as canvas or Binca (used for cross stitch) are stiff enough already, but this also makes them hard to cut. Fabrics can be stiffened by starching or using a spray, but a cheap and effective method is to paint the fabric with PVA glue. A thin layer of glue spread over one side will produce a stiff fabric that can still be draped and shaped. Plain fabric can be

Figure 4.27 A simple triangular framework used to make a model swing. The triangular side pieces provide strong structures which maintain their shape even when a top bar is added from which to hang the swings.

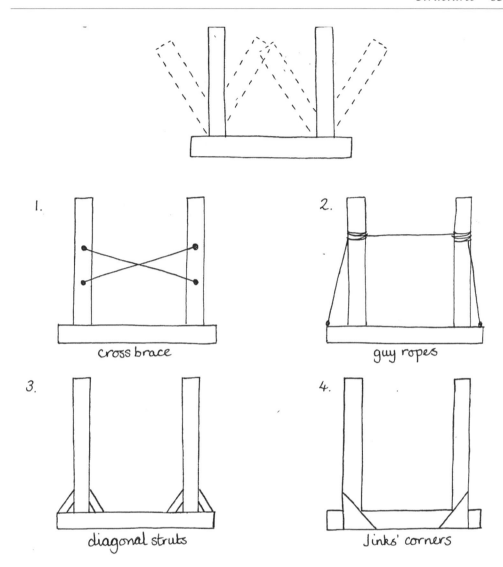

1. cross brace
2. guy ropes
3. diagonal struts
4. Jinks' corners

Figure 4.28 Reinforcing and supporting structures.

Figure 4.29

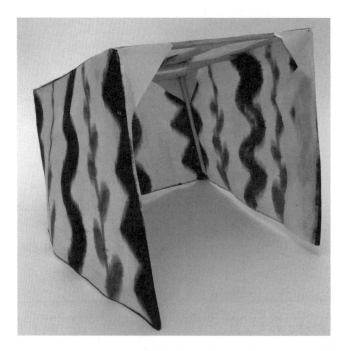

Figure 4.30 A shelter for the Headmaster and his wife for Sports Day. It is covered in PVA-stiffened cotton decorated in the school colours.

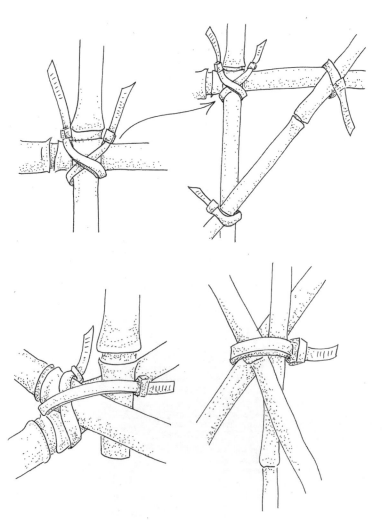

Figure 4.31 Joining bamboo using cable ties

decorated before the glue is added. Watered down PVA (1 part PVA: 1 part water) spreads more easily and still gives a well stiffened fabric, but it will cause felt pen decorations to run if applied on top.

Working with frameworks is a great opportunity to allow the children to make large structures. Bamboo canes make an ideal building material and they can be held together effectively with plastic cable ties (Figure 4.31). Use two cable ties to connect two structural canes together. Then support and strengthen the joint using a small diagonal strut. Very thin bamboo can be bent, gently, to provide a gentle curve to a structure, if necessary.

If no bamboo canes are available, rolling up pages from a broadsheet newspaper can provide an alternative building material, but the rods will be shorter and are more inclined to bend when a cable tie is tightened around them.

To avoid injury, cut off the long end of the cable tie when it has been tightened. Challenge children to make a scale model with skewers and then replicate the design, full size, in bamboo. You may have to suggest a suitable scaling factor.

THINGS TO CONSIDER

1 Modelling clay is not an ideal fixing material as it is liable to move and change shape, but it is useful for building prototypes and testing structures before they are glued more firmly into place.

2 Although bamboo can be bought cheaply, you may be able to get a free supply of canes if you know anyone with a bamboo hedge. Most gardeners will be only too pleased to pull some shoots out. The longer they stay in the ground, the stronger the stems are.

3 A local building site will provide excellent examples of frameworks in use, from scaffolding to roof struts. Remember to warn children of the dangers of these places.

Finishing and decorating

All models and structures need finishing. This might be essential, to cover up the printing on cardboard boxes or to disguise poor joints, but finishing a product should also provide it with an attractive and eye-catching exterior.

There are various methods of decorating and finishing structures (Table 4.1).

Table 4.1

Paint	• Poster paints come in a variety of colours and will cover many surfaces well. The paint can be flaky if applied too thickly and will tend to crack off if the surface is bent, so use at the end of the project.
	• Household emulsion paint is a useful material for covering over the printing on cartons prior to more appropriate decoration. There are paints available that are water-based and don't produce unpleasant solvent odours. Emulsion paint works well on thick card and wood and provides a surface that can be decorated (as parents of small children will know) with pens, paints or stickers. Hang on to half-used cans from home decorating.
Pens	• Felt pens are convenient, easy to use and come in a huge variety of colours. A disadvantage for larger models is that the cheaper pens quickly run out with extended use. Felt pen ink will spread on wood and can spoil careful detail. The ink easily rubs off onto damp hands, so apply varnish or PVA glue after decorating, to protect the finish.
	• Permanent markers work very effectively on wood and card. However, they can also permanently mark school property and uniforms, so should be used with caution.
	• Ball point pens are useful for marking in details such as faces or control panels, but are not advisable for covering large areas.
Fabric	• Fabric, especially felt, can be glued onto wood and card using PVA glue. Glue can soak through to show through on the outer surface, so some care is needed.
	• Double-sided tape is an alternative and effective way to secure fabric but it only works well on smooth fabric (silk, ribbon) as the hairs of rougher fabrics (felt) tend to pull away from the tape.
	• Stitching the fabric around the structure or lacing it in place can provide an alternative way to attach fabric to structures.
Découpage	• Découpage is the art of decorating an object by gluing coloured paper scraps onto it. The object is covered with layers of scraps from magazines, tissue paper, wrapping paper or purpose-manufactured papers. Each layer is sealed with varnish. It is a simple and effective way to decorate wooden or card items. Découpage provides an added advantage to e.g. picture frames as it will also strengthen the structure of the frame.
Stickers	• There are thousands of stickers available and some may provide that extra bit of realism required, such as a face or some control panels, lettering or even go-faster stripes.
Varnish	• Varnish adds a shine and professional finish to a product. Many varnishes contain solvents and care should be taken if using them in school. Varnish needs time to dry and touching it before it is hard will spoil the gloss. Varnish can be painted on with a brush or sprayed on from a can. This is best done outside.
	• PVA glue produces a child-friendly varnish-like finish.

IDEAS FOR PROJECTS

JUNK MODELLING	• scrap challenge – use the junk to make a vehicle or protect an egg dropped from an upstairs window • pet dens
CARDBOARD MODELLING	• desk tidy • scale models of houses, castles and vehicles • toys and homes for small pets
WOODWORK	• photo frames • desk tidy • frameworks for model buildings or theatres • props for school plays
CONSTRUCTION KITS	• prototypes and mock-ups for all projects
FRAMEWORKS	• shelters, tents and homes • playground equipment
PLASTICS	• desk tidy
FABRICS	• tents and shelters

© 2016, *The Really Useful Primary Design and Technology Book*, E. Flinn and S. Patel, Routledge

CROSS-CURRICULAR LINKS

LITERACY	• build a puppet theatre • build a scene from a book, e.g. Goldilocks • make props and scenery for the school play
NUMERACY	• measuring and marking • 2D and 3D shapes and nets • scale models
SCIENCE	• names of trees and uses for the wood they produce • properties of materials used for building structures
GEOGRAPHY	• research the countries that produce wood for carpentry and look at the types of trees grown • look at the ways in which people in poorer countries recycle junk materials to make useful items
HISTORY	• buildings and vehicles throughout history have been made using wood • make model castles or houses to investigate the architecture of the period • follow the development of structural building materials (concrete, iron, glass, etc.) through the ages
RS/RE	• places of worship often have beautifully carved wood on screens, seats or ceilings • examine the architecture of places of worship to look for interesting building materials (marble, stone, etc.) and for supporting structures
MUSIC	• make junk musical instruments – shakers, rattles, etc. • look at the structures of instruments and investigate how the shape and material affects the sound they make
PSHEC	• use knowledge of structures to build shelters for emergency services to use in times of flood or earthquake

© 2016, *The Really Useful Primary Design and Technology Book*, E. Flinn and S. Patel, Routledge

HOW TO MAKE SOME OF THE MODELS ILLUSTRATED IN THIS CHAPTER

Card desk tidy

Base:

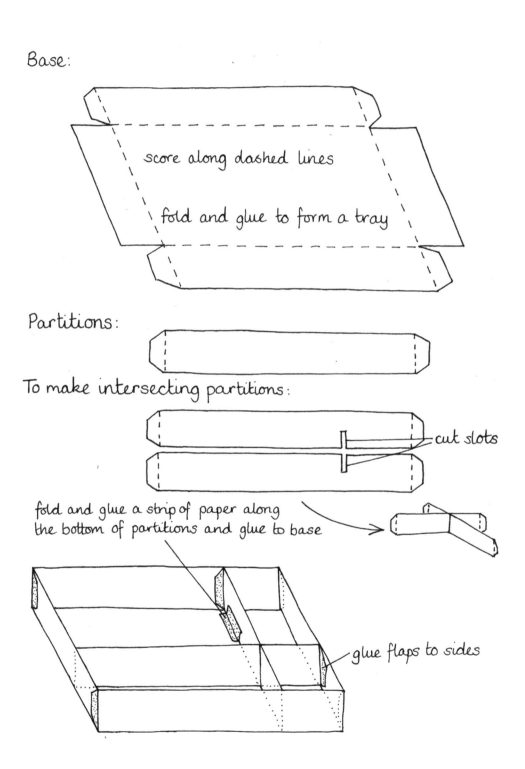

score along dashed lines

fold and glue to form a tray

Partitions:

To make intersecting partitions:

cut slots

fold and glue a strip of paper along
the bottom of partitions and glue to base

glue flaps to sides

© 2016, *The Really Useful Primary Design and Technology Book*, E. Flinn and S. Patel, Routledge

Food box nets

For a full-size sandwich box, enlarge this Figure by 200 per cent. The 2 cm line should be approx. 4 cm long.

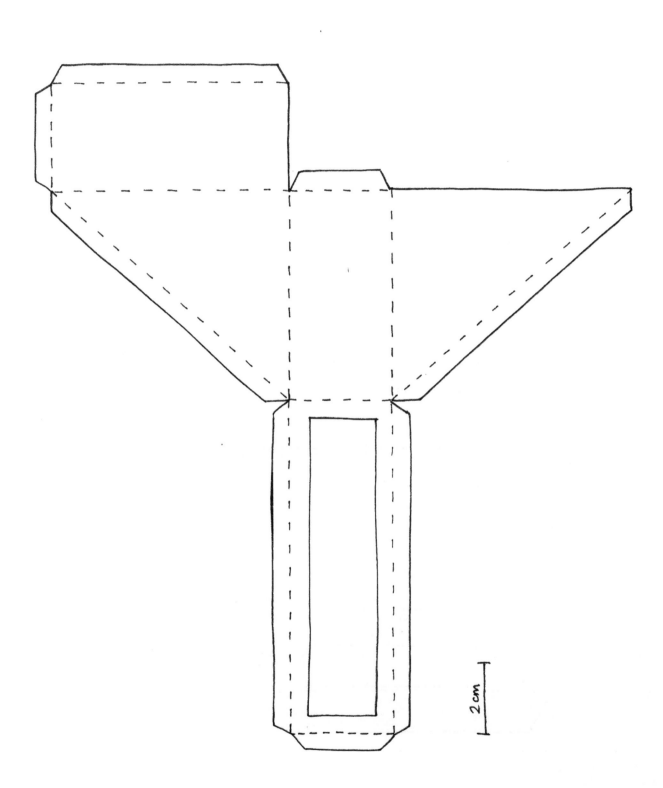

2 cm

© 2016, *The Really Useful Primary Design and Technology Book*, E. Flinn and S. Patel, Routledge

Box with hinged lid

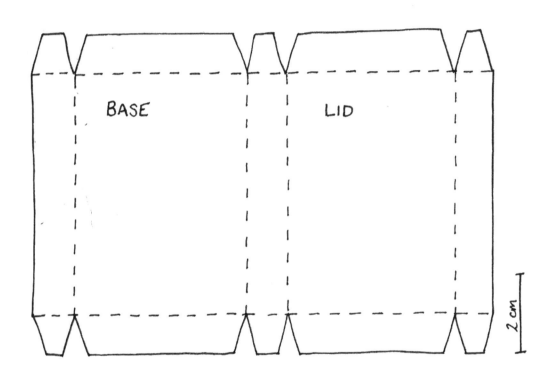

BASE

LID

2 cm

© 2016, *The Really Useful Primary Design and Technology Book*, E. Flinn and S. Patel, Routledge

Table and chair nets

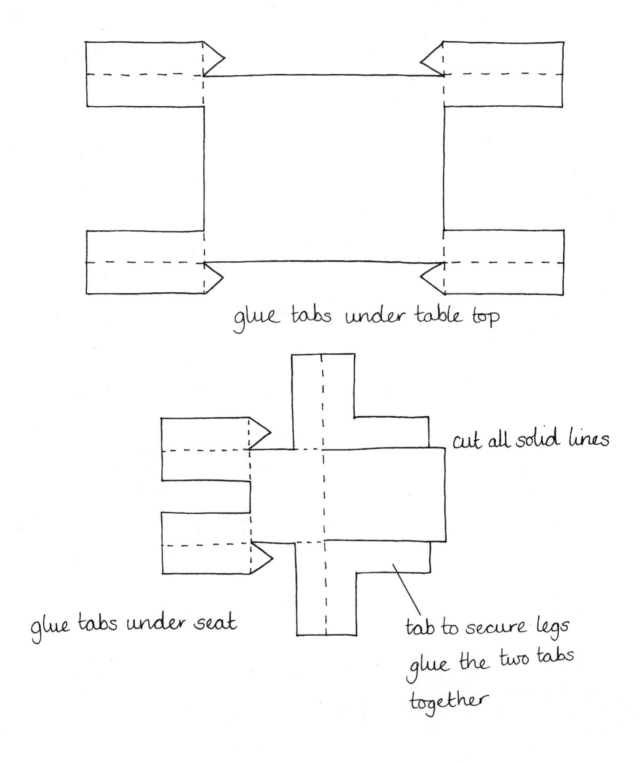

glue tabs under table top

cut all solid lines

glue tabs under seat

tab to secure legs
glue the two tabs
together

© 2016, *The Really Useful Primary Design and Technology Book*, E. Flinn and S. Patel, Routledge

Wooden table and chair

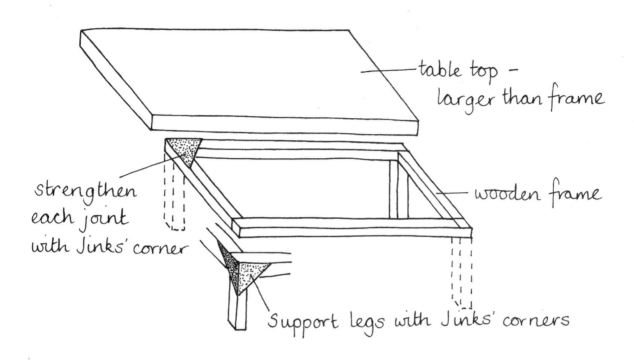

table top – larger than frame

strengthen each joint with Jinks' corner

wooden frame

Support legs with Jinks' corners

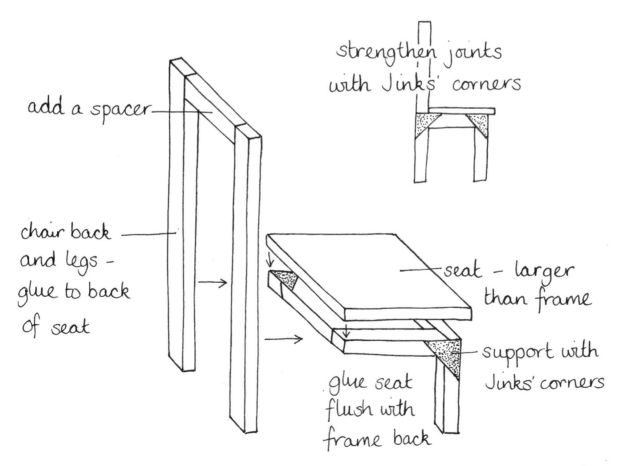

strengthen joints with Jinks' corners

add a spacer

chair back and legs – glue to back of seat

seat – larger than frame

support with Jinks' corners

glue seat flush with frame back

© 2016, *The Really Useful Primary Design and Technology Book*, E. Flinn and S. Patel, Routledge

Wooden house

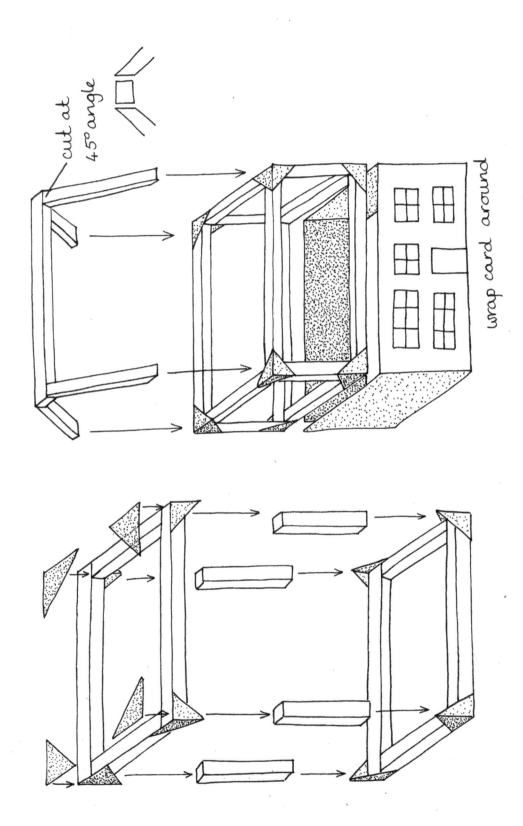

cut at 45° angle

wrap card around

© 2016, *The Really Useful Primary Design and Technology Book*, E. Flinn and S. Patel, Routledge

Wooden desk tidy

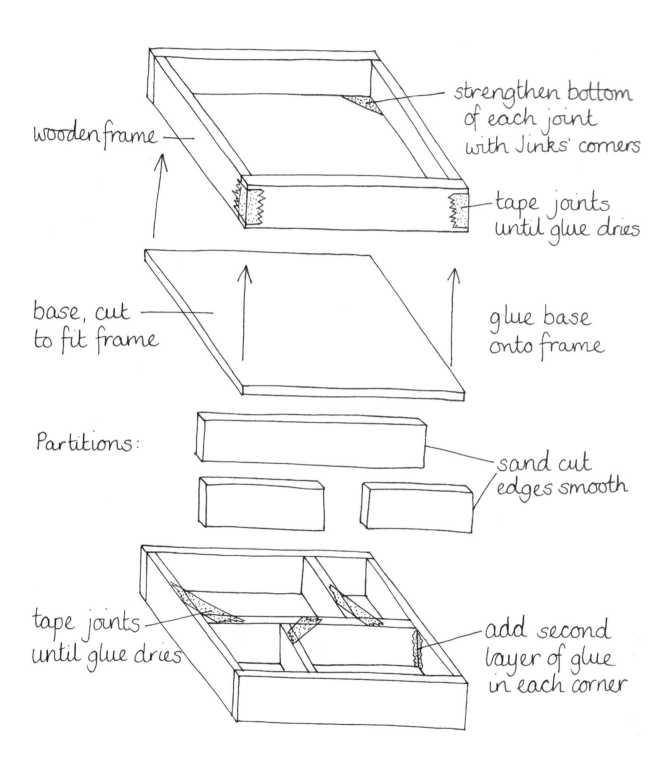

wooden frame

strengthen bottom
of each joint
with Jinks' corners

tape joints
until glue dries

base, cut
to fit frame

glue base
onto frame

Partitions:

sand cut
edges smooth

tape joints
until glue dries

add second
layer of glue
in each corner

© 2016, *The Really Useful Primary Design and Technology Book*, E. Flinn and S. Patel, Routledge

Découpage

3. Spread glue all over

4. Stick on scraps

5. Spread glue all over

6. Stick on more scraps

7. Repeat until scraps cover surface

8. Spread a final layer of glue

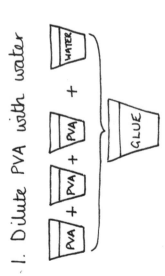

1. Dilute PVA with water

PVA + PVA + PVA + WATER

GLUE

2. Cut scraps of coloured paper

© 2016, *The Really Useful Primary Design and Technology Book*, E. Flinn and S. Patel, Routledge

LESSON PLANS

KS1

Design and build a desk tidy using wood, cardboard or junk.

KS2

Build a full-size shelter which can be packed flat when not in use.

STRUCTURES: KS1 LESSON PLAN

Session	D&T skills	Lesson outline	Resources	Differentiation
1	Research	**Introduction** Discuss the arrangement of the classroom and ask the children how they know where to find things. Introduce the idea that it is easier it is to find things when they are in labelled trays or cupboards. Ask children how easy it is to find things on the messy table. **Main session** Using catalogues or appropriate Internet sites, ask the children to look at what is available to keep a classroom tidy. They should make a list of the different organisation methods they find. As the selection of storage furniture and equipment is huge, help the children by asking them to search for something specific such as ways to keep lunch boxes tidy, or ways to store painting equipment. The children can feed back their findings to the rest of the class. Depending on the resources available, it may be possible to make a chart of all the different ways there are to do the same thing (for example, pencils can be stored in pots or trays or boxes or pencil cases). Ask children which ways of storing things they think are most useful. Is it better to be able to see what is in a box or tray? **Plenary** Return to the messy classroom table and ask how to make it more organised. Explain that the children will be designing and making an organiser to keep things tidy on their tables. Discuss what this organiser might need to hold.	• A messy table (or photo) • School suppliers' catalogues or Internet sites.	This is a visual activity so EAL children should be able to take part. The specialist vocabulary includes the names of most common classroom equipment. Ask HA to note down the costs of the items; this can be used later on to compare to the cost of making their own product.
2	Design and make a mock-up	**Introduction** Show the children the selection of items normally found on their table. Explain that they will be designing and making a tray to hold the equipment for their table. **Main session** In groups, children produce a design for a tray for their table. This may have different sections within it, or it may consist of various tubes and boxes. Provide the children with a piece of paper which shows them the area of their tray. Using this as a pattern, they can draw in the section dividers or positions of the boxes and tubes. Ask the children to use a construction kit to build their design to produce a mock-up.	• A selection of the equipment normally found on the children's tables • Paper patterns to show the area of the organiser tray (A4 is ideal for this)	This activity requires team work and compromise, so support those children who struggle with these concepts. LA may find handling the junk boxes and tubes will help them visualise the storage space available.

© 2016, *The Really Useful Primary Design and Technology Book*, E. Flinn and S. Patel, Routledge

Session	D&T skills	Lesson outline	Resources	Differentiation
		<u>Plenary</u> Discuss the children's ideas and any problems they have had. Explain to the children that they have a choice of materials to make their organiser from – show them the card and wood and any suitable junk items. Ask them to think about what material will be best suited to their design.	• Construction kits • Examples of the materials available for constructing the organiser (card, junk, wood)	Extend: HA by providing some odd-shaped pieces of equipment such as scissors, or small items like paper clips.
3	Design	<u>Introduction</u> Remind the children of the materials they can use. Discuss the properties of the materials. Show the nets for the cardboard boxes and/or discuss how to make a similar box in wood. <u>Main session</u> In groups, children complete a proper design of their organiser. This should show the structure, materials and decoration. Sizes of the various compartments should be included. The children should prepare a story board to show the order in which they will do things. <u>Plenary</u> Each group shows their design and talks the rest of the class through their decisions about shape, material, etc.	• Wood, stiff card and junk materials (tubes, small pots and boxes) • Open box nets of appropriate sizes. • Design sheets, storyboard frames. • Isometric graph paper for 3D drawing.	As above. To help with the storyboard, encourage children to think about their mock-up and the order in which they built it. HA could try drawing a 3D view of their design using isometric paper.
4	Make	<u>Introduction</u> Explain to the children the importance of following their designs accurately. Ask the children about the equipment they will need and any health and safety aspects they need to consider. <u>Main session</u> Children work in groups to make their organiser. Encourage them to follow their story board and do things in a sensible order. <u>Plenary</u> Ask the children about their plans – were they able to follow their story board or were things in the wrong order? Encourage discussion of problems and solutions as this will help others too.	• Wood, saws, bench hooks, sand paper, rulers, pens for marking, glue (either a glue gun or PVA) • Stiff card, scissors, rulers, PVA glue and spreaders, pegs, paper • Nets of open box of the correct size • Junk items	Assist children with cutting as appropriate. LA may need help folding and sticking the box net – have a ready assembled one to help them. Provide a finished wooden box to help with assembly. HA should be encouraged to cut as accurately as possible so that the internal sections fit snugly.

© 2016, *The Really Useful Primary Design and Technology Book*, E. Flinn and S. Patel, Routledge

STRUCTURES: KS1 LESSON PLAN *continued*

Session	D&T skills	Lesson outline	Resources	Differentiation
5	Make	Children continue to make their organisers and finish them off with appropriate decoration.	As above • Finishing materials: paints, pens, tissue for découpage, stickers	As above.
6	Evaluate	**Introduction** Return to the messy classroom table. Ask the children what they hoped to achieve with their organisers. Discuss what evaluating a product entails. **Main session** Children fill their organisers as they have planned. They should evaluate their design and product by considering how well their organiser works. They can think about the ease with which the equipment can be packed away and also how easy it is to pick out a pencil or rubber. They should think about how strong their organiser is – will it last a week? A month? A term? Finally they can look at the finish/decoration and decide whether it is suitable, of good quality and able to withstand regular use. Children should also note down changes they made to their design during the manufacture, and any changes they would make if they could do it all again. **Plenary** The children can evaluate each other's products by pointing out what they think are the good design features.	• Picture of messy classroom table • Evaluation sheet • Pencils, rubbers, glue sticks, etc. to go in the organisers	LA may need help with evaluation: if necessary, record their thoughts for them. Provide HA with approximate costs of the materials used. They can compare this to the prices of commercially available organisers. Ask them to consider why they are more expensive.

© 2016, *The Really Useful Primary Design and Technology Book*, E. Flinn and S. Patel, Routledge

STRUCTURES: KS2 LESSON PLAN

Session	D&T skills	Lesson outline	Resources	Differentiation
1	Research	**Introduction** Discuss with the children how natural disasters such as earthquakes, tsunamis and volcanic eruptions can mean that many people are suddenly made homeless. Use charity and news websites to find data about the numbers affected by recent disasters. **Main session** Ask the children to find out what the most essential needs are for such people (food, water, shelter, sanitation). The children should try to find out where help for affected people comes from and how essential equipment is delivered. Many disaster sites are in remote areas or are made remote by the scale of the disaster, so much of the aid is air-lifted in. Children may be aware of weight restrictions on commercial flights, so they will understand the logistical problems of delivering aid. After a discussion, make a list of the items the UK sends to disaster-struck areas. **Plenary** Collate all information into a large table. Show how aid is divided into various categories such as shelter, food and health. Explain to the children that they are going to focus on designing a shelter that can be used to protect people from wind, rain and sun.	• Photos or video of recent or notable natural disasters • Data from charities about the numbers of people affected and the time it takes to restore normal services • Computers, laptops or tablets for research	Be aware throughout that children or their families may have experienced life as a refugee from either natural disasters or war. If necessary, change the scenario to a fantasy world or space trip to colonise a distant planet. Ask LA to look at pictures of camps for survivors and make a list of what they can see there. They can compare it to a photo of an unaffected town or village. HA can extend their research to cover food and medical aid too. They could also find out about the costs of sending aid to disaster-hit countries.
2	Design	**Introduction** Set the scene: a disaster has struck in a remote area. A shelter is needed to house families of 4–6 people. The shelters must be resistant to strong winds, torrential rain and hot sun. They must fold flat for transport but must be quick and easy to assemble. Show the children the bamboo canes and explain that they will form the framework of the shelter. Show them how a cable tie works. **Main session** In groups, children discuss and design their shelters. They should consider the size and shape of the shelter. At this point in the design process, the children should produce two or more possible designs which can be tested. They can use their knowledge of frameworks to help them to make a strong structure, but must also think about how it can be folded flat for transport.	• Pictures from a natural disaster • Bamboo canes (or newspaper rolls) of various lengths, cable ties • Design sheets, metre sticks, examples of the materials available for prototype making (skewers, lolly sticks, dowels, string, plastic bags, paper, fabric, card, pins, pegs)	Groups will have to learn the art of compromise. Help children who find this hard. Encourage pairs to design their own shelters at this stage. Provide labelled photos of the materials for EAL children. LA could concentrate on the protection from either rain or wind.

© 2016, *The Really Useful Primary Design and Technology Book*, E. Flinn and S. Patel, Routledge

STRUCTURES: KS2 LESSON PLAN continued

Session	D&T skills	Lesson outline	Resources	Differentiation
		<u>Plenary</u> Introduce the concept of a prototype. Explain why designers make prototypes and show the children the materials they can use to make their prototype shelters for testing the next session.		Challenge HA to incorporate a safe place to cook (outside the main shelter, but still protected from the elements).
3	Design and make a prototype	<u>Introduction</u> Recap the explanation of a prototype and the conditions that the shelters need to withstand. <u>Main session</u> Following their designs from the previous session, the groups assemble their prototype shelters. These can be glued together or elastic bands used to represent cable ties. It is hard to rig a shelter securely on a table, so provide a suitable surface into which tent pegs or stakes can be driven: a square of turf, a box of damp sand or a piece of pin board can be used for this, or the prototype can be erected outside on a suitable patch of grass. Once the shelters have been manufactured and all glue is dry, test them. Each shelter is subjected to a blast from the fan and a deluge of water. Using a desk lamp as the sun, check that the inside of the shelter is shady. Once their shelters have been tested, children should note down any problems, any failures and their thoughts on repairs and alterations. <u>Plenary</u> Discuss what the test results showed. Ask children to explain why testing of prototypes is so important. Ask them to think about what would have happened if they had made a full-size shelter and sent it to the disaster without testing it first.	• Table fan, watering can, desk lamp (with filament bulb, not an energy-saving one) thermometer • Skewers, lolly sticks, dowel, string, plastic bags, paper, fabric, card, pins, pegs, elastic bands, glue (either PVA, with spreaders or glue guns) • Turf, box of sand or pin board for erecting shelters	Assist children with poor fine motor skills to glue components. Lolly sticks and dowel are easier to use than skewers. Use modelling clay to hold the components together and put tape over the top. HA may be able to design a test for heat protection. Provide thermometers and lamps and allow them to investigate. Assist groups who find discussion and compromise hard. Provide them with score cards so that it is clear which model has performed best when they come to choose next session.

© 2016, *The Really Useful Primary Design and Technology Book*, E. Flinn and S. Patel, Routledge

Session	D&T skills	Lesson outline	Resources	Differentiation
4	Make	**Introduction** Recap previous session. Each group should decide which of their designs was the most successful and be prepared to make a full-size version of it. Remind them of the criteria for success and of the requirement that the shelter be flat packed and easy to assemble. Demonstrate how to join the bamboo canes with cable ties. **Main session** Allow the groups some time to discuss which of their designs they will use and to make any adjustments to the design in the light of the prototype testing. Once all groups are ready, move to the hall or playground and hand out the bamboo and cable ties. Encourage children to follow their designs. This session should be focused on building the framework; it is not necessary to erect a stable structure yet; the children need to demonstrate the flat pack nature of their design. **Plenary** Each group demonstrates their framework to the rest of the class, showing how it will be erected. Feedback from the teacher and pupils on each design can help with final adjustments.	• Bamboo canes of various lengths, cable ties, dowels, string, rope, washing line, tent pegs or similar, pegs, staples, tape • Large sheets, tarpaulins, plastic bin bags	Lots of adult supervision is required for this activity. Where possible, assign an adult to each group. LA may benefit from having the prototype model available as well as the design when they are building the framework. Challenge HA to make the disassembled shelter fit in to a particular area: tape out a 2x1 m rectangle on the floor and insist that the whole shelter fits inside.
5	Make	**Introduction** Recap the conditions the shelter must withstand. **Main session** Children erect and cover their frameworks in their choice of material. They should ensure that the shelter is securely anchored to the ground. Once completed, the shelters can be tested: • hold on to the framework and shake it well (wind) • empty a bucket of water over the shelter (rain) • ask the group to lie down inside their shelter: is there room for them all? • if possible, leave the shelters up on a sunny day with thermometers inside and out (sun and heat)	• Bamboo canes of various lengths, cable ties, dowels, string, rope, washing line, tent pegs or similar, pegs, staples, tape • Large sheets, tarpaulins, plastic bin bags • Bucket of water or hose, thermometers • Camera • Clipboards, paper and pencils	As above. Children will require help to cover the framework with a tarpaulin. Take photos to assist LA with evaluation, and ask them for their thoughts on the success of the design straight away and record these.

© 2016, *The Really Useful Primary Design and Technology Book*, E. Flinn and S. Patel, Routledge

STRUCTURES: KS2 LESSON PLAN *continued*

Session	D&T skills	Lesson outline	Resources	Differentiation
		It is most exciting if the children can stay inside their shelters for the testing unless they are going to get hurt by falling bamboo or soaked with water. Take photos or video of the testing to support children when they are evaluating. Children should record or grade the results of each test immediately. Plenary Children discuss their successes and failures. Agree on a scoring system to use for evaluation.		
6	Evaluate	Introduction Using photos or video from the previous session, discuss the success of the shelters. Emphasise the criteria for a successful shelter and remind the children of the scoring system. Main session In groups, the children evaluate their shelter, taking into account the design brief. Plenary Compare the children's designs to the tents and shelters used by charities in disaster areas. How are they the same and how do they differ? If possible, find out the cost of a single shelter.	• Evaluation sheets and score cards • Photos or video of shelters • Charity/news websites showing refugee camps and similar	Use photos and record of comments to help LA evaluate. HA could consider the time taken to erect the shelter and the cost of each shelter.

© 2016, *The Really Useful Primary Design and Technology Book*, E. Flinn and S. Patel, Routledge

5 Textiles

Textiles are used to manufacture clothes as well as to provide structure to frameworks. The flexible nature of fabrics means that they can be cut and shaped to fit complicated shapes. Modern textiles have 'super properties', such as fire resistance, temperature regulation and knife/bullet proofing thus extending their uses to more than simply covering something.

WHY TEACH TEXTILES?

There are several compelling reasons why we should teach textiles:

- It provides children with the opportunity to develop fine motor skills (utilising small muscles) by cutting, drawing around templates, sewing, etc.
- It offers activities which promote hand–eye coordination (the ability of the visual system to process information in order to coordinate and control the movement of our hands to accomplish tasks).
- It reinforces the skill to follow multi-step instructions such as learning to sew a new stitch.
- Research by New York University has found that sewing activities engage relaxation responses, which includes lowering blood pressure, calming breathing and reducing body temperature (Reynolds, 2000).

INNOVATORS AND KEY EVENTS

Children in KS2 need to be taught about how key events and individuals in D&T have helped shape the world (Department for Education, 2013).

Some key events

The industrial revolution

Before the industrial revolution, textiles were mainly made in people's homes; consequently, it was known as a cottage industry. Many people spent their whole lives turning raw cotton into threads using a spinning wheel. The threads were spun one at a time and they were then woven on looms in order to make fabric. The process was extremely laborious. Sir Richard Arkwright decided that there must be some way to speed up the process and came up with a machine that was partly based on how clocks work; it controlled the process of spinning cotton fibres and used a water wheel to power the machine. The first Water-Frame was made in 1771 and could easily be replicated. As long as there was a supply of raw cotton, huge quantities of fabric could be produced. This had never been possible before.

The start of waterproofing fabric

The Mackintosh is a waterproof raincoat made from rubberised fabric. It was invented by Charles Macintosh (hence the name, though many writers add the letter k: this variant spelling 'Mackintosh' is now standard) and it was first sold in 1824.

The start of electronic textiles

Electronic textiles (e-textiles) are innovative textile materials that incorporate digital components (including small computers) and electronics directly into the textile itself. Many smart clothes involve the use of e-textiles and remain comfortable as the wires and hard electronics are eliminated, so all you feel is the textile.

Figure 5.1
Charles Macintosh

Key individuals

Heribert Bauer

The snap fastener (also called press stud or popper) is commonly used as an alternative to buttons for fastening clothing. It consists of a pair of interlocking discs made out of metal or plastic; a circular lip under one disc fits into a groove on the top of the other which are held in place once force is applied. Snap fasteners were first patented by the German inventor Heribert Bauer in 1885.

Joseph Shivers

Spandex (aka Lycra) is an anagram of the word 'expands'. It is a synthetic fibre known for its unique properties such as its elasticity; it can regain its shape after being stretched to 600 per cent of its original size. This new fibre was developed in 1949 by Joseph Shivers and his colleagues. It quickly replaced the use of natural rubber (used at the time in a range of garments) as it is breathable, stronger and more durable. Because of its many functional features, it is still popular today and is found in many garments such as swimwear, exercise wear and underwear.

Figure 5.2
Joseph Shivers

George De Mestral

The invention of Velcro (an easy-to-use fastener) was inspired by the burdock burr, a tiny seed covered in hundreds of 'hooks' which naturally catches onto the microscopic loops that cover fur, hair and clothing. George De Mestral (a Swiss mountaineer/inventor) first got the idea when he and his dog became covered in burrs after taking a walk; he was fascinated by the way the burrs clung so securely to his trouser legs. This led to the creation of Velcro, which was patented in 1955.

SUBJECT KNOWLEDGE

Textiles are a type of cloth or material that consists of yarn, which is a continuous strand of twisted threads of natural or synthetic material, such as wool or nylon. Textiles are produced by knotting, weaving, knitting, crocheting, or pressing fibres together.

Beware when using the words fabric, cloth and material; although they are similar in meaning, they do have subtle differences.

- *Fabric* refers to any material made by weaving, knitting or felting, etc. that may be used in the production of further goods, such as garments.
- *Material* refers to the chief ingredients that make up the cloth or textile.
- *Cloth* is also a *fabric* but often refers to a finished piece of fabric used for a purpose such as tea towels and dishcloths.

Methods of textile making

Weaving

Weaving is a method which involves interlacing two distinct sets of yarns or threads at right angles to form a fabric or cloth.

Woven fabrics are made up of a weft, a warp and a selvedge. The *weft* is the yarn going across the width of the fabric, the *warp* is the yarn going down the length of the loom, and together they form a simple criss-cross pattern. The *selvedge* is the side of the fabric where the wefts are doubled back to form a non-fraying edge (see Figure 5.4).

In order to understand the procedure of weaving, children could use natural materials such as twigs, flowers, large leaves (joined together), etc. to create a sensory weave using the school's railings as a large loom.

Figure 5.3 Fabric weave

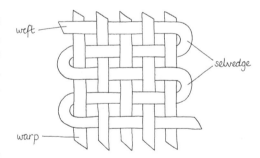

Figure 5.4

Looms

Children can make their own looms either out of card or from a wooden frame (see Chapter 4 Structures).

When creating a circular weave, you must use an odd number of strings (see Figure 5.5). The first inner circle is slightly tricky but once you have mastered that, the rest is easy.

Advantages of weaving

It is easy to create, you can use many different materials and you can differentiate by using different sizes of material, for example thick paper for less able children and thinner paper for more able children. Children can also weave with any material. When it comes to looms, there are many quick and easy ways of making them (see Figures 5.6 and 5.7) but if you don't have time you can always tape the ends of your material to the table and weave without a loom.

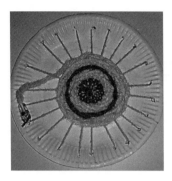
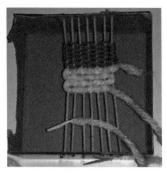

Figure 5.5
Circular weaving using a paper plate

Figure 5.6
Weaving using a cardboard box loom

Figure 5.7
Weaving using a paper loom

Disadvantages of weaving

All the strips of material need to be even, which can be time consuming. Many children find the process complicated so lots of adult support will be needed.

Felting

Felt is produced by shrinking or matting fibres together using moisture, heat and pressure to form a dense fabric that can be cut without fraying the edges. Felt can be made from natural fibres such as wool or synthetic fibres such as acrylic. There are several methods of felting, the easiest to do in school is wet felting.

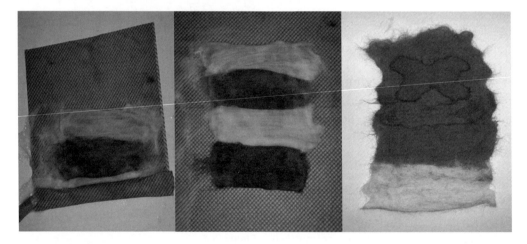

Figure 5.8 Felting

Advantages of felting

It is a really enjoyable activity and it results in a useful and attractive end product.

Disadvantages of felting

Be warned – wet felting is very messy!

Macramé

Knotting, also known as macramé, involves using knots such as the square knot to form a fabric or cloth.

Advantages of macramé

You can make a variety of products such as jewellery, key rings and belts, many of which you cannot make from other textile making methods.

Disadvantages of macramé

It takes a long time to create a large textile. It is very difficult to rectify a mistake.

Figure 5.9
Macramé bracelet made from string

Knitting

Knitting is a method which involves manipulating thread or yarn to create consecutive rows of loops, called stitches. As each row progresses, a new loop is pulled through an existing loop. The active stitches are held on a knitting needle until another loop can be passed through them. There are various stitches, the easiest being garter stitch (knitting every row) and purl (knitting stitch backwards).

Advantages of knitting

Children can make a huge variety of different items which can vary in the level of difficulty, from knitting a scarf to knitting a teddy bear. You can also make it easier for children by providing them with thick needles and chunky yarn.

Disadvantages of knitting

Children will need one-to-one support if they are learning for the first time. Children (and adults!) will need lots of patience when rectifying mistakes.

Crocheting

Crocheting involves using a special needle called a crochet hook to draw the thread or yarn through intertwined loops, like knitting, except that crocheting also requires the thread or yarn to be wrapped around the hook one or more times. This process creates stitches which look similar to knots.

Advantages of crocheting

It is easier to create circular items such as hats, circular coasters and place mats by crocheting as opposed to knitting.

Disadvantages of crocheting

As with knitting, children will need one-to-one support if they are learning this for the first time and children (and adults!) will need lots of patience when rectifying mistakes.

Figure 5.10 Crochet square

NATIONAL CURRICULUM (2014)

In Primary D&T, the topic 'Textiles' is introduced in KS1 as construction materials which children need to select according to their characteristics. In KS2 children are expected to choose these materials according to their functional properties and aesthetic qualities.

Types of fabric

Woven and non-woven fabric

Most fabrics are made by weaving or knitting yarns. However, non-woven fabrics are made by bonding or felting fibres together. A fabric's appearance, properties and end use can be affected by the way in which it was constructed.

Natural fibres made from plants

See Table 5.1.

Table 5.1 The properties of natural fibres made from plants

Fabric	Used for	Properties
Cotton	Jeans, T-shirts, school shirts, bed sheets and towels	Cotton comes in many forms, so its properties vary. For example the cotton in jeans will have very different properties from the cotton in school shirts. Therefore this list of properties is relevant for most cotton: • cool to wear • very absorbent, dries slowly • soft • durable • frays easily • easiest fabric to dye • becomes stronger when wet • low cost • strong
Linen	Summer clothing, tea towels and tablecloths	• fresh and cool to wear • very absorbent, dries quickly • stiffer to handle • durable • can be dyed • expensive • creases easily

Natural fibres made from animals

See Table 5.2.

Synthetic fibres

See Table 5.3.

Table 5.2 The properties of natural fibres made from animals

Fabric	Used for	Properties
Wool	Jumpers, suits, scarves, shawls and blankets	• warm to wear • absorbent • dries slowly • breathable • repels rain • soft or coarse • can shrink when wet • not durable • can be spun into a yarn • can be dyed • expensive • easy to felt • if used in felt it will not fray
Silk	Evening wear, shirts and ties	• warm to wear • absorbent • soft • durable • strongest of the natural fibres • can be dyed • expensive

Table 5.3 The properties of synthetic fibres

Fabric	Used for	Properties
Viscose	Coats, dresses, linings and shirts	• low warmth • absorbent, dries slowly • soft • not durable • can be dyed
Acrylic	Jumpers, fleece jackets, scarves, hats and blankets	• warm to wear • non-absorbent, dries quickly • durable • stiff • difficult to dye
Nylon (Tactel)	Active sportswear, fleece jackets, tights, socks and seat belts	• warm to wear • breathable • repels rain • soft or coarse • durable • can be dyed • strong
Polyester	Raincoats, fleece jackets, towels and medical textiles	• non-absorbent, dries quickly • soft • very durable • difficult to dye • low cost

The two most useful materials for school use are felt (it is cheap to buy and can be used in many projects such as puppets, wallets and brooches) and cotton (it is easily sourced, e.g. lost property box, and can be used in many projects such as clothing, bags and slippers).

When choosing materials for projects, children should be able to explain why they have chosen a particular material and in KS2 children need to choose these materials according to their functional properties and aesthetic qualities (Department for Education, 2013). Therefore it is important to teach the necessary and precise vocabulary, which children sometimes confuse.

Table 5.4 Properties of materials

Aesthetic properties	Functional properties	Comfort properties
Colour	Durability	Warmth
Handle	Strength	Absorbency
Appearance	Water resistance	Softness
	Cost	

KEY SKILLS

Before starting a textiles unit, it is useful to know whether the children have the following skills:

- drawing designs (see Chapter 2 The Design Cycle)
- drawing around templates
- cutting
- sewing (including threading a needle and tying a knot)
- evaluating (see Chapter 2 The Design Cycle)

Differentiation for key skills

Drawing around templates

- Children can either create their own templates or you can provide them.
- For children with poor fine motor skills you can laminate their template so that it is easier for them to draw around it.
- Pin templates to fabric to make the cutting easier and more accurate.

Cutting

- Provide left-handed scissors for those who need them.
- If children struggle cutting around a template, provide them with a fabric wheel cutter/rotary cutter, but be aware of safety issues.

Sewing

- Threading a needle can be made harder or easier depending on the size of needle given. For children who struggle with this skill, provide them with large needles and wool instead of embroidery thread.
- Tying a knot – if this is too difficult children can sellotape the end or overstitch several times.

- Sewing stitches can be simplified by providing children with fabric which has ready-made holes in it. You can make these yourself with a hole punch or buy fabric with pre-punched holes.

Methods of joining textiles

- glue: use fabric glue or PVA
- staple: make sure that the ends are folded around (to create a hem) and be aware of health and safety issues
- sewing: backstitch, running stitch or blanket stitch

Pattern pieces and seams

In KS2 children should be given the opportunity to create 3D products using pattern pieces and seam allowances. A seam is where you stitch to join two or more pieces of fabric together and the seam allowance is the distance between the seam line and the cut edge of the fabric.

It is important to follow the seam line lines accurately so that fabric pieces line up correctly in order to achieve a professional finish. It is useful if children can use a grading ruler but if you don't have one, children can use an ordinary ruler. With this, they mark the seam allowance width at intervals along the seam and then draw a line through all the points. How much seam allowance to add mainly depends on the type of product you are making. For example, if you are making a bag, you will need wider seams as these will need to be stronger, whereas for puppets you want to avoid bulky seams which would affect the final shape.

Methods of marking textiles

The following tools are options for marking textiles:

- pencil/felt-tip/biro: shows up well on lots of fabrics but may not wash out
- washable pens: good alternative to the above as they will come out in the wash (but do check first!)
- chalk pencil: easy to use and rubs off fairly easily

According to the National Curriculum (2014) children in both Key Stages should be able to select from a (wide for Key Stage 2) range of tools and equipment to perform practical tasks. In order to do this, provide children with a range of marking tools and scraps of various fabric so that they can trial them and decide on their tool. Their decision will depend on whether it is sufficiently visible and whether it stains the fabric permanently (this may not be a problem, as children could decide that this is a decorative feature by incorporating it into their design).

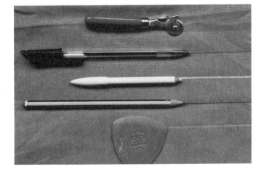

Figure 5.11 Marking fabric

Methods of decorating textiles

Dyeing

This involves changing the colour of fabric (see Tables 5.1–5.3 for which fabrics which can be dyed). An easy and fun method for dyeing is tie-dyeing. The process typically consists of twisting fabric and binding it with string or rubber bands, followed by application of dye(s).White areas are left where the fabric was bound.

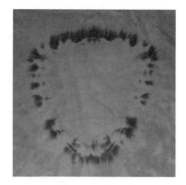

Figure 5.12 Tie-dyed fabric

Health and safety considerations

• Wear rubber gloves and an apron to keep the dye from getting on to skin or clothes.

Top tips for tie-dyeing

• Don't use water that is boiling or very hot, as this will prevent the dye from setting properly.
• Adding salt to your dye mixture makes the colour appear more vibrant.
• You can mix dye colours to make other colours.

Figure 5.13 Appliqué

Appliqué

The word *appliqué* comes from the French word *appliquer*, meaning *to put on*. Appliqué is a technique in which pieces of fabric are 'put on' to a base fabric, these are then sewn or glued in place. Many different types of fabric and thread can be combined to add to the appearance (i.e. texture/colour) and structure (i.e. strength through reinforcement).

Embroidery: This is the use of stitches to create patterns on fabrics. There are many different stitches, from simple back stitches to raised knotted three-dimensional stitches. Beginners can practice drawing a simple design on to a piece of fabric and filling it in with stitches they know, such as satin stitch.

Figure 5.14 Embroidery

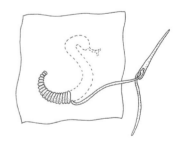

Figure 5.15 Embroidery

Beads and sequins

The application of beads and sequins by sewing is a quick and easy way to enhance the appearance of any fabric.

Figure 5.16 Sewing with beads

Figure 5.17 Sewing with sequins

Textile printing

The easiest form of printing is block printing. Block printing uses a stamp to create a pattern on fabric by dipping the stamp into paint and then printing it onto fabric. Stamps can be made from all sorts of objects, such as dice, buttons, corks, etc., or you can make your own from potatoes (cut the potato in half and cut out a shape with a knife) or use a cotton reel, cover with Blu Tack and make patterns with a pencil – see Figure 5.18).

Figure 5.18 Textile printing

Types of stitches

Running stitch

Running stitch is easy to do but it is weak and it can gather if pulled.

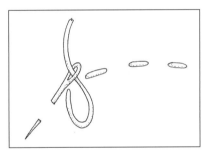

Figure 5.19 How to do running stitch

Back stitch

Back stitch is also easy to do although it takes longer. It is stronger than running stitch so can be used to join textiles or can be used for emphasising outlines.

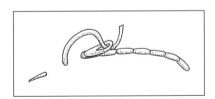

Figure 5.20 How to do backstitch

Whip stitch

Whip stitch is simple to do and can be used to join two pieces of materials together.

Blanket stitch

Blanket stitch has a range of uses, it is decorative and it can prevent the fraying of edges, however it is more complex to create. The first stitch is the most difficult so you could do this for children and let them continue the pattern once you have modelled this. For how to do a blanket stitch, see Figure 5.22.

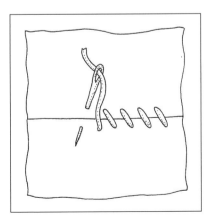

Figure 5.21 How to do whip stitch

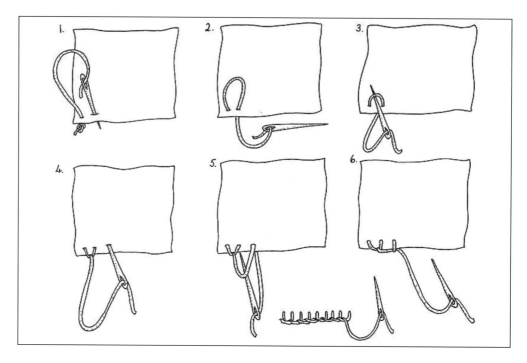

Figure 5.22 How to do blanket stitch

Chain stitch

Chain stitch is a decorative stitch, which is formed by creating a series of looped stitches, to form a chain-like pattern.

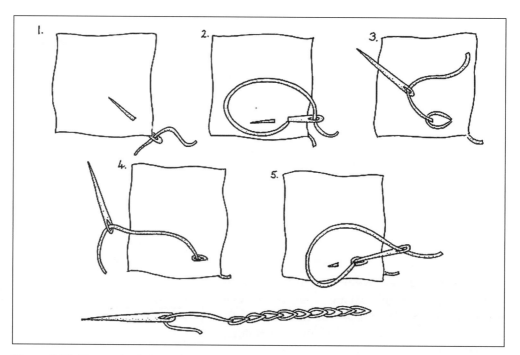

Figure 5.23 How to do chain stitch

Cross stitch

Cross stitch is a decorative stitch which is formed by pairs of diagonal stitches of the same length, being crossed in the middle to form an X. If this is the first time children are learning how to create this stitch, use fabric with an open weave, such as Binca as it helps to keep stitches even and accurate.

Figure 5.24 Cross stitch

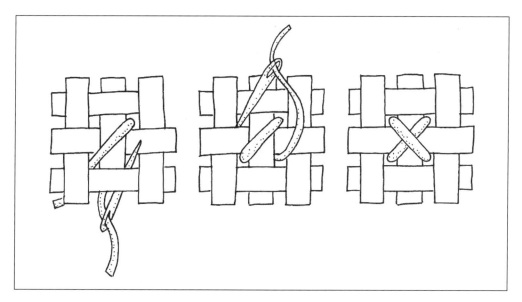

Figure 5.25 How to do cross stitch

Health and safety considerations

When carrying out a risk assessment for this activity, teachers will need to consider the materials, tools and equipment being used. In addition, the following points should be noted:

- needles are very sharp: handle with care or use plastic needles
- take care with the storage of sharp objects, e.g. pins and needles
- felt pads with lines drawn on are useful for storing and checking needles; ongoing work with needles attached can be stored in re-sealable bags
- when using dyes: wear safety clothing, such as gloves and aprons
- to avoid trip hazards make sure walkways are kept clear, ensure all bags and chairs are tucked under tables

THINGS TO CONSIDER

- Non-fraying fabric such as felt will be easier for children to use for textile projects. However, you can prevent fraying by applying glue/nail varnish or cutting fabric with zigzag scissors.

- Binca is useful for practising basic sewing techniques.

- Use needles that are appropriate for the fabric and thread, e.g. small needles for silk, as you see the holes made by the needle, whereas you can get away with larger needles when using other fabric such as cotton and felt.

- To avoid wasting fabric, the children could be given pieces of fabric that are approximately the right size. Discuss appropriate use of materials with the children and demonstrate placing templates in strategic positions so that the least amount of fabric is wasted (most children will naturally go straight for drawing in the middle of the fabric).

- The amount of adult support for textile projects will depend on the previous experience of the children. Use carousel activities to offer more support for sewing.

- When demonstrating stitching use dark thread on light fabric.

- YouTube clips or using a visualiser on the interactive whiteboard are useful resources if you want to demonstrate how to create a particular stitch to the whole class.

- To help children stitch in straight lines or follow a pattern, draw lines on light fabric and get children to follow the line with chosen stitches.

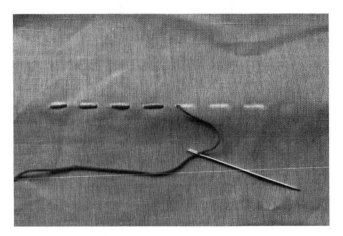

Figure 5.26
Demonstrating running stitch using dark thread on light fabric

IDEAS FOR PROJECTS

Main skill	Suggested material	Project ideas
SEWING	• embroidery thread • cotton • scrap material • felt	• puppets • bags, e.g. book bag • purses/wallets • costumes for Christmas show/ end of Year 6 show • a carrier belt (see lesson plan)
WEAVING	• paper • plastic • ribbon • thread • fabric • twigs • almost anything!	• place mats • bags • bracelets • belts • circular rug (using a hula hoop) • sensory weaves • lanterns
KNITTING	• wool	• scarves • bags • headband
MACRAMÉ	• embroidery thread • cotton twine • leather • string	• key rings • bags • bracelets • belts
CROCHETING	• wool • string	• hats • place mats • bags
FELTING	• wool felt	• jewellery • hats • slippers • bags
APPLIQUÉ	• all of the above	• make a whole class collage

© 2016, *The Really Useful Primary Design and Technology Book*, E. Flinn and S. Patel, Routledge

CROSS-CURRICULAR LINKS

LITERACY	• writing for different purposes and audiences, e.g. puppet show script • speaking and listening: performing a puppet show • writing instructions: how to make e.g. felt • evaluating products • explaining design decisions
NUMERACY	• measuring accurately, e.g. for seams and patterns • scale drawing of design • creating symmetry and patterns, e.g. textile printing
SCIENCE	• properties of materials • shadow puppets
GEOGRAPHY	• look at where products such as puppets are found in the world, how they differ and how they are similar
HISTORY	• look at puppet shows from the past; compare and contrast • look at how products such as bags have changed over time • look at methods such as felting and compare how these have changed over time • research how key events in D&T have helped shape the world, e.g. industrial revolution • research how key individuals in D&T have helped shape textiles, e.g. Charles Macintosh, Joseph Shiver, Heribert Bauer
RS/RE	• puppet show could have a religious theme
MUSIC	• creating music for the puppet show • create music for a fashion show to showcase final products
PSHEC	.• puppet show to illustrate the SEAL theme 'getting on and falling out'
COMPUTING	• use CAD to design products • use the Internet to research • stop-action puppets and animation • discover how technology has had an impact on the designing and making of products, e.g. CAD, CAM
MFL	• puppet show in French/Spanish/German

© 2016, *The Really Useful Primary Design and Technology Book*, E. Flinn and S. Patel, Routledge

HOW TO MAKE SOME OF THE MODELS ILLUSTRATED IN THIS CHAPTER

How to make a puppet

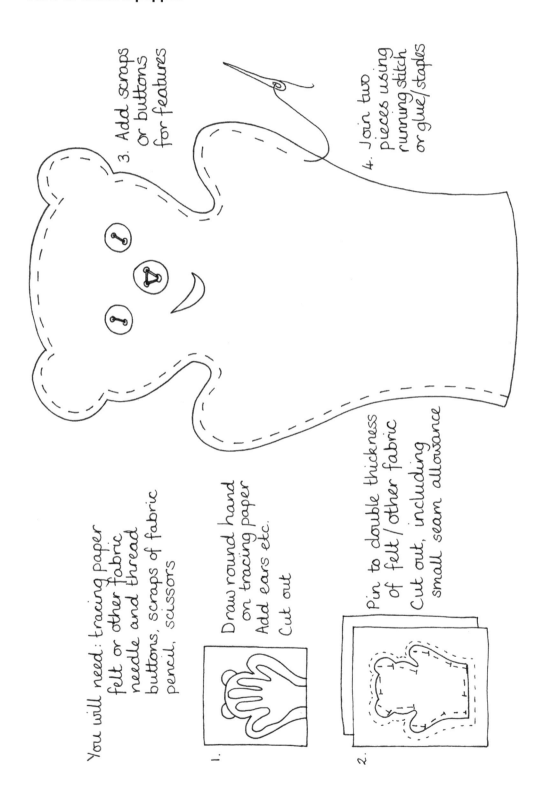

3. Add scraps or buttons for features

4. Join two pieces using running stitch or glue/staples

You will need: tracing paper felt or other fabric needle and thread buttons, scraps of fabric pencil, scissors

1. Draw round hand on tracing paper Add ears etc. Cut out

2. Pin to double thickness of felt / other fabric Cut out, including small seam allowance

© 2016, *The Really Useful Primary Design and Technology Book*, E. Flinn and S. Patel, Routledge

How to make a book bag

Things you will need:

newspaper

patterned fabric

needle and and cotton thread

plain fabric

pins

scissors

fabric chalk or pencil

ruler

tape measure

1. Make a prototype out of newspaper (or other paper).

62cm

40 cm

42cm

4cm

© 2016, *The Really Useful Primary Design and Technology Book*, E. Flinn and S. Patel, Routledge

How to make a book bag *continued*

2. Use the pieces as templates. Cut a main piece from the lining, another from the patterned fabric and four handles (two of each fabric).

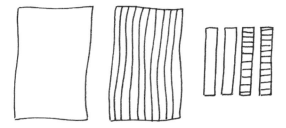

3. Match patterned and lining fabric pieces in pairs, 'right' sides together. Mark 1 cm seam allowance. Pin and sew along three sides, leaving one long side of bag open and a gap in each handle.

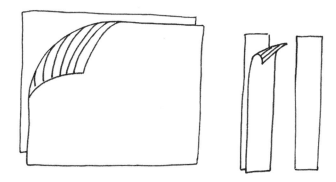

4. Turn bag inside out, using a ruler to poke the corners. Turn unstitched edges of both sides in at the seam allowance and pin.

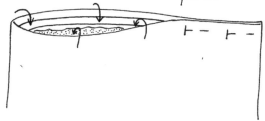

© 2016, *The Really Useful Primary Design and Technology Book*, E. Flinn and S. Patel, Routledge

How to make a book bag *continued*

5. Fold the bag to shape, lining inwards, pin, and over stitch the sides, using thread to match fabric.

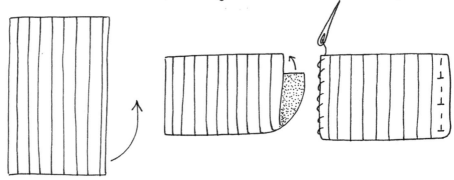

6. Turn handles right side out, using a pencil to poke the fabric through. Tuck in the unstitched edges and sew up the gap.

7. Measure and mark where to attach the handles. Make sure they are not twisted, then sew in place.

© 2016, *The Really Useful Primary Design and Technology Book*, E. Flinn and S. Patel, Routledge

How to make a carrier belt

Things you will need:

newspaper

fabric (same both sides, or plain)

needle and cotton thread

pins

scissors

tape measure

ruler

fabric chalk or pencil

1. Make a prototype out of newspaper.

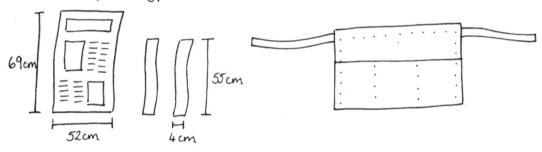

69cm

52cm

55cm

4 cm

2. Use the pieces as templates. Cut two straps and one main piece from the fabric.

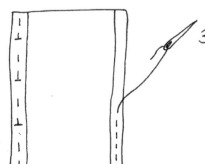

3. Mark 1cm seam allowance on the long sides of the main piece. Fold, pin and stitch the seams.

© 2016, *The Really Useful Primary Design and Technology Book*, E. Flinn and S. Patel, Routledge

How to make a carrier belt *continued*

4. Mark a line across the fabric,
   36 cm from the bottom edge.

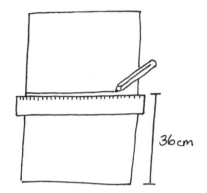

36cm

5. Fold fabric to match the bottom edge to the marked line, then fold again along the marked line.

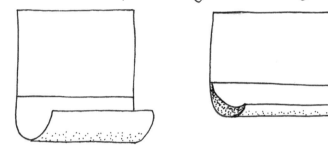

6. Pin and sew along both sides, making the pocket.

7. Choose the number and size of sections for the pocket and mark on the fabric using fabric chalk or pencil. Sew along these marks.

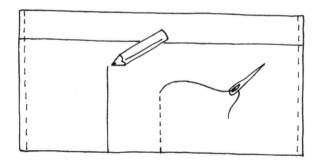

© 2016, *The Really Useful Primary Design and Technology Book*, E. Flinn and S. Patel, Routledge

8. Fold the straps in half lengthways and sew to join edges.

9. Pin and sew straps to back of the carrier belt.

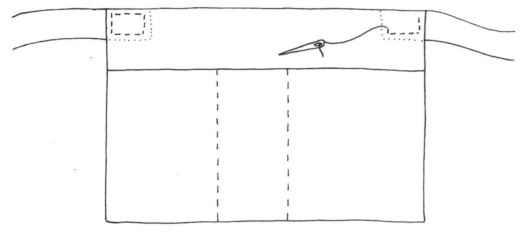

10. Fold top edge of carrier over and sew, securing the straps.

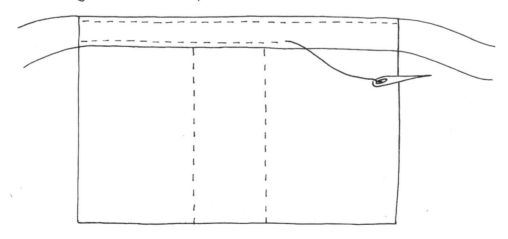

Children can customise their designs to carry their special items.

© 2016, *The Really Useful Primary Design and Technology Book*, E. Flinn and S. Patel, Routledge

How to tie dye

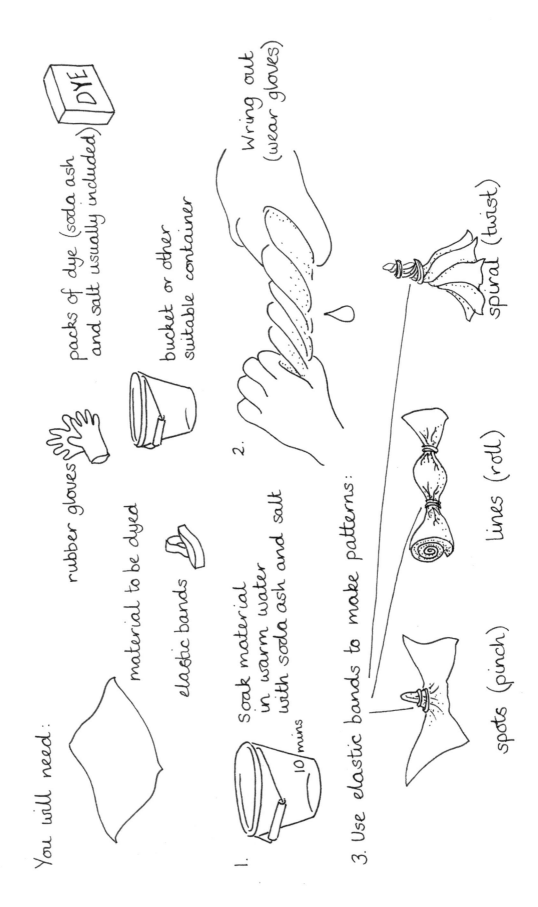

You will need:

material to be dyed

rubber gloves

elastic bands

packs of dye (soda ash and salt usually included)

bucket or other suitable container

DYE

1. Soak material in warm water with soda ash and salt

10 mins

2. Wring out (wear gloves)

3. Use elastic bands to make patterns:

spots (pinch)

lines (roll)

spiral (twist)

© 2016, *The Really Useful Primary Design and Technology Book*, E. Flinn and S. Patel, Routledge

LESSON PLANS

KS1

Design and make an appliqué display

Depending on your class's needs you could make an advent calendar style appliqué where there is a pouch for each child, and it could be used as the behaviour chart so that each pouch holds traffic light cards or marbles. Or, you could make a large wall hanging to store each child's plimsolls for PE.

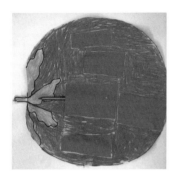  

KS2

Make a carrier belt

TEXTILES: KS1 LESSON PLAN

Session	D&T skills	Lesson outline	Resources	Differentiation
1	Research	**Introduce the problem:** The teacher keeps finding children's pencils on the floor so she/he has decided that the class is going to make a wall hanging to hold everyone's pencils. Ask children what they think a wall hanging is. Show the class some examples. Discuss which ones they like and why. Provide opportunities for children to examine a selection of appliqué. *How have the materials been put together? How might we join our material together? Who might it have been made for? How well has it been made?* *What do they think the word appliqué means?* Explain that it means to sew or stick pieces of material on to a piece of fabric to form pictures or patterns. Encourage the children to come up with some themes for their wall hanging. Give some examples, e.g. mini-beasts, rainforests, under the sea, etc. The theme could relate to your class name or topic. It could be that you or the children decide to make a wall hanging for each table rather than one for the whole class. Allow time for children to sketch some of their initial ideas for themes. Share children's ideas and as a class choose the theme. **Plenary** Introduce the design cycle, explain that the lesson we have done is our research. *What did our research involve us doing? What will we do next lesson (design our appliqué wall hanging)?*	• Examples of appliqué and a wall hanging • Picture of the design cycle	<u>Support</u>: children to sketch one idea. <u>Extension</u>: encourage children to sketch a few ideas.

© 2016, *The Really Useful Primary Design and Technology Book*, E. Flinn and S. Patel, Routledge

Session	D&T skills	Lesson outline	Resources	Differentiation
2	Design	Ask children what they are going to be designing and making in D&T. Ask children what appliqué means and which theme you have decided on. *What is going to be the purpose of the wall hanging? How will this affect the size of the pouch?* Refer back to the Design Cycle – ask children what they did last lesson. *What will they do this lesson?* Show images of the chosen theme. Model how to design a wall hanging with pouches for each child or a wall hanging for each child. Demonstrate to the class that they need to label the colours and features on their design. Plenary Choose some children to show their designs. Get the class to evaluate the designs: *Is there a pouch for each child? Is the pouch large enough? Does it fit in with the chosen theme? Have they labelled the colours and features?*	• Templates for design • Picture of the design cycle • Colouring pencils	Support: provide a template of the wall hanging. Extension: encourage children to draw their design without a template.
3	Design and make a mock-up	Tell the children that they are going to make a mock-up. Explain what this is. Ask why they think designers do this. Using the IWB, let children practice layering templates on top of each other. Discuss which templates will look best on the pouches (ones which are small enough to fit on the front of the pouch). Discuss which colours look best together. Show the class the resources that they will have on their table: a square of coloured paper (10 cm by 10 cm works well); a template of the pouch; shapes which match your theme, e.g. palm tree, ladybird, fish (these should be smaller than the pouch so that they can be stuck onto the front of the pouch); glue; scissors. Children should have their designs out and use these to inform their mock-ups. Write down the steps and model to the class how they will make their mock-up. 1 Choose a coloured square. 2 Choose a coloured pouch. 3 Choose a shape. 4 Cover one side of the shape with the glue and stick it onto the front of the pouch.	• Scissors • Coloured paper square • Coloured paper shapes • Template of a pouch • Glue • Sequins • Felt tips • Children's designs from last lesson • Large pieces of sugar paper	Support: use templates provided. Adult support with joining. Extend: challenge children to design and cut out their own shapes for the pouch, or provide pictures with, for example, the face of a cat for children to cut out and use as pouch.

© 2016, *The Really Useful Primary Design and Technology Book*, E. Flinn and S. Patel, Routledge

TEXTILES: KS1 LESSON PLAN continued

Session	D&T skills	Lesson outline	Resources	Differentiation
		5 Glue the edge of the pouch and stick it in the MIDDLE of the square. 6 Decorate your mock-up with felt tips/sequins. **Plenary** Allow each table to hold up their mock-ups and show the rest of the class. Ask children what the design brief is. *Do they meet the brief? How will they know?* Test the mock-ups by putting a pencil in the pouch. Does it hold? Children to self assess their mock-ups. If creating a whole class wall hanging, stick these onto a large piece of sugar paper (could be shaped or painted to fit in with your theme, e.g. waves of sea, tree, leaf, etc.). If creating table wall hangings, provide each table with a large piece of sugar paper (again this can be shaped to fit in with your theme). Let the children experiment with arranging the pouches on the template. Discuss which arrangements look best and allow children to stick down their pouches.		
4	Make	Remind children of the last lesson and get children to look at their mock-up and discuss if any changes need to be made. E.g. *Was the pouch stuck down correctly so that a pencil could fit in?* Tell children that they will start making their wall hanging in this lesson and that they are going to focus on the skills of drawing around a template and cutting out. Model drawing around a template and show that they must: • keep the template still • make sure they have drawn all the way around the template before removing it • press hard on the pen so that they can see the marks once the template is removed	• PVA glue • Pins/Blu Tack • Biscuit cutters • Cardboard templates • Biros/felt tips • Scissors • Felt	<u>Support</u>: pin/Blu Tack or hold the cardboard cut outs onto the paper and material for the children. <u>Extend</u>: use more complex shapes to draw around.

© 2016, *The Really Useful Primary Design and Technology Book*, E. Flinn and S. Patel, Routledge

Session	D&T skills	Lesson outline	Resources	Differentiation
		Focused practical task 1 Provide children with paper which has a range of lines (straight, curved, zigzag, etc.) to cut along. **Focused practical task 2** Using cardboard templates or biscuit cutters, children practise drawing around these accurately and then cutting them out. **Focused practical task** Repeat tasks 1 and 2 on fabric. Use biros or felt tips to draw with. **Plenary** Children to assess how accurately they can draw around templates and cut out. Share tips and strategies. Tell children that next lesson they will be making the appliqué wall hanging.		
5	Make	Ask children what skills they learned in the last lesson. *What do they need to remember when drawing around a template?* (keep it still until they have finished, draw all the way around the template, press hard on the pen so that they can see the marks). Write down the steps and model to the class how they will make their part of the wall hanging. 1 Choose a coloured square of fabric. 2 Draw around the template on to your fabric for your pouch and cut this out. 3 Choose a template to draw around for the appliqué and cut out. 4 Cover one side of the shape with the glue and stick it onto the front of the pouch. 5 Glue the edge of the pouch and stick it in the MIDDLE of the square. **Plenary** Children to show their pouches. Look back at the steps: *Have they completed each step? Which was the most challenging/easiest step? Why?*	• PVA glue • Felt • Needle and thread • Biscuit cutters • Cardboard templates • Biros/felt tips • Scissors • Pins/Blu Tack • Felt squares 10 cm by 10 cm • Children's designs	<u>Support</u>: pin or hold the cardboard cut outs onto the fabric for the children. <u>Extend</u>: support children to sew their pouch on using running stitch.

© 2016, *The Really Useful Primary Design and Technology Book*, E. Flinn and S. Patel, Routledge

TEXTILES: KS1 LESSON PLAN continued

Session	D&T skills	Lesson outline	Resources	Differentiation
6	Evaluate	Refer children back to the Design Cycle. Discuss what they have done for each part of the cycle. What will they be doing in this lesson? Get children to compare their appliqué to their design: *Is their pouch different from their original design? Why do they think they have made changes?* *What was their design brief? Do they think the wall hanging meets the design brief? How do we know? Allow children to test out their pouches. Can it hold their pencil? Which ones do they like the most? Why?* As a class, produce the success criteria for their pouch: • it can hold a pencil • it fits in with the theme • the fabric is joined securely • it looks attractive Get children to use the success criteria to self assess their product. You could provide this as a tick list for children to complete. If children were given more time, *what would they do differently or add? How could they make pouches stronger?* Plenary Discuss where the best place would be to display the wall hanging/s. *What do they need to consider? (Can children reach their pouch, is it easy to get to?)* Ask children who the user is and what the purpose is. If the school has a sewing machine you can sew the pouches together and reinforce with cardboard or sew/glue onto fabric.	• Design cycle • Design brief • Children's designs • The wall hanging/s • Success criteria for each child	<u>Support</u>: use the tick list. <u>Extend</u>: encourage children to write a wish for how their product could be improved.

© 2016, *The Really Useful Primary Design and Technology Book*, E. Flinn and S. Patel, Routledge

TEXTILES: KS2 LESSON PLAN

Session	D&T skills	Lesson outline	Resources	Differentiation

1	Research	Provide the context: Someone (e.g. child/friend of teacher) has broken their leg and they are going to be on crutches for some time. They need to carry some essential items around with them. As part of differentiation you could give different ability groups different items that their product has to carry, or children could choose their own. Items could include a mobile phone, water bottle, pencil case, purse, etc.
		
		Show a range of different carrier belt products (e.g. money belts, tool belts, rucksacks, carrier belts) that could carry the necessary items. Evaluate the carrier belts in terms of benefits (carrier belts carry items on the front of the body so items are easy to access) and drawbacks (e.g. money belts can only carry very small items so no good for our needs). Explain that we will base our designs on the carrier belt as they best fit the design brief.
		
		Provide aprons on each table. Get children to find out:
		
		Where is there stitching? What type of stitching is used? Why do you think that particular stitching was used? What could you fit in the pouch? How could you make it easier to find items? (smaller separate pouches)
		
		What is the purpose of the part of the aprons which covers the chest? Do we need this part? (no) Which are the essential parts? (tie around waist and pouch) What are the aprons made from? Why are these good materials? Could they be made from any other materials?
		
		Plenary
		Show children the Design Cycle. Discuss why research is important. *How has it helped children with their task?*
		
		What will come next? Which part of the Design Cycle is most important? (all) Why?
		
		Introduce children to some famous textile inventors (see beginning of this chapter). Discuss the importance of designing and making something which has a function, a purpose, a clear user and is innovative. Check that children understand these terms.
			• Items/images of:
			  – money belts
			  – tool belts
			  – rucksacks
			• Apron for each table
			• If possible crutches or a picture of person on crutches
			• Your chosen items, e.g. water bottle, mobile phone, pencil case
			• Picture of the design cycle
				Support: design and make a holder which has one pouch.
				
				Extend: design and make a holder which has more than one pouch and can hold a particular item, e.g. water bottle.

© 2016, *The Really Useful Primary Design and Technology Book*, E. Flinn and S. Patel, Routledge

TEXTILES: KS2 LESSON PLAN continued

Session	D&T skills	Lesson outline	Resources	Differentiation
2	Design	Ask children: *What are they going to be making in their D&T lessons? What is its purpose? Who is the user? What is the function?* Ask children what they did in the last lesson. *So what will they be doing today?* Discuss why children need to design their carrier belts before they make them. Ask children what features a design needs to include. Model how to design a carrier belt including all the essential features. Remind children that the design should fill the page. Discuss and show children what materials will be available. Success criteria: • clear labels: type of stitch, materials, purpose of each section • appropriate size of design, it should fill the page • clearly show the sections • colour/pattern of material <u>Mini plenary</u> Choose a child's design and as a class assess it using the success criteria. Give children time to use the success criteria to peer assess each other's design. *What have children done well? What could they improve on?* Next ask children to write a step by step guide for how to make their carrier belt. Model how to do this. This can link to writing instructions in Literacy. There can be pictures, bullet points for each step or both depending on the children's ability or the user's needs. <u>Plenary</u> Choose some children's step by step guides. *What is good about it? Have they missed any steps? Why are step by step guides useful? What will we be doing in the next lesson?*	• Paper • Pencils • Rulers • Templates • Materials that will be available to make the product.	<u>Support</u>: provide templates of shapes for the straps, main part of carrier belt and section. <u>Extend</u>: use an exploded diagram (see Chapter 2 The Design Cycle).

© 2016, *The Really Useful Primary Design and Technology Book*, E. Flinn and S. Patel, Routledge

Session	D&T skills	Lesson outline	Resources	Differentiation
3	Design and make a prototype	Tell the class that they will be making a prototype based on their initial design. Discuss what a prototype is and why designers use them. Ask the children how many pattern pieces they will have (two for the straps, one for the main part of carrier belt). Then demonstrate how to draw, cut and stick together the pattern pieces. Highlight the importance of being accurate as this will affect the final shape. If children already know how to do running stitch allow them to use this, as it is quick and enables you to see the shape and size of the carrier belt and its sections. Otherwise children can use newspaper and glue/sellotape the templates together. Plenary Children to show their prototypes and describe what has worked well and any changes they need to make. Check that straps are long enough and that section sizes are appropriate for their design brief.	• Glue/Sellotape • J cloths • Thread and needles • Newspaper • Scissors	Support: adult support to help draw and cut out templates. Use newspaper and sellotape. Extend: use J cloths and simple stitching.
4	Make	Ask children what skills they are going to need to make their carrier belt (draw around a template, cut out and sew). Explain that this lesson will focus on practising these skills so that they are the best that they can be for the final product. Model how: • to thread a needle • to sew the running stitch (once children have mastered this move on to the backstitch and, depending on ability, decorative stitches such as whip and chain stitch) • to finish stitches using a knot or overstitching the last stitch Focused practical task Practise how to: • thread a needle • use a ruler to draw a straight line on their material and accurately sew along the lines • stitch accurately and neatly (choose stitch according to ability/experience) • finish stitches either by tying a knot or sewing over the last stitch several times	• Needles, thread • Binca or scrap material such as felt or cotton • Rulers • Scissors • Needles	Support: practise the running stitch. Depending on children's needs you can provide Binca, a pre-threaded needle, a larger needle and wool. Extend: practise decorative stitches such as chain and whip stitch.

© 2016, *The Really Useful Primary Design and Technology Book*, E. Flinn and S. Patel, Routledge

TEXTILES: KS2 LESSON PLAN *continued*

Session	D&T skills	Lesson outline	Resources	Differentiation
		Plenary Discuss the purpose and benefits of particular stitches. *Which stitches would be best for the product?* (backstitch as it is the strongest) Share different strategies to thread the needle and to finish stitches. Self assess their skills: draw around a template, cut out and sew.		
5	Make (you will probably need two lessons for this)	Tell the children that they will be making their carrier belt in this lesson. *What will they need to help them?* (step by step guide, design and materials) If possible have an adult on each table (you could invite parents in for these lessons). Remind children of the importance of being accurate and go through the steps to make their carrier belt: 1 Draw the templates of their carrier belt on the material (straps x2, main part of carrier belt). 2 Pin on the pouches. 3 Stitch the pouches on. 4 Stitch the straps (make sure that they are long enough and securely fastened). 5 If time, decorate their carrier belt using appliqué. **Plenary** Children to share any problems that they had during the making and how they will or have overcome them. *Have their original designs changed? If so why? Do they think famous D&T designers such as Sir James Dyson made changes to his original plans?*	• Children's step by step guide and their design • Needles, thread • Scrap material such as felt or cotton • Rulers • Scissors	Support: adult support with drawing the template and cutting it out. You could provide webbing for the straps so that they don't need to sew around the edges. Extend: use decorative stitches such as chain and whip stitch and/or appliqué. Children can think of ways to customise it to carry special items.

© 2016, *The Really Useful Primary Design and Technology Book*, E. Flinn and S. Patel, Routledge

Session	D&T skills	Lesson outline	Resources	Differentiation
6	Evaluate	Refer children back to the Design Cycle. *What will they be doing in this lesson? What was their design brief? Do you they think the product meets the design brief? How do they know?* Allow children to test out their carrier belts and the carrier belts of others in the class. *Can it carry the specified items? Which do they like the most? Why?* As a class, produce the success criteria for their carrier belt: • it has straps which tie around the body • it can carry several items • items are accessible • it is comfortable to wear Use the success criteria to self assess their carrier belt. Tell children that they are going to write a review of another child's carrier belt. Discuss what should be included in the review; write this up in a list so that children can refer back to it. Provide a list of technical vocabulary to use, such as strength, compartment, names of all stitches, comfortable, secure, etc. Plenary If children were given more time, *what would they do differently or add? How could they make straps more comfortable? How could they make sections stronger?* Discuss the Industrial Revolution and get children to think about the impact of this on textile production today.	• Design Cycle • Copy of the design brief	Support: provide sentence starters and key vocabulary for the review. Extend: encourage children to write about whether the product is innovative and whether it is a gimmick (see Chapter 2 The Design Cycle).

© 2016, *The Really Useful Primary Design and Technology Book*, E. Flinn and S. Patel, Routledge

REFERENCES

Department for Education, (2013). *National Curriculum Primary Handbook.* [online] UK Government. Available at: www.gov.uk/government/collections/national-curriculum [Accessed 3 January. 2016].

Reynolds, F. (2000). Managing depression through needlecraft creative activities: A qualitative study. *Arts Psychotherapy*, *27*(2): 107–44.

6 Mechanisms

A mechanism is a device which takes one type of motion or force, and produces a different one. The role of a mechanism is to make a job easier to do. Some common mechanisms are sliders, levers, linkages, gears, pulleys and cams. Other mechanisms include pneumatics and hydraulics.

WHY TEACH MECHANISMS?

- We live in a mechanised world but the mechanisms we depend on are rarely visible. Looking at simple mechanisms in D&T gives children an understanding of how many machines work.
- The most complex robots in factories rely on cams, levers and linkages to work, so the children are learning a useful, job-related skill.
- Assembling mechanisms helps with the development of fine motor skills and enables children to understand how to plan in 3D.

INNOVATORS AND KEY EVENTS

Children in KS2 should to be taught about how key events and individuals in D&T have helped shape the world (Department for Education, 2013).

Some key events

3500 BC – The wheel

In 3500–3200 BC an unknown Mesopotamian used two solid potter's wheels turned on their sides and joined with an axle to make the first wheels. In 800–600 BC Celts invented the pivoted axle, which allowed easier steering. The pneumatic tyre was patented by Robert William Thomson in 1846 (and reinvented in 1888 by John Boyd Dunlop). By 1967, the first alloy wheels appeared on racing cars, which improved speed and steering.

300 BC – Gears invented

Gears were first used in China in 300 BC in watermills and in mechanisms for arming crossbows. In about 100 BC the Antikythera Mechanism was made in ancient Greece. It used metal gears with wedge-shaped teeth. It is thought that this instrument was a type of mechanical analogue computer used to calculate the movements of stars and planets in astronomy. Gears were not seen again in Europe until the 1100s; however, the technology was used in the Middle East to make calendars and astronomical devices such as astrolabes.

1650 – Start of the study of hydraulics

The French mathematician Blaise Pascal showed, in the 1650s, that liquids cannot be compressed (squashed). In the late 1700s, Joseph Bramah used Pascal's principles of hydraulics to invent a hydraulic engine to pump beer from the cellar to the bar of a London tavern. In 1883 the London Hydraulic Power Company was set up. Hydraulic power was used to raise lifts, theatre curtains and Tower Bridge. These days, hydraulic pistons are used to raise the platforms known as cherry pickers which are used for maintaining street lights and overhead cables.

Some key individuals

Archimedes (287–212 BC)

The Greek mathematician and inventor Archimedes lived on the island of Sicily and wrote many influential works on mechanics. He is credited with being the first person to describe levers and pulleys in mathematical terms. He designed machines to help fight invading Roman ships, including one which, through a series of pulleys, could capsize the ship.

Al-Jazari (1136–1206)

The Persian inventor Al-Jazari was chief engineer at the Artuklu Palace in Anatolia. He invented water-raising machines which used gears, cams and suction pumps. He also produced water clocks, candle clocks and many automata, including a musical robot band, a drinks-serving waitress and a hand washing device with figures which appear offering soap and towels. In 1206 he wrote *The Book of Knowledge of Ingenious Mechanical Devices*, in which he gives detailed instructions about how to make many of his inventions.

SUBJECT KNOWLEDGE

- At KS1 children should be taught to explore and use mechanisms (for example levers, sliders, wheels and axles) in their products.
- At KS2 children should be taught to understand and use mechanical systems in their products (for example, gears, pulleys, cams, levers and linkages).

Sliders

Sliders can be used to make objects move. In simple terms, a push or pull on one end of a rod results in the other end moving.

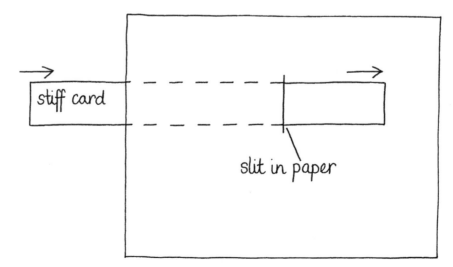

Figure 6.1 A simple slider

Figure 6.2

If there is an object attached to one end of the rod, it will move as a result of this force, making a very simple, but satisfying, moving toy. A stiff rod of card or plastic can be inserted into slots in a piece of cardboard. The card is decorated with the background picture, and the moving object is attached to the end of the slider. As the slider moves, the object will move in relation to the background picture (Figure 6.2). A guide strip stuck on the back of the card makes the movement of the slider smoother and holds it in place.

It is possible to have a more ambitious route for the slider to follow, as shown in Figure 6.3. A strong and stiff slider is used to pull the worm along a wiggly path. Take care when gluing the backing paper in place that there is enough room for the slider to move.

Figure 6.3

Moving objects can be attached to sliders with glue, like the flower in Figure 6. 2. However, if they are to move along a trail like the worm in Figure 6. 3, it is easier to attach them with a split pin. Sometimes it spoils the effect to have the head of the split pin showing. There are two ways round this:

1   glue the moving object on top of the split pin – this is hard if it is a small object;
2   make a card linker – it works like a split pin but is easier to disguise (Figure 6.4).

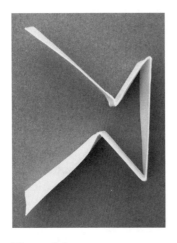  

Figure 6.4
A card linker folded ready, attached to the moving object, and fully assembled in a moving picture

Sometimes, sliders need to be invisible as they are just being used to move a component, but often, the slider forms an important and visible part of the finished project.

The slider in Figure 6.5 has part of each message written on it; the rest of the message is written on the guide strip.

In a magic picture (Figure 6.6), as the slider is pulled out, the picture magically becomes coloured. The slider is made in two layers, one transparent and one opaque. A card guide strip lies between the two layers, covering up the coloured layer until the slider is pulled out of the frame.

Figure 6.5 A sliding message card

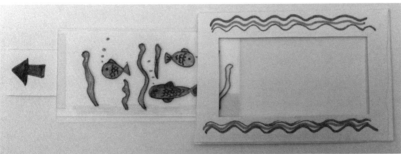

Figure 6.6 A magic picture

A pop-up puppet (Figure 6.7) is a slider mechanism in 3D. Pushing and pulling the rod (slider) reveals and hides the puppet. A dowel is attached to the head of the puppet and passes through the box and out at the end. As the rod is pulled, the fabric puppet folds up and fits inside the box.

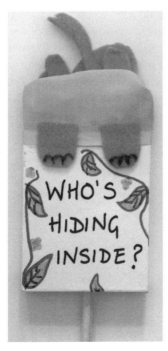

Figure 6.7

THINGS TO CONSIDER

1   Will the slider be visible? If so, will it form part of the picture or will it have to be disguised in some way?

2   How far is the moving part going to move? Is the slider long enough for the complete movement?

Levers

A lever is a simple machine consisting of a rigid bar or rod pivoted at one point along its length (this is called the pivot or fulcrum).

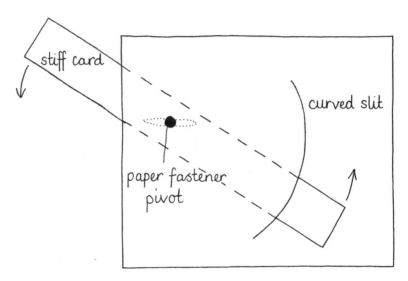

Figure 6.8 A simple lever

A force on one end of the lever produces a response (movement) at the other end. The movement will be in the opposite direction to the original force. So a push *down* results in a movement *up* or a pull *left* results in a movement *right*. Depending on the position of the pivot, the movement can be magnified or diminished (Figure 6.9).

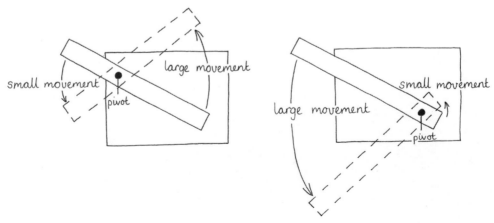

Figure 6.9

Figure 6.10

To magnify a movement, place the pivot near the end where the force acts.

To diminish the effect, place the pivot far away from the force.

In Figure 6.10 the pivot is close to the end of the lever, so a big movement creates quite a small movement of the crocodile's jaw. In this cardboard model, the lever is pivoted using a paper fastener.

Construction kits contain rods and clips that can be used to make a pivot, so 3D levers can be made.

The catapult in Figure 6.11 is a 3D lever. It works very effectively, tossing the ping pong ball about 5 m. Changing the position of the pivot will change the ball's trajectory.

Figure 6.11

THINGS TO CONSIDER

1 Is it possible to disguise the pivot? If so, how can you ensure it won't get stuck or catch on things?

2 The lever will move in a circle around the pivot; you will need to cut a curved slot.

Linkages

By combining the mechanisms of sliders and levers, linkages are produced.

Linkages allow a motion to be directed elsewhere. For example it may cause wheels on a vehicle to turn as a result of a motor spinning somewhere within that vehicle. Linkages can also be used to produce several movements from a single input force. Linkages rely on a series of connectors joined by moving and fixed pivots (Figure 6.12).

A fixed pivot attaches the linkage mechanism to the non-moving base or support. The linkage mechanism can move but only about the pivot.

A moving pivot connects two rods and allows them to move freely, as they are not held on the base.

In the portcullis model in Figure 6.13, the middle paper fastener is a fixed pivot. The ones on either side are moving pivots. Pulling the arm down will cause the gate to lift up vertically.

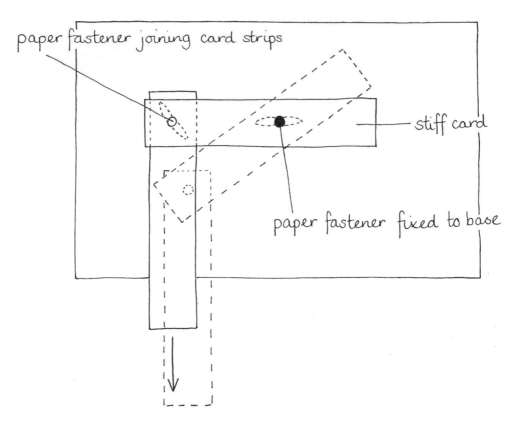

Figure 6.12 A simple linkage

Figure 6.13

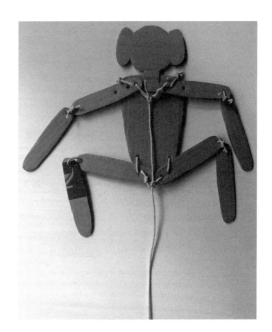

Figure 6.14

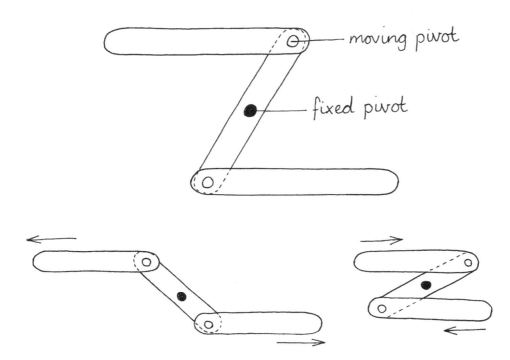

Figure 6.15a

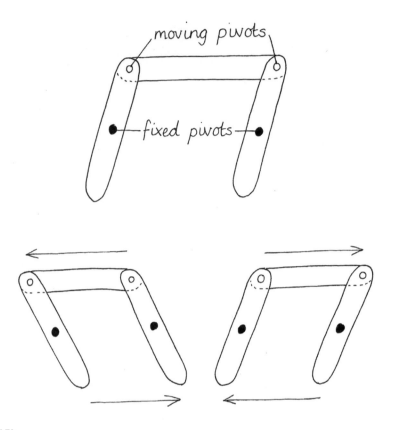

Figure 6.15b

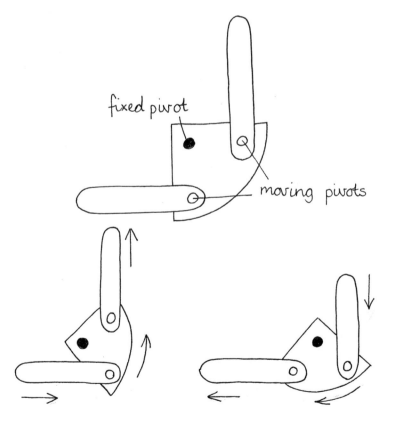

Figure 6.15c

Figure 6.14 shows the reverse of a monkey puppet, showing the string linkages coupled together so that the arms and legs move up and down together when the string is pulled.

By joining two or more rods together with pivots, more complicated and more distant movement can be achieved.

A reverse-motion linkage (Figure 6.15a) changes the direction of motion. So pushing the rod to the left would result in a movement to the right.

A parallel-motion linkage (Figure 6.15b) creates an identical parallel motion. Pulling one rod to the left moves the other rod to the left too.

A bell-crank linkage (Figure 6.15c) changes the direction of movement by 90°. Pulling the rod to the left causes a downwards movement.

THINGS TO CONSIDER

1 Linkages are quite complex to put together. It helps to attach them in a particular order; make a prototype first.

2 Is the base of your model rigid enough to hold the fixed pivots firmly?

3 Linkages made with string or thread (e.g. in a puppet) can get tangled. Is there a way you could prevent this?

Wheels and axles

Wheels allow things to move. Models are much more exciting with moving parts and model vehicles are better if they move forwards and backwards smoothly. A wheel is generally mounted on an axle which allows the wheel to roll. The axle also provides a means of attaching the wheels to the vehicle.

There are two basic methods to get a model to roll on wheels: fixed axles or fixed wheels.

Fixed axles

The axle is fastened firmly to the chassis or frame of the vehicle. It can't move but wheels mounted on it spin round freely. The simplest example of this is a wheel attached to a model with a split pin.

This method works effectively if the wheels are retained by the sides of the chassis. A cotton reel on a dowel is an example of a successful fixed axle system (Figure 6.16). Cotton reels are threaded onto dowels which are fastened securely to the framework or chassis. The cotton reels can move freely and the vehicle will roll forwards if given a gentle push.

Figure 6.16

It is hard to link this wheel-axle arrangement to a motor because the free movement of the wheel makes any linkage (be it gears or pulleys or elastic bands) difficult to connect firmly. However, these systems are simple to make and accuracy of assembly is not as important as it is for the fixed wheel system.

Fixed wheels

In a fixed wheel model, the wheel is fixed firmly to the axle, and the axle is mounted so that it spins freely (Figure 6.17). Thus, the wheel and axle will turn together. Many construction kits use this method; the axles spin inside a special clip or a hole in the base unit and the wheels are clipped or screwed firmly to the axle. Using this approach, the wheels can be fixed inside or outside the chassis; the length of the axle being the only limiting factor.

These models can be more easily motorised, as gears and pulleys can also be attached to the axle and will spin round at the same speed as the wheels. Vehicles with fixed wheels will move in a straight line, provided the axle has been mounted correctly (at right angles to the sides of the vehicle).

Figure 6.17

Mounting axles on models

Axles should be attached firmly and, as far as possible, at right angles to the direction of movement. There are various ways to mount the axle on the chassis of a vehicle. Figure 6.18 show a few ideas, but be innovative and use what is to hand.

Figure 6.18

Fixing wheels to axles

Wheels on fixed axles need to spin, so they should only be held lightly in place, with a small washer or pin on the axle to stop the wheel falling off.

Fixed wheels can be glued to the axle. Place a blob of glue on the axle and slide the wheel slowly over it; the glue should spread neatly into the joint and hold the wheel in place. Add a thread of glue to either side of the wheel for added strength (Figure 6.19). Construction kit wheels may have a tiny anchoring screw which can be tightened until the wheel is held firmly (Figure 6.20). It is worthwhile adding one or two washers between the wheel and the axle support. This helps the axle to spin more smoothly (Figure 6.21).

Figure 6.19

Figure 6.20

Figure 6.21

THINGS TO CONSIDER

1 Wheels and axles can be fiddly to fix and to mount correctly. Construction kits have well designed parts which fit together correctly and may be easier to use until the children have developed their skills.

2 Cutting decent wheels from card or wood is hard. This is an occasion where it is worth buying in resources.

Gears

Two or more gears in a row are called a gear train. The number and size of the gear wheels will affect the speed and direction of spin. Two identical gear wheels, meshing together, will turn in *opposite* directions but at the *same* speed (Figure 6.22).

If there are an odd number of gears in a train the outermost two will rotate in the same direction (Figure 6.23). Note that the size of the middle gear, or idler, is unimportant. The two identical gears on either side now turn at the same speed and in the same direction.

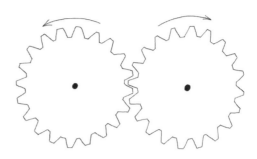

Figure 6.22

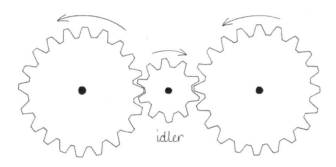

Figure 6.23

Gears can be used to do two important tasks:

1 they can change the speed of rotation;
2 they can change the orientation of rotation by 90°, that is, horizontal to vertical or vertical to horizontal.

Two gears of different sizes, meshing together, will turn at different speeds (and in different directions). The smaller gear will always turn faster. To calculate the difference in speed, count the teeth. In Figure 6.24, the big gear has 60 teeth, the small gear has 20. The tooth ratio is 60:20 or, simplifying, 3:1. This means that the small gear will turn three times for every complete rotation of the larger gear. Therefore, the larger gear will rotate three times slower than the smaller gear. Although the larger gear is rotating slowly, its torque or turning force is increased. This effect is particularly useful when using small motors for powering vehicles. The motor spins fast, but it lacks the torque to turn wheels. Fixing a small gear wheel to the motor and meshing it with a much larger

Figure 6.24

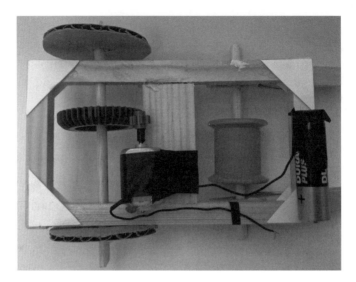

Figure 6.25

Figure 6.26

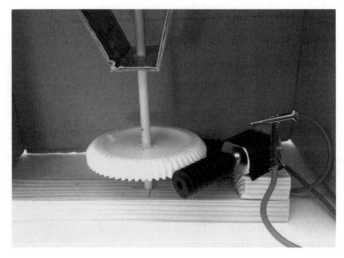

Figure 6.27

Figure 6.28

one on the axle of the vehicle will cause the torque to be increased while the turning speed slows (Figure 6.25). The vehicle will move.

Worm gears (Figure 6.26) convert a large movement into a tiny movement. A whole rotation of the worm gear only moves the wheel round by one cog. This is another useful way to change the speed of rotation. Figure 6.27 shows a spinning planes model. The model is motorised, using a worm gear on the motor to turn the mechanism. As the screw (or worm) can't be moved by the gear wheel, worm gears are good to use in hoists and cranes because the load will not fall back when the motor stops.

Gear wheels at right angles to each other change the orientation of the movement (Figure 6.28). This can be useful if the mechanism or motor used for turning can't be fitted in so that the gears mesh neatly next to each other.

THINGS TO CONSIDER

1 Gears must mesh correctly; if you are making gears from scrap, how can you ensure that this happens?

2 Everything must be held firmly in place, so think about the base that the gears are to be mounted on.

3 To motorise a model the gear on the motor needs to be tiny and the linked gear as big as possible, otherwise the motor will spin ineffectually.

Pulleys

A pulley is a wheel fitted to an axle, allowing it to spin freely. The edges of pulley wheels often have a channel in which a rope or belt fits. Pulleys can play a similar role to gears in moving machines. They can be linked to a motor and used to transfer the turning force of the motor to an axle wheel elsewhere on the model or to change the speed or direction of the motion.

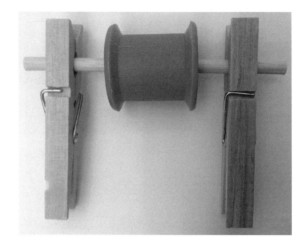

Figure 6.29

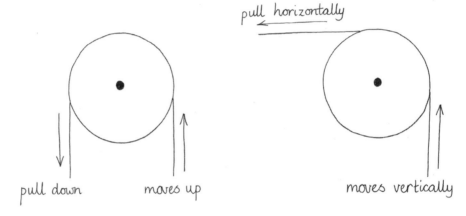

pull horizontally

pull down   moves up   moves vertically

Figure 6.30

Figure 6.29 shows a simple pulley made from a cotton reel mounted on a dowel. Two pegs have been used to hold the dowel securely and these can be easily fastened to models.

Pulleys can be used to:

1 change the direction of a force;
2 change the speed of rotation;
3 multiply the effect of the force (so a small force can be used to move heavy loads).

A single pulley, spinning on an axle, can change the direction of a pulling force (Figure 6.30). This is particularly useful for hoisting flags or hauling up buckets from wells where the pulling force needed (upwards) is difficult (flags) or dangerous (wells) to carry out.

Figure 6.31
The lighthouse keeper can use a pulley to hoist up his rations

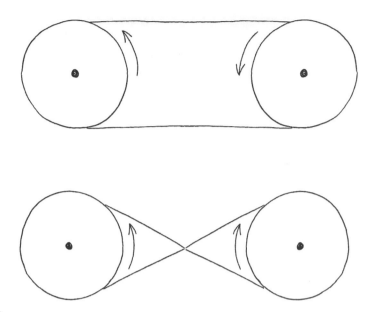

Figure 6.32

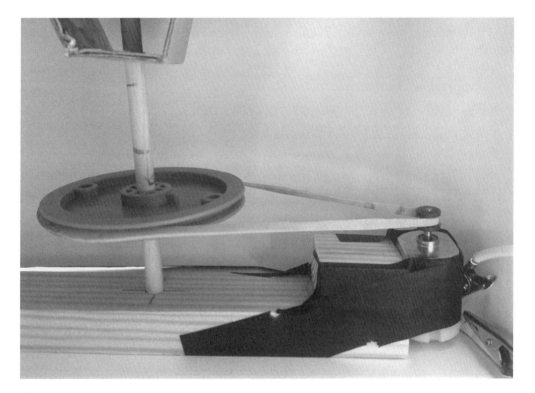

Figure 6.33

If two pulleys are linked together with a belt, they both turn the same way. To get the wheels to turn in opposite directions, simply cross over the linking belt (Figure 6.32).

Pulleys can be used to make something rotate. Like gears, a smaller pulley wheel will spin faster than a large one if they are connected with a drive belt.

Figure 6.33 shows a spinning model powered by pulleys linked to the motor.

The motor and main axle must be held firmly in place or the main axle will be pulled towards the motor due to the tension in the belt. In this example, the motor is taped to the same block of wood into which the spinning axle has been inserted.

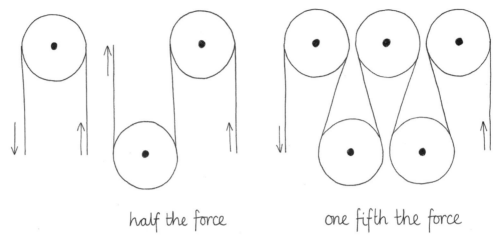

half the force   one fifth the force

Figure 6.34

A pulley system with two or more units can be used to magnify a force. In simple terms, the more pulleys there are, the easier it will be to move a heavy load. Because of the way the pulleys share the force, the addition of each extra pulley reduces the total force required to move the load (Figure 6.34).

Of course, the more pulleys there are in a system, the longer the rope connecting them has to be, and the longer the free rope at the end of the task.

THINGS TO CONSIDER

1 How is the pulley to be fastened to the model?

2 The base on which the pulleys are mounted will need to be sturdy if heavy things are to be moved.

3 If using a multiple pulley system to move a heavy load, think about the amount of string or rope which needs to be threaded through the system. Will this cause a problem as the load is hoisted?

Table 6.1 A comparison of gears and pulleys

Gears	Pulleys
Hard to make from junk as the teeth have to mesh accurately	*Easy to make from junk, e.g. cotton reels*
The gears mesh together closely; there is no belt required to hold them in contact with each other	The belt connecting the two pulleys tends to pull them together, so the axles are under a lot of strain and the pulley wheels may not be straight
Two gears together only ever turn in opposite directions	*Two pulleys together can turn the same way or in opposite directions*
No drive belts	Drive belts (elastic bands) weaken and snap
Have limited uses in model-making as they have to be mounted very accurately in order to mesh properly	*Versatile; can be used in many different model-making situations as the belt can bridge any size of gap*

Gears and pulleys carry out some of the same roles. There are advantages and disadvantages to each system (Table 6.1).

Cams

Cams convert rotation to linear movement.

A cam is a shaped piece of metal or plastic fixed to a rotating shaft. A cam mechanism has four parts: cam, shaft, slide and follower (Figure 6.35). The shaft rotates, turning the cam. The follower is a rod that rests on the edge of the cam. The follower is free to move up and down, but is prevented from moving from side-to-side by the slide.

The follower's movement depends on the shape of the cam. If the cam is perfectly round and the shaft is in the centre of the cam, the follower won't move. If the cam is not round or the shaft is not central, the follower will rise or fall. How the follower moves is determined by the shape of the cam and the position of the shaft.

Some of the popular cam shapes for model-making are: eccentric (off-centre), pear-shaped and snail (Figure 6.36). Each

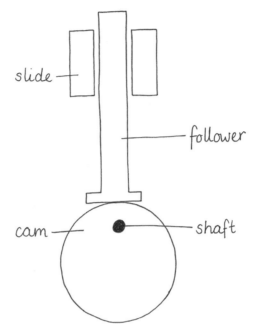

Figure 6.35

of these causes the follower to move in a particular way. The follower may move up or down, or remain stationary (dwell) for a time.

The eccentric cam is circular, but the rotating shaft is off-centre, which affects how it turns. This type of cam produces a smooth, symmetrical rise and fall motion in the follower, which never pauses to dwell (Figure 6.36a).

The pear-shaped cam causes the follower to dwell until the pointed part of the cam approaches. Then the follower is pushed up and, as the point passes, falls before the cycle starts again (Figure 6.36b).

The shape of the snail cam causes the follower to rise smoothly and then drop suddenly at the top of the rise (Figure 6.36c).

To help children to understand the movement produced by different shaped cams, make some small demonstration models (Figure 6.37).

There is friction acting between the edge of the cam and the follower, so the follower will spin round as it moves up and down. While this can add interest to some moving toys, it may be a problem in some cases. To prevent spinning it is best to use a follower with a square cross-section in a straight-edged slide.

Assembling cam machines can be quite hard. The cam must be directly under the follower, which must be able to move freely in the slide. Making a thick cam (two or three commercial card cams stuck together) allows for some sideways movement of the follower. The slide can be formed from an extra strip of card glued across the inside of the box (see Figure 6.38b), or a piece of card can be folded and stuck directly under the hole through which the follower passes (Figure 6.39, left image). A very effective and simple slide can be made from a plastic drinking straw, glued firmly into the hole for the follower (Figure 6.39, left image). A thick wooden frame for the cam mechanism provides an excellent support for the follower but needs to be drilled accurately (Figure 6.39, right image).

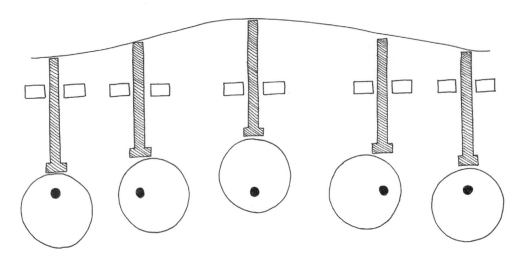

Figure 6.36 a Eccentric cam

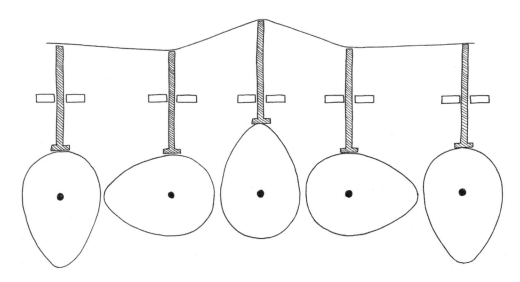

Figure 6.36 b Pear-shaped cam

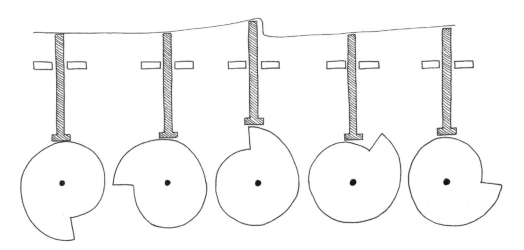

Figure 6.36 c Snail cam

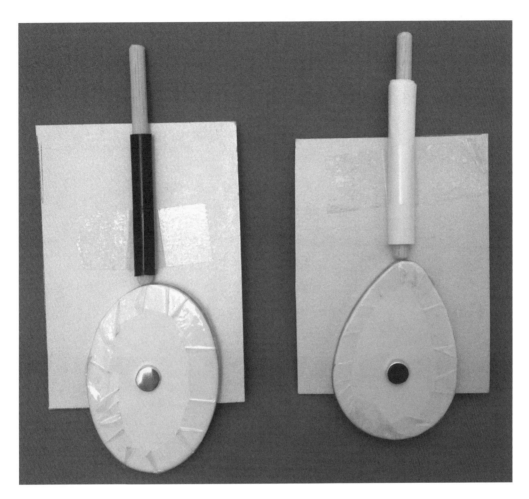

Figure 6.37

Figure 6.38 A cam toy made from scratch – even the cams were cut out of a piece of cardboard rather than bought ready-cut

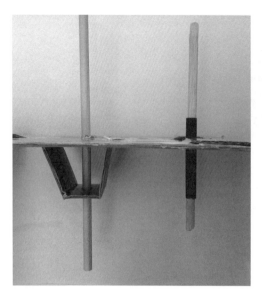
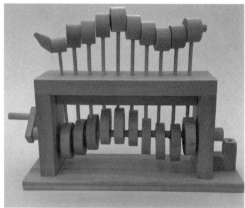

Figure 6.39

Figure 6.40

While cam mechanisms are generally found in 3D moving toys, they can also be used to make 2D moving pictures (Figure 6.40). In this example an eccentric cam is controlling the movement of the owl. The follower is connected, with a moving pivot, to the cam wheel. As the wheel is turned the follower describes an eccentric motion around the central (fixed) pivot.

THINGS TO CONSIDER

If making a moving cam toy using a box to hold the mechanism:

1 make sure the box is large enough for the follower to move up as far as it needs;

2 mount the cams on an axle which gives them clearance all round. Some cams are thicker on one side than the other (e.g. snail, pear-shaped), so make sure they don't hit the edge or bottom of any box;

3 a successful cam machine is one which is assembled with accuracy, so consider buying a kit with pre-punched card or wood.

Pneumatics (and hydraulics)

Pneumatic systems use the energy stored in compressed air to do work. In simple terms, air can be pushed from one container to another and in doing so something can be made to move. For example, the monster's mouth in Figure 6.41 opens as a balloon inside is inflated.

Figure 6.41

Air is a gas; this means it can flow freely and it can be compressed (squashed). Compressed air produces a force which acts on the sides of the container. For example, as air is pushed into a bicycle tyre, it exerts an increasingly strong force on the sides of the tyre until the tyre feels firm. Continued pumping would increase the force even more and might lead to the tyre bursting (think about balloons). Compressed air systems can be used to lift heavy objects. This can be demonstrated by placing a balloon under some books before inflating it. As air enters the balloon, the books rise up. A single balloon attached to a 20cm^3 syringe can easily raise three standard paperback books (Figure 6.42).

Figure 6.42

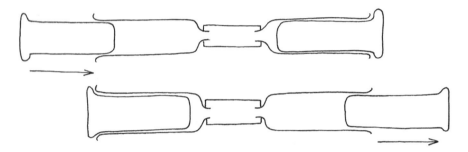

Figure 6.43

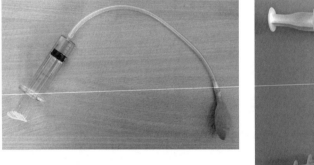 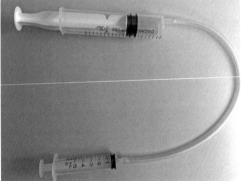

Figures 6.44

Air flows freely along tubes, so pneumatic systems can be controlled from a distance (Figure 6.43). The air in a storage container can be pushed along any length of tubing until it reaches a second container which it inflates (a balloon), or moves (a syringe). If required, the air can then be drawn back through the tubing to the storage container.

Many model systems use syringes and plastic tubing to create a pneumatic system. Syringes are strong and easy to use and fit tightly onto the plastic tubing (Figure 6.44). A simpler method involves taping a balloon onto a squeezy bottle (Figure 6.45).

Using different sized containers at each end of the system can magnify or diminish the effect. A small movement in a big container is converted into a large movement in a small one (Figure 6.46). This can be used very effectively in moving models where a small syringe is hidden inside a model and controlled using small movements of a large syringe which is much easier to manipulate (Figure 6.47).

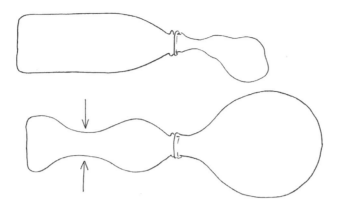

Figure 6.45

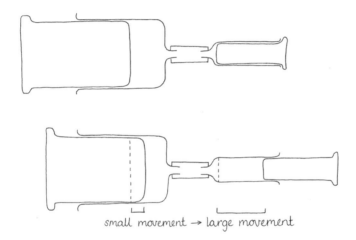

small movement → large movement

Figure 6.46

Figure 6.47

In the pneumatic walker in Figure 6.47 there is a small syringe inside the body of the caterpillar which pushes the legs apart and pulls them together as the large, controlling syringe is pushed in or pulled out. These walkers work best on carpet as they need friction to stop the legs sliding.

Hydraulic mechanisms work in an identical way but instead of air, the system is filled with a liquid: either water or a hydraulic fluid (which contains antifreeze and other chemicals). Systems can be set up in the same way with the same results.

THINGS TO CONSIDER

1   Everything needs to be airtight; a leak at any point will cause loss of pressure. Tape joints tightly and carefully.

2   Old syringes are often not airtight. Some grease around the rubber seal of the plunger may help.

3   If using different-sized syringes, make sure that the volume of air/liquid pushed through doesn't cause the plunger of the smaller syringe to pop out.

4   When using balloons, blow up fully once before use, they will then inflate more easily.

5   Think carefully before creating and using a hydraulic system. Leaks can be rather more dramatic when liquids are involved.

IDEAS FOR PROJECTS

SLIDERS/LEVERS	• moving pictures • greetings cards • story books • simple puppets
LINKAGES	• moving pictures • moving vehicles • puppets
GEARS	• motorised vehicles • spinning toys or models
PULLEYS	• cable cars • transport systems • motorised vehicles and spinning models
CAMS	• 3D moving toys • moving pictures
PNEUMATICS/ HYDRAULICS	• moving toys • machines to help people, e.g. remote control to open a door

© 2016, *The Really Useful Primary Design and Technology Book*, E. Flinn and S. Patel, Routledge

CROSS-CURRICULAR LINKS

LITERACY	• moving pictures to illustrate a story • puppets, with moving arms and legs to act out stories • writing instructions – how to make a moving model
NUMERACY	• sliding pictures of problem and solution • volume measurements in pneumatics designs • simple ratios to calculate the effect of different-sized gears
SCIENCE	• pulleys, gears and levers in upper KS2 • links to forces, e.g. moving heavy loads (pulleys), moving distant loads (pneumatics) • moving models of skeletons and/or particular joints • moving shadow puppets
GEOGRAPHY	• interactive local map, with pull-out information sliders
HISTORY	• moving vehicles, from Roman chariots to Mars Rovers • models of wells and cranes • lifting of heavy weights (pyramid building, coal mining) or heavy sails (Viking ships), using pulleys to reduce force required
RS/RE	• moving picture cards for celebrations • moving pictures to illustrate key stories in religious texts
MUSIC	• Swanee whistles (sliders in 3D) • percussion-playing machines (see lesson plan)
PSHEC	• moving toys designed for children with particular needs, e.g. poor vision, poor coordination

© 2016, *The Really Useful Primary Design and Technology Book*, E. Flinn and S. Patel, Routledge

HOW TO MAKE SOME OF THE MODELS ILLUSTRATED IN THIS CHAPTER

Sliding message card

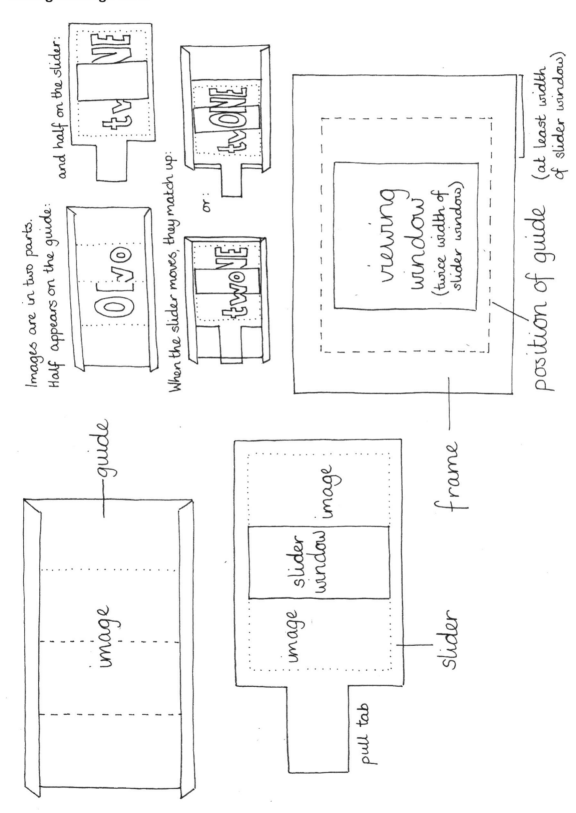

Adapted from *New Pop-Up Paper Projects* by Paul Johnson (Routledge)

© 2016, *The Really Useful Primary Design and Technology Book*, E. Flinn and S. Patel, Routledge

Magic picture

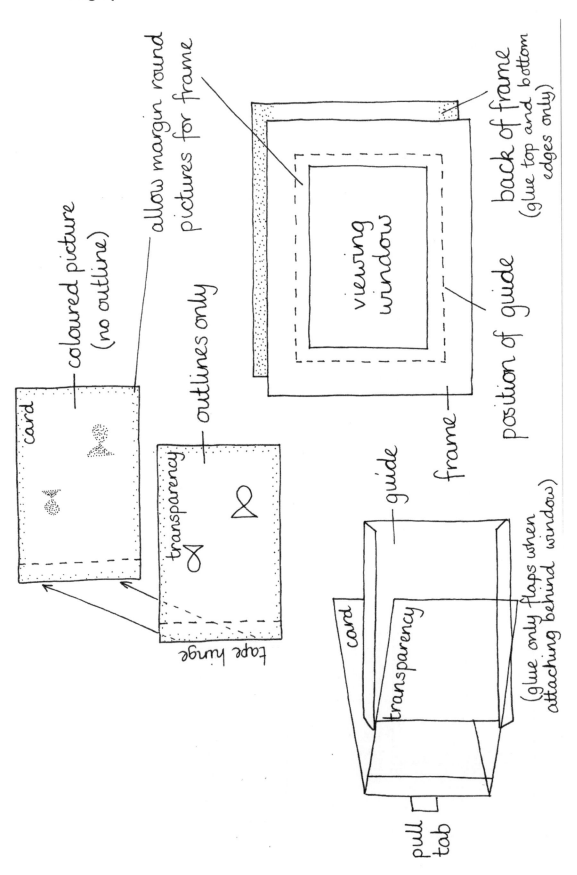

allow margin round pictures for frame

coloured picture (no outline)

outlines only

card

transparency

tape hinge

back of frame (glue top and bottom edges only)

viewing window

position of guide

frame

guide

card

transparency

(glue only flaps when attaching behind window)

pull tab

© 2016, *The Really Useful Primary Design and Technology Book*, E. Flinn and S. Patel, Routledge

Pop-up puppet

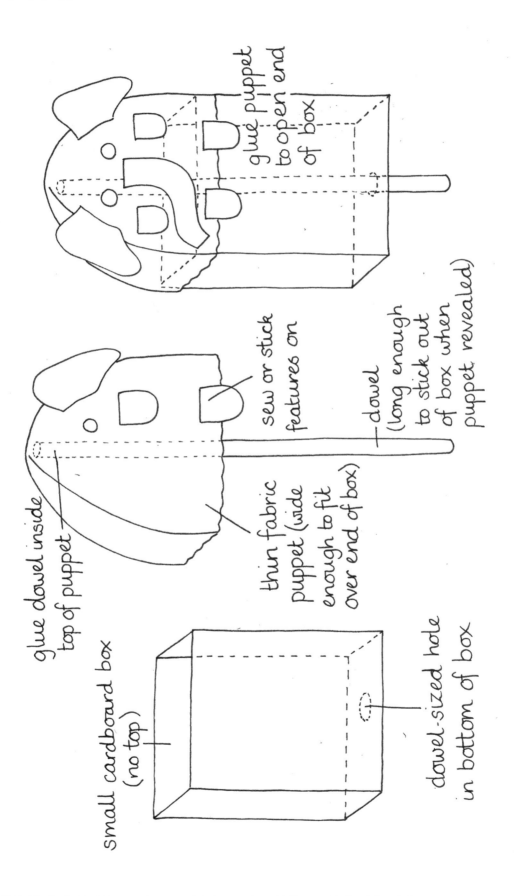

glue puppet to open end of box

sew or stick features on

dowel (long enough to stick out of box when puppet revealed)

glue dowel inside top of puppet

thin fabric puppet (wide enough to fit over end of box)

small cardboard box (no top)

dowel-sized hole in bottom of box

© 2016, *The Really Useful Primary Design and Technology Book*, E. Flinn and S. Patel, Routledge

Cam demonstrator

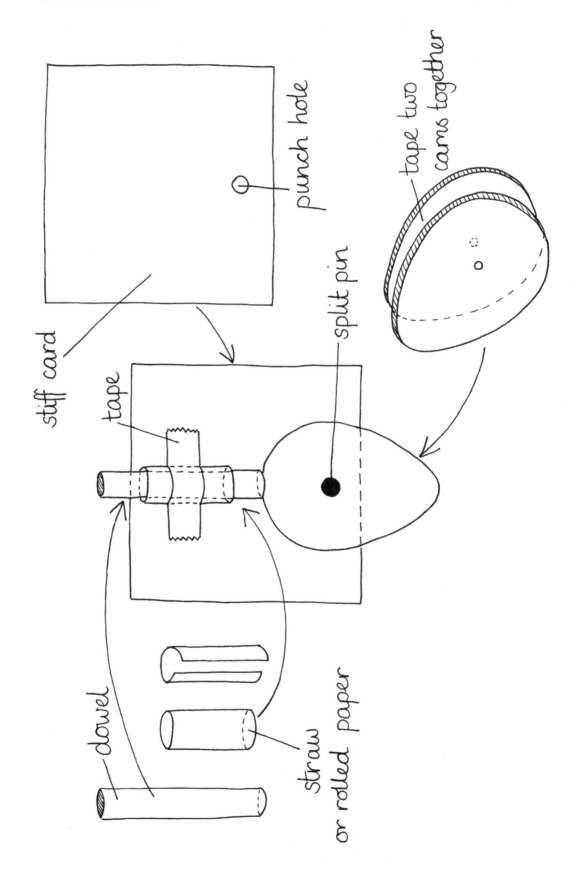

stiff card

punch hole

tape two cams together

split pin

tape

dowel

straw
or rolled paper

© 2016, *The Really Useful Primary Design and Technology Book*, E. Flinn and S. Patel, Routledge

Cam card

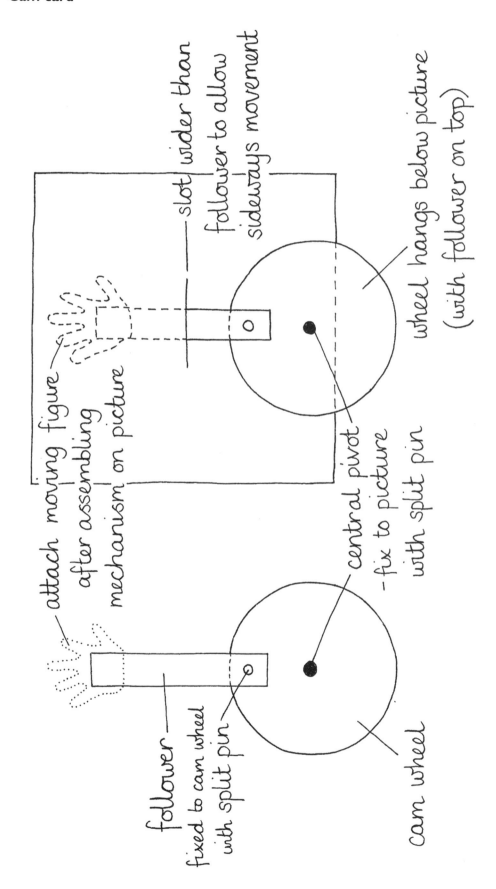

attach moving figure after assembling mechanism on picture

slot wider than follower to allow sideways movement

wheel hangs below picture (with follower on top)

central pivot – fix to picture with split pin

follower fixed to cam wheel with split pin

Cam wheel

© 2016, *The Really Useful Primary Design and Technology Book*, E. Flinn and S. Patel, Routledge

Pneumatic monster

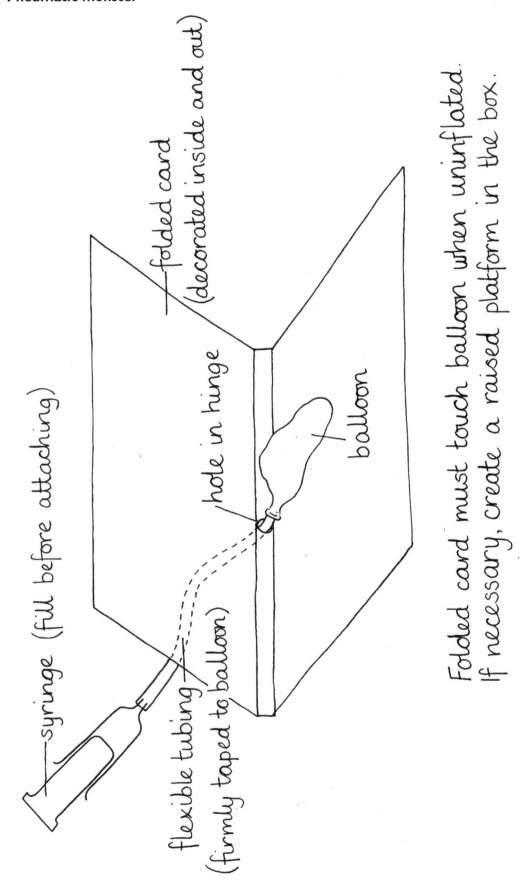

folded card
(decorated inside and out)

hole in hinge

balloon

syringe (fill before attaching)

flexible tubing
(firmly taped to balloon)

Folded card must touch balloon when uninflated.
If necessary, create a raised platform in the box.

© 2016, *The Really Useful Primary Design and Technology Book*, E. Flinn and S. Patel, Routledge

Pneumatic walker

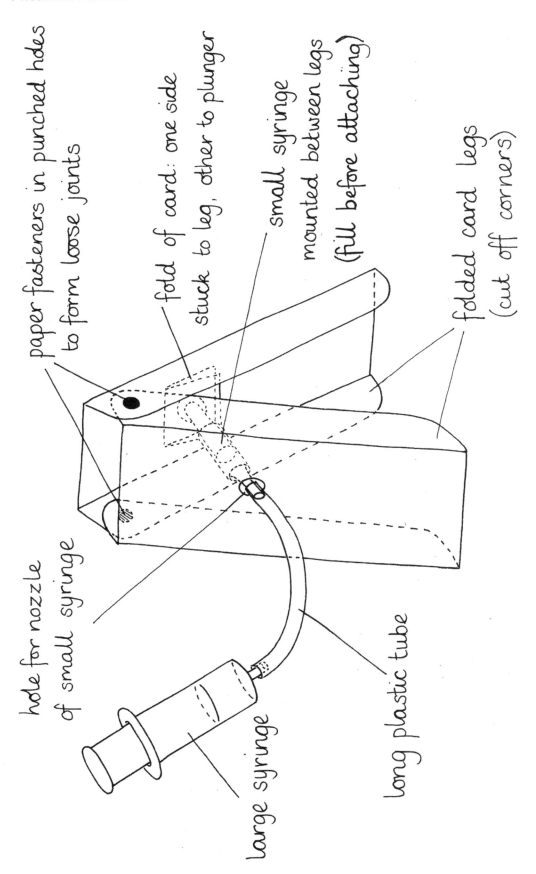

paper fasteners in punched holes to form loose joints

fold of card: one side stuck to leg, other to plunger

small syringe mounted between legs (fill before attaching)

folded card legs (cut off corners)

hole for nozzle of small syringe

large syringe

long plastic tube

© 2016, *The Really Useful Primary Design and Technology Book*, E. Flinn and S. Patel, Routledge

LESSON PLANS

KS1

Make a moving picture and then use your knowledge to make a page for an interactive book.

KS2

Investigate how cams can change circular movement to linear movement and use your knowledge to make a mechanical musical instrument.

 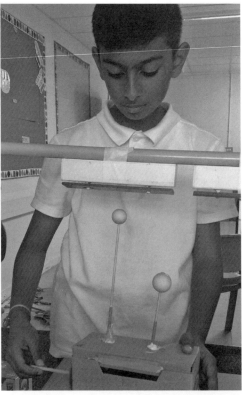

MECHANISMS: KS1 LESSON PLAN

Session	D&T skills	Lesson outline	Resources	Differentiation
1	Research	**Introduction** Show the children a variety of interactive books, e.g. pop-up, lift the flap, moving pictures. Ask the children to suggest why these books may be more fun than an ordinary book. Listen for ideas that suggest that the children are thinking about interacting with the book, making the story more interesting. **Main session** Allow the children to investigate some interactive books. Ask them to try to find out how the moving parts work. This will inevitably mean the books will be taken to pieces, so make sure that this is possible. If this isn't possible, then have some working examples of moving pictures that the children can examine. In groups or pairs, the children should try to draw the mechanism involved, with any annotations to help explain. **Plenary** Discuss the various mechanisms the children have investigated (sliders, levers, wheels, flaps). Did they notice that the moving part was only a small part of the whole picture? Read a suitable story to the children. Ask the children to think about how each page could be illustrated with a moving picture. Show an example of a page. Pick out a few points in the story and start to talk about which bit could move.	• Moving picture books • Old pop-up and moving picture books or examples of different mechanisms • Paper and pencils • A suitable (non-moving) story book	All children can take part in the activities regardless of their ability. Ask HA to draw and annotate various different mechanisms. LA can choose one mechanism to draw and then try to explain how it works. Consider the vocabulary children will need.
2	Design and make a prototype	**Introduction** Read the chosen story again. Remind children that they will be making a moving picture to illustrate the story. However, first of all, they all need to make a *prototype* – explain what this is and why designers make them. The children will use a slider or a lever to make something move. Show them a finished product and go carefully through the parts of the mechanism, showing how things join together.	• Card • Sliders/levers cut to length • Paper fasteners (if required) • Glue • Coloured pens/pencils	HA may find this easy, so give them the opportunity to assemble the mechanisms themselves. Ask them to think about where the slot should be cut in the background picture, let them

© 2016, *The Really Useful Primary Design and Technology Book*, E. Flinn and S. Patel, Routledge

MECHANISMS: KS1 LESSON PLAN *continued*

Session	D&T skills	Lesson outline	Resources	Differentiation
		<u>Main session</u> Children make their own simple moving picture following instructions. <u>Plenary:</u> The children demonstrate their moving pictures. Discuss with them the important questions to consider when planning and making a moving picture: • *What will move?* • *How will it move?* • *What will the mechanism be?* • *How will the mechanism be connected to the picture?* • *Will they need to cut holes in the background picture?*		decide how to mount the mechanism. LA may need help in assembling the components of the picture, to fasten components and to cut slots in appropriate places.
3	Design	<u>Introduction</u> Re-read the story. Remind the children that they will be making a moving picture to illustrate one of the pages. <u>Main session</u> Provide each group with the page of the story they will illustrate. Give them the words or a photocopy of the page. The children should decide what part of the picture will move, making sure it is relevant to the story. They should design the background as well as the moving part. Their design should include diagrams to show how the mechanism will work and how the moving part will be connected. You might decide that it is worthwhile providing a set of components for the children to assemble rather than allowing them to make everything from scratch. The children should produce a *mock-up* – a copy of the page, with words and pictures in place but without the movement. <u>Plenary</u> The children show their mock-ups and explain what will move and the mechanism they plan to use.	• Pages or text from the book chosen • Planning pro-forma, or plain paper for sketches of the design • Pens, pencils • If required: components of the mechanism and an assembled model	HA may work fast, with a clear idea of their finished page, while LA designers may struggle to get their ideas down on paper. Provide some examples of plans to help.

© 2016, *The Really Useful Primary Design and Technology Book*, E. Flinn and S. Patel, Routledge

Session	D&T skills	Lesson outline	Resources	Differentiation
4	Make	<u>Introduction</u> Recap the design brief. Ensure that the children will orient their pages correctly. Discuss where the binding will be and how this might affect the design of the page. <u>Main session</u> Using their designs, the children make their page. They should draw and colour the background as well as assembling the moving parts. If there is a character that appears throughout the book, you can provide a template of the character so it remains the same on all the pages. <u>Plenary</u> Discuss with the children whether they have kept to their design. Ask about technical problems and their solutions. Children with unsolved problems can ask the rest of the class to comment on ways to solve them.	• Thin card, scissors, rulers pens, paints, mechanism components • Example of assembled mechanisms • Templates of any key characters	Help with cutting and assembly may be required by children of all abilities. Use all adults in the class to help. Children may require help in realising their designs – make sure you have checked the designs for potential problems.
5	Make	Children continue to make and finish their page. They should ensure that the moving part moves and that the mechanism is not visible. Encourage them to produce a professional-looking finished product.	As above	As above

© 2016, *The Really Useful Primary Design and Technology Book*, E. Flinn and S. Patel, Routledge

MECHANISMS: KS1 LESSON PLAN *continued*

Session	D&T skills	Lesson outline	Resources	Differentiation
6	Evaluate	**Introduction** Collate the completed pages and read the children their version of the story, working the mechanisms as you go. Explain what evaluation is and why it is important. **Main session** Each group should evaluate their page. Ask the children to consider the following: • *Does the picture illustrate the story well?* • *Does the moving part move smoothly and correctly?* • *Is the moving part linked to the text on the page?* • *Is the mechanism strong enough to be used many times? Are there any parts of the picture that they are not satisfied with?* • *How would they change it if they had to make it again?* Children can record their thoughts in writing, as a score or verbally. Mount each picture carefully so that the mechanisms work and assemble the pages to make a book. Think at the start of the project about how to bind the book, as binders cannot bind the long edge of A3. Make sure the children leave the bound edge free from levers, etc. If you have a large class, you may find you end up with more than one book. This is a perfect opportunity for some more evaluation and a chance to discuss how two identical stories can be so different when many designers work on the project.	• The finished pages, evaluation pro-forma or plain paper for evaluation • Prompt cards suggesting what factors the children should think about • Binder – preferably one that allows spiral or ring binding (only staple in the last resort!)	Provide prompt cards and assistance for LA or EAL children. Ask HA to explain how to solve any mechanical issues and to comment on whether another moving part could be added successfully to the picture.

© 2016, *The Really Useful Primary Design and Technology Book*, E. Flinn and S. Patel, Routledge

MECHANISMS: KS2 LESSON PLAN

Session	D&T skills	Lesson outline	Resources	Differentiation
1	Research	<u>Introduction</u> Show a picture or film of a mechanical instrument and discuss how old these toys are. Have any children ever seen one in action? Do they know how they work? <u>Main session</u> Show the children some pictures or films of mechanical instruments (or even visit a museum). Ask them to look at the movement of the characters on old musical boxes and to consider what might be causing them to move in that way. They should list the different movements that they can see and also make a note of the instruments being played. Encourage the children to draw their ideas of the mechanism. <u>Plenary</u> Children feed back about their research. Most of the machines will involve rotary motion and up-and-down motion and most of the instruments played are percussion ones. Discuss why this is. Introduce mechanisms; remind the children about their knowledge of levers and wheels, etc.	• Interactive whiteboard able to show films from the Internet • Videos of working mechanical musical instruments Suggested link: www.morrismuseum.org/the-guinness-collection-of-instruments-automata/	Cams can be difficult to understand. Provide as many different resources as possible – some children will find a video better than a model and others might need a diagram to help them. EAL children should not be at a disadvantage because the cam vocabulary will be new to all children. However, they may need help with the vocabulary to describe motion (up, down, side-to-side, etc.)
2	Design and make a prototype	<u>Introduction</u> Show a cam toy and explain all the different components and their roles. Discuss with the children how turning a handle can produce an up-and-down movement. Show the children the different shaped cams available. Discuss why they are different shapes. <u>Main session</u> The children should make some small cam models (see Figure 6.37). They can compare the movements and relate this to the shape of the cams. <u>Plenary</u> Ask the children how the cam models could be used to play a percussion instrument. Discuss the fact that the cams won't work if turned upside down and the implications this has for designing a machine to play a percussion instrument.	• Videos of cam machines in action: www.timber kits.com/ (they also produce a worksheet and school kit) • A cam toy • Cardboard cams of different shapes, thin dowel, plastic drinking straws (through which the dowel will slide freely), paper fasteners, cardboard, tape, scissors • Instructions for making a simple cam machine	Assembling the cam models is fairly simple, help children to ensure that the tape is smooth round the edge of the cams. Ask HA children to predict the motion of the follower before making the cam model. The snail cam has the most obvious shape – motion link, LA children may find this cam easiest to understand.

© 2016, *The Really Useful Primary Design and Technology Book*, E. Flinn and S. Patel, Routledge

MECHANISMS: KS2 LESSON PLAN *continued*

Session	D&T skills	Lesson outline	Resources	Differentiation
3	Design	**Introduction** Explain that the children will be making a machine to play a percussion instrument, using a cam mechanism. Show the children the instruments available. Ask the children to decide how each instrument can be made to make a sound. **Main session** In groups, the children should decide what they would like their machine to do, e.g. hit a chime bar or bang a drum. They should consider the force required to make the instrument sound. They need to think about what the beater/drum stick will be made from and how heavy it might be. Once they have made decisions about the instrument, the children should move on to consider the cam mechanism. Allow some group discussion, then talk to the whole class about the problem with the cam. Remind them that the cam cannot be turned upside down. Discuss solutions (the simplest solution is to suspend the instruments above the machine). The finished design should show how the cam will strike the instrument as well as how the axle and turning handle will be assembled. This mechanism is best built inside a rigid cardboard box. **Plenary** Chose groups which have produced very different designs to present their ideas.	• A selection of percussion instruments: wood block, chime bar, drum, tambourine, triangle, cymbal • Suspend one chime bar from a broom stick or metre stick for the children to test their cam • Examples of the beaters and drum sticks normally used to play the instruments • Paper and pencils • A functioning cam machine showing how the axle, cam and follower are set up Provide examples of: • appropriate boxes to house the mechanism • materials available for making the beaters • cam shapes available	Provide a simple cam machine for children to look at and try out. LA children may struggle to see how an instrument can be played 'upside down' so they may need to investigate. HA children could be encouraged to produce a machine which beats in a rhythm. This might involve using more than one cam or designing a new cam shape.

© 2016, *The Really Useful Primary Design and Technology Book*, E. Flinn and S. Patel, Routledge

Session	D&T skills	Lesson outline	Resources	Differentiation
4	Make	**Introduction** Recap the design brief. Encourage the children to use their designs as they build their machines. Ask them to consider the order in which they assemble their machine. **Main session** Using their designs, the children make their machine. Once the machine has been assembled, it is worthwhile testing it out before any final gluing takes place. **Plenary** Give children the opportunity to talk about the problems they have encountered.	• Cardboard boxes, dowel, cams, glue (for card and for wood), straws, materials for beaters (plastic beads, wooden beads, plastic bottle tops, cotton wool), hole punch, scissors, saws and bench hooks, sandpaper • A chime bar suspended on a broom handle, for testing the machines	LA may need assistance assembling their machines from their designs. Provide some examples of cam machines for the children to look at, if you can. HA: see below.
5	Make	Children finish making their machine and make any adjustments as necessary after testing it.	As above	HA: see suggestions for session 6. LA: as above.
6	Evaluate	**Introduction** Discuss with the children the importance of evaluation and decide on the criteria to be considered. **Main session** All machines should be demonstrated. The groups consider how successfully their design has worked. They should record in their evaluation if they made any changes to their design during the assembly process and as well as noting how well their machine played the instrument. There is an opportunity here for filming the machines working. The children could use the films to spot problems or to trouble-shoot. **Plenary** Discuss how the machines could be made better. • *Is it possible to play a tune?* • *Is it possible to play a rhythmic accompaniment to a popular song?*	• Percussion instruments, broom handle, clamps, strong string • Camera or other filming device • Evaluation sheets, with prompts if appropriate	HA could consider how to change their designs to allow a drum to be hit in a conventional manner (i.e. with the drum stick *above* the drum). This is possible using the equipment suggested. LA children could consider how to add a second beater to their machine to produce a more interesting rhythm.

© 2016, *The Really Useful Primary Design and Technology Book*, E. Flinn and S. Patel, Routledge

7 Electronic systems

Electricity is a form of energy that can move along wires in a flow called an electric current. This has made it one of the most useful scientific discoveries ever. These days, it is used to power everything from lights to computers and mobile phones. The flow of electricity can be controlled by switches and resistors so that its effect can be moderated, increased or turned off altogether.

WHY TEACH ELECTRONICS?

- In an electricity-reliant world, it is essential that children gain an understanding of how electronic systems work.
- Studying electronic systems in D&T should build on and help to reinforce the knowledge gained in Science lessons.
- Through their understanding of circuits, children will also develop a respect for the power and potential hazards of electricity in their everyday lives.
- Fine motor skills are developed as children learn how to build a circuit with thin wires and tiny components.

INNOVATORS AND KEY EVENTS

Children in KS2 should to be taught about how key events and individuals in D&T have helped shape the world (Department for Education, 2013).

Some key events

1799 – The battery

In 1791, Alessandro Volta showed that a circuit of two different metals and brine (salty water) can produce an electric current. In 1799, Volta produced the Voltaic pile, the first battery. It consisted of a stack of zinc and copper separated by brine-soaked paper discs. When wires were connected to each end of the stack an electric current was generated; the higher the pile, the bigger the current.

1962 – The light emitting diode (LED)

The LED was developed by Nick Holonyack Jr., working in the General Electric research labs in the USA. The LED is an energy-efficient device which emits coloured light. LEDs are very bright, work more efficiently than filament bulbs and do not get hot. The first LED emitted red light; eventually LEDs in other colours were also produced. LEDs are widespread and are rapidly replacing all filament and fluorescent bulbs.

1941 and 1954 – The solar panel

Russell Ohl invented the solar cell in 1941. However, solar power technology dates back to the Industrial Revolution, when solar energy plants were developed to heat water that created steam to drive machinery. By 1954, the first working solar panel was produced by Bell Labs in the USA. It was only able to convert three per cent of the sun's energy into electricity. Recently, solar panels have been manufactured that can convert 30 per cent of the sun's energy.

Some key individuals

Michael Faraday (1791–1867)

Despite having very little formal education, Michael Faraday was one of the most influential scientists of his time. He was the son of a blacksmith and was apprenticed to a bookbinder in London. While in London, he attended lectures at the Royal Institution (RI) and wrote, illustrated and bound a book from his lecture notes. He was eventually taken on as assistant to Humphrey Davey and worked with him at the RI. While there, Faraday invented the electric motor and the dynamo and investigated electromagnetism. He was elected Director of the RI in 1825, when he initiated the Christmas Lectures which still run today.

Joseph Swan (1828–1914)

Joseph Swan ran a chemist's shop in Newcastle and did scientific research in his spare time. In February 1879, Swan produced the first successful light bulb, just ahead of Thomas Edison, who was working on the same thing in the USA. Swan's light bulb contained an incandescent filament; that is, a wire that heated up and glowed when an electric current passed through it. As Edison's bulb was more commercially viable, Joseph Swan's achievements have been somewhat overlooked.

Sir Charles Parsons (1854–1931)

Born in London, the son of the Third Earl of Rosse, Parsons trained as an engineer, working for several firms in the north of England. He developed the steam turbine engine and an electricity generator in the late 1880s. He went on to design a turbine powered ship, the *Turbinia*, which was faster than any ship in the Royal Navy. Steam turbines like the ones developed by Parsons are still used to produce most of the world's electricity.

SUBJECT KNOWLEDGE

In Primary D&T, electronic systems are introduced in KS2. This corresponds to the introduction of circuits and conductors in Science. It would be extremely useful to incorporate some electrical system work into D&T lessons at the same time as the children meet the concept in Science. Children should be taught to understand and use electronic systems in their products (for example, series circuits incorporating switches, buzzers and motors).

Voltage, current and resistance

Voltage is a measure of the energy available for the components in the circuit. Energy is required to make bulbs glow, motors spin and buzzers buzz. The power supply (battery, mains, etc.) provides this energy to the electric charge flowing round the circuit.

Current is a measure of the speed of the flow of the electric charge (electrons) which carries the energy around a circuit. A low current is one where the flow is very slow and a high current corresponds to a fast flow. In circuits with a high current, more energy can be delivered to a component than in a circuit with a low current. The more energy that is provided, the brighter a bulb will glow (or the faster a motor will spin, or the louder a buzzer will buzz). With a fixed power supply like a battery, it is hard to change the amount of energy (volts) available. In order to regulate the brightness, speed and volume of components, it is usual to change the current instead.

The size of the current in a circuit can be determined in several ways.

- The cell or battery provides a kick to push the electric charge around; this is called the Electromotive Force (emf) and is measured in volts. The bigger the kick from the battery, the faster the flow, so D batteries with high voltages (6 V) will produce a higher current than a single AA cell (1.5 V).
- Components in a circuit such as bulbs, buzzers and motors cause resistance, which will slow down the current. The more components there are, the larger the effect. Three bulbs in a row might slow the current so much that there simply isn't enough energy delivered for any of them to glow (Figure 7.1). This is a common problem when children build circuits; they like to include as many different components as possible and end up with a circuit that does nothing!

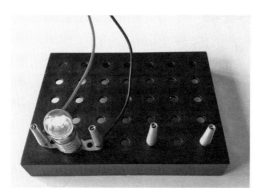 

Figure 7.1

- A variable resistor (rheostat) can be used to adjust the size of the current in a circuit. Common real-life variable resistors include a dimmer switch for lights or a volume control on a stereo.
- A switch in a circuit can prevent the current from flowing altogether.

To summarise:

- current: speed of flow, measured in amps
- voltage: energy provided to components, measured in volts
- resistance: impedance to the flow, measured in ohms

THINGS TO CONSIDER

1 It is not necessary for the children to understand all of this, but it is perhaps useful to know why previously good buzzers have suddenly gone quiet or why two bulbs will light up but five won't.

2 The greater the current, the hotter the circuit can get.

3 The more components there are in a circuit, the faster the battery will run down.

Electrical components

At KS2, the components the children should be familiar with are:

Bulb: produces white light when a current flows through it. There are some numbers stamped on the metal part just below the glass bulb which give information about the energy required to light the bulb. If the bulb is marked 6 V, it isn't going to be very bright in a circuit with a 1.5 V cell. If it is marked 1.5 V, then it will probably blow in a circuit with a 9 V battery.

Figure 7.2

LED (light emitting diode): produces light when a current flows through it. Diodes are 'one-way' controllers, which means electricity can only pass through them in one direction. Take care to put them the correct way round in a circuit (or: if it doesn't light up the first time . . . turn it around!). LEDs produce a variety of coloured light: white, red, yellow and green are the most common.

LEDs require a very small current to work. Attaching them to a battery can cause them to blow. When an LED blows, the coloured top bit can shoot off with some force. You must put a resistor in the circuit. You can buy LEDs already linked to a resistor.

Figure 7.3

Motor: spins round when a current flows through it. Once again, these components are affected by their orientation in a circuit. Connecting the motor one way will make the motor spin clockwise; reversing the connectors (or the battery) will make it spin anti-clockwise. Motors are generally marked as requiring 6 V. However, it is possible to run them with a 1.5 V cell; they won't go as fast as they could, but that may be an advantage.

Figure 7.4

Buzzer: makes a noise when current flows through. Some buzzers buzz; others squeak. Some buzzers must be linked the correct way round in a circuit. Look for red (+) and black (−) connecting wires. The red wire should be linked to the + end of the battery.

Figure 7.5

Switch: makes and breaks a circuit. The default position is usually OFF, which avoids unnecessary use of the battery and saves energy as a result. Pressing the button down will switch the circuit ON. This is a push switch, the simplest of many different switches (Figure 7.6).

Switches will be covered in more detail later in the chapter.

Figure 7.6

Cell/battery: provides the energy for the circuit. 'Battery' is a collective term for a number of 1.5 V cells. Thus, one AA 'battery' should really be called a cell. Two AA cells linked together would form a battery. A 9 V battery consists of six 1.5 V cells.

Figure 7.7

Connectors: usually wires, used to link up components in a circuit. Some connectors may be equipped with crocodile clips, or push connectors. Wires are covered in a coloured plastic insulating sheath. You will need to cut away a bit from the ends of freshly cut wire in order to expose the metal core. The colours of wires aren't important (they are all the same inside) but generally, red indicates positive and black negative for connecting purposes. This can be useful for connecting buzzers or LEDs in the correct orientation.

Figure 7.8

THINGS TO CONSIDER

1   If the children have already done a Science unit on electrical circuits, they may be used to using components from a kit, which are often assembled on to plastic or metal bases to be easy to connect. Electrical components for D&T will not be assembled onto bases but will have tiny connecting arms or wires which must be attached securely to each other to make a functioning circuit. Make sure you are aware of the differences between the Science and D&T resources.

2   All circuit components are delicate and easily damaged. Store them safely and hand them out only when required; don't let them lie around on tables throughout a lesson.

Building circuits

The key to building a successful circuit is to keep things as simple as possible. Draw out the arrangement of components; think about how to link them and how many wire connectors will be needed. A useful rule of thumb is that, for a simple series circuit, the number of connecting wires should be the same as the number of components (Figure 7.9).

The components should be linked together in a circle. Arrange the components and connectors in a large circle on the table so that it is possible to see what is going where. If the wires start to get tangled up it gets very confusing.

If two or more components are to be used in a circuit (a motor and a bulb, for example) there are two ways to build the circuit.

A *series circuit* (Figure 7.10) uses fewer connectors and is simple to build, but the current running through the circuit will be greatly reduced by resistance and the components may not function satisfactorily.

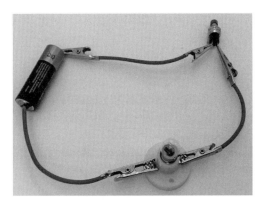

Figure 7.9

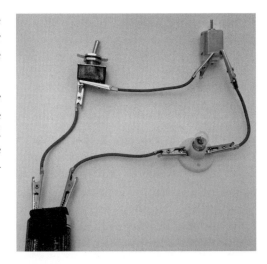

Figure 7.10

A *parallel circuit* (Figure 7.11) uses more wire and is complex to build successfully, but the components will work well.

In a series circuit, the components are connected in a single loop. If the bulb blows, the motor will stop spinning. In the circuit in Figure 7.10, one switch controls the bulb and a motor.

In a parallel circuit, the components are connected in two loops. In Figure 7.11, the electricity running to the bulb bypasses the motor and the current to the motor not flow through the bulb. The switch is still used to control both components, but if the bulb should blow, the motor will continue to spin.

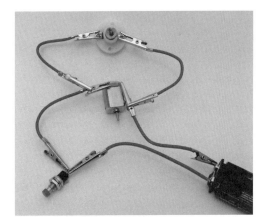

Figure 7.11

Joining components

If you are fortunate enough to have connectors with clips on the ends, then they can easily be attached to the components.

If you have to cope with lengths of wire then make sure there is a sufficient length of bare wire at each end (1 cm is the minimum). If the wire is made of lots of thin strands, then twist them tightly together between thumb and forefinger before starting. To join two connecting wires twist the two ends together tightly (Figure 7.12). Fold the joint back against the insulated part of the wire. Then tape the joint with electrical tape. If the tape also covers a short length of the insulated wire, the joint is less likely to be pulled apart during rough handling.

Figure 7.12

If using bulb holders with small screw connections, wrap the stripped wire once round the screw before tightening it.

Connecting a bulb without a holder into a circuit is complex. The wires must touch the side and the bottom of the bulb. Tape can be used to hold the wires in place but it comes unstuck very easily and it can be extremely frustrating to get the wires to stay in place while taping. Using some

Figure 7.13

modelling clay and silver foil, it is possible to produce a home-made bulb holder, which will be easier to work with and which holds the wires and bulb firmly in contact (Figure 7.13). This can be used as a temporary solution but for a really reliable connection, use commercial bulb holders.

Figure 7.14

If wires are not available, aluminium foil will make an excellent connector for circuits. It can be cut to an appropriate length and taped carefully to a piece of card to produce a circuit board. As tape is an insulator, foil wires can be criss-crossed over each other without there being any short circuit problems. This is an ideal way to make a quiz board (Figure 7.14).

Conductive play dough (Figure 7.15) can be used as a tactile if temporary way to build circuits. The dough can be moulded into any shape and the circuit components are pressed into the dough in order to complete the circuit. The dough must be damp to work as a conductor (see p. 187 for recipe).

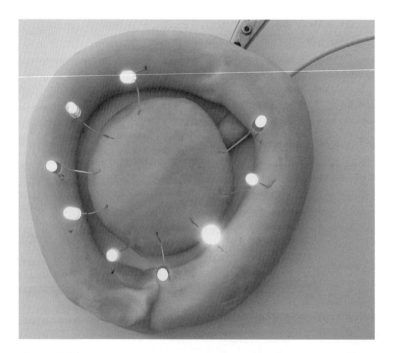

Figure 7.15

If stored in an airtight container, the dough will last for several weeks. Mixing the same ingredients together without cooking also produces conductive dough but more flour is needed to make it into a solid lump and the texture is not as smooth and flexible. The cooking step takes no longer than 10 minutes and is worth the extra time. The dough has a high resistance so use a minimum of four AA cells linked together. Buzzers, motors and bulbs don't work very well at all but this is an occasion where LEDs can be safely used without resistors in the circuit. The longer leg of the LED should be in the dough connected to the + terminal of the battery. The LEDs should link two pieces of dough, rather than being pushed into one lump. Think of the dough as replacing wires in the circuit.

Children who enjoy making circuits from unusual components may also find the Makey Makey kits interesting (see Chapter 8 IT Control and Monitoring). The creators of Makey Makey have produced a system which can turn everyday objects into 'keys', to control any software normally controlled by keyboard or mouse. Linking Makey Makey with Scratch allows children to design their own interactive games using very simple equipment.

Figure 7.16 shows a prototype of a video camera trap using Makey Makey and Scratch. If a human (or other animal) touches two adjacent foil keys with a foot, hand or paw, an alarm sounds and the video camera is turned on.

For more information go to: www.makeymakey.com.

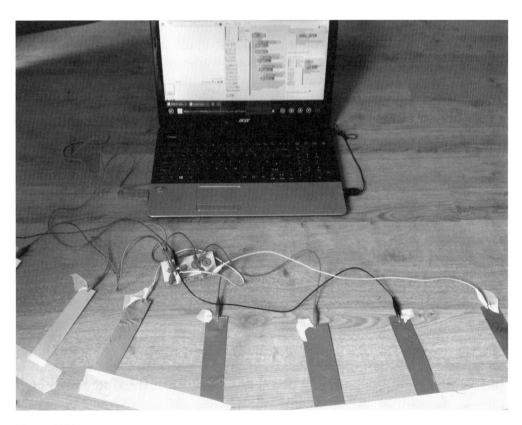

Figure 7.16

THINGS TO CONSIDER

1 Circuits are delicate things and too much energetic handling will loosen and eventually break the joints. Consider how to keep the circuits protected, e.g. by placing them inside a box, by fastening switches and bulbs firmly to a rigid surface.

2 Even in a simple circuit with one AA cell and a bulb, the wires can get hot very quickly. Discourage children from holding connections together with their fingers. Invest in some battery and bulb holders and some clip-on connectors.

3 Children who are keen may try to investigate and build circuits at home, using parts from broken toys, etc. Be sure they are aware of potential hazards such as capacitors which can store a charge and give a nasty electric shock (they are found in disposable cameras, among other things). Discourage home electronics unless the parents are happy to supervise.

4 Circuits are not normally held together with twisted wires and tape. If you are able to find a circuit board somewhere (an old computer is a good starting point), show the children how the components are soldered into place. If they continue with D&T in secondary school, they may learn how to do this.

Circuit diagrams

Drawing pictures of circuits is time consuming and can lead to confusion as components from different suppliers may look very different to each other. Thus, the conventional way of drawing circuits is to use standard symbols for components. A circuit diagram doesn't look anything like the real circuit, but it is easy to see how the components have been joined together. The most common circuit diagram symbols are shown in Figure 7.17.

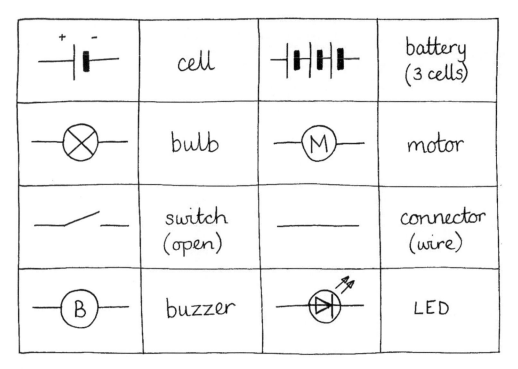

Figure 7.17

Circuit diagrams should be drawn using a ruler to make sure the lines are straight and the corners are right angles. Children may find this difficult to start with but soon realise how much easier it is than having to sketch the actual circuit. Circuit diagrams are easy to draw if the circuit is laid out in front of the children, but they find it very hard to build a circuit following a diagram. It may help to have a diagram and a photo of the completed circuit side by side (Figures 7.18, 7.19 and 7.20).

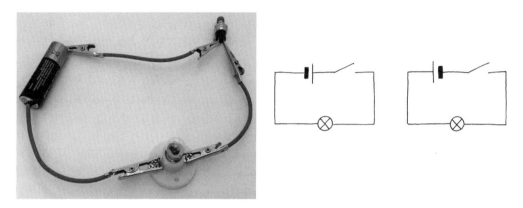

Figure 7.18

Be careful when drawing circuit diagrams. Although both diagrams in Figure 7.18 show a functional circuit, the one on the right has the cell drawn in the wrong orientation (this doesn't matter for a bulb, but it would matter for LEDs).

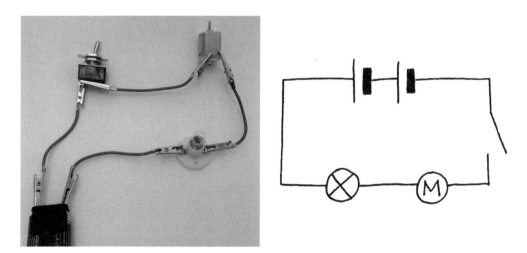

Figure 7.19

The circuit may not look exactly the same as the diagram. The circuit in Figure 7.19 is identical to the diagram, but oriented differently. Children can find this very confusing. Encourage children to focus on the order of the components rather than the shape of the circuit.

Parallel circuit diagrams look much less complex than the real thing (Figure 7.20).

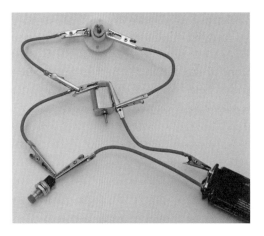
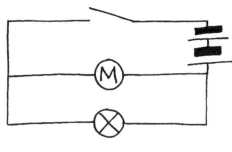

Figure 7.20

THINGS TO CONSIDER

1 Circuit diagrams are covered in KS2 Science.

2 Following a circuit diagram to build a circuit with a 1.5 V cell, a bulb and a few wires does not make you a qualified electrician – stress the importance of leaving home electricals to the experts.

3 Children may be able to use their electronics skills in other D&T sessions, in order to make models move or light up. Encourage them to use circuit diagrams in their plans.

Switches

In its simplest form, a switch is two conductors held apart by an insulator. There is usually a mechanical way of bringing the two conductors together to allow the current to flow.

Switches are easy and cheap to make and children love to use their own switches rather than the commercial ones. Figure 7.21 shows a simple but functional foil and card switch. The switch in Figure 7.22 is made using a peg. With the card in place, the switch is OFF; pulling out the card turns the switch ON.

Given the opportunity, some foil and imagination, children can invent their own switches. In Figure 7.23, there is a foil connector under the plane. When it lands on the runway, it makes contact with the foil-covered block and the bulb lights up.

Figure 7.21

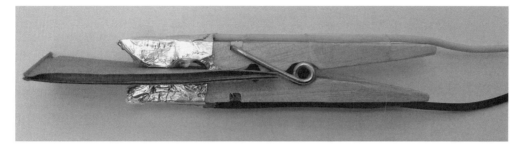

Figure 7.22

Figure 7.23

There are many different ready-made switches to buy. The shape and colours will depend upon the manufacturer and there are several different types you might come across.

1 **Push switch** (Figure 7.24): these are generally 'push to make' (or NO – Normally Open) switches, which means they are in the OFF position until they are pushed (the foil and card switch is one of these). Releasing the lever or button stops the current again. These are battery-saving switches as they can't be left on accidently. There are also 'push to break' (or NC – Normally Closed) switches that remain ON until pushed. Connect a wire to each leg.

2 **Toggle switches** (Figure 7.25 and 7.26): these can be set in the ON or OFF position. Some toggle switches have several connectors because they can be used to control several circuits. Try to avoid using these if possible; connection can be confusing, with some circuits being ON when the switch indicates OFF. In general, always connect wire to a central leg and another leg on the same side.

Figure 7.24

Figure 7.25

Toggle switches are designed to be hidden from view. There is a nut securing the ON/OFF label. Undo the nut and remove the ON/OFF label. The switch lever can then be poked through a hole in the model and fastened in place with the nut. The rest of the switch is hidden inside the model (Figure 7.26).

Figure 7.26

3 **Reed switches** (Figure 7.27): delicate and rare in a primary school, but an excellent switch to show the children.

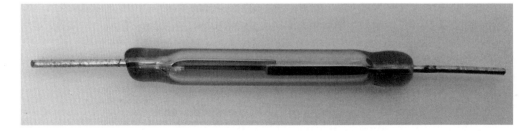

Figure 7.27

Reed switches have two thin conductors assembled very close together and protected by a glass tube. The conductors are made from a magnetic metal, so when a magnet is brought up to the side of the switch, the two strips become magnetised and attract each other, completing the circuit. When the magnet is removed the conductors spring apart, breaking the circuit. Reed switches are often found in appliances that switch off when the cover is closed (for example an e-book reader or a mobile phone).

4 **Switches with more than two connectors** (Figure 7.28): some switches are designed to control several circuits at once. Avoid using them if you can, but if it is unavoidable, here are some hints:

The switch in Figure 7.28 can be either push to make OR push to break. One wire from the circuit connects to the left-hand COM leg, and the other wire is either connected to the middle NO leg (off until pushed) or to the right-hand NC leg (on until pushed).

The switch in Figure 7.29 has the potential to control four different circuits. Connect one wire to a central leg. The other wire should be connected to a leg on the *same* side.

Figure 7.28   **Figure 7.29**

Switch terminology

There may be useful connection information printed on switches:

– *COM* (Common). This connector works with any other and should always be used.
– *NO* (Normally Open). Connecting the second wire here means that the switch will be OFF unless pressed, flicked, etc.
– *NC* (Normally Closed). Connecting the second wire here means the switch will be ON unless pressed.

Making switches for a particular task

Once children have an understanding of how a simple switch works, they should be able to design a switch for a particular task. Popular electronics projects often focus on burglar alarms: that is, switches which turn on an alarm without the operator realising.

Pressure switches (Figure 7.30) and tilt switches (Figure 7.31) can be used to monitor the position of an object; if it is moved, then the alarm sounds.

Once children understand the theory behind a switch, they can start to use their knowledge to make simple games.

In the golf game in Figure 7.32, as the golf ball rolls into the cup (suspended below the table) the bulb lights up to signal a successful putt. There is a simple pressure switch at the bottom of the cup which is turned on by the weight of the ball.

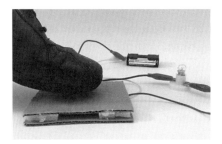

Figure 7.30

Figure 7.31

Figure 7.32

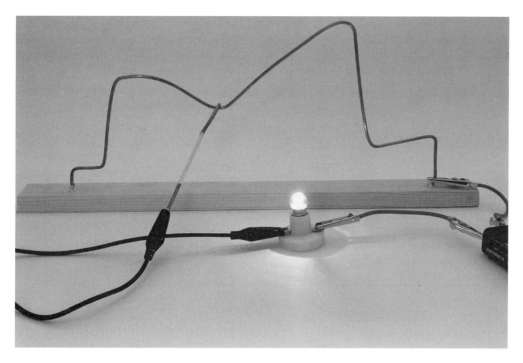

Figure 7.33

Steady-hand games are a form of simple switch. These games rely on the players keeping two conductors apart. A shake of the hand which causes the two conductors to touch will set off a buzzer or light a lamp.

In a traditional steady-hand game (Figure 7.33), the metal loop must be moved along the wire from one end to the other. Touching the wire causes an alarm to sound or a bulb to light. The steady-hand game in Figure 7.34 challenges the player to pick the apples from the tree, using the tweezers, without setting off the alarm. The apples are placed in small pots fastened under each hole. If the metal tweezers touch the sides of the hole, a circuit is completed, causing the buzzer to make a sound.

Computer programming languages use binary code (a series of 0s and 1s). The code signals whether an electronic switch should be on (1) or off (0). Following a series of binary instructions enables a computer to carry out a particular task. A simple version

Figure 7.34

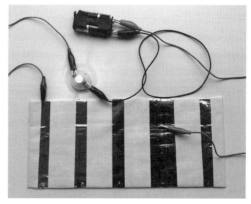

Figure 7.35

of a binary code program can be made with some foil and masking tape (Figure 7.35). This program causes the circuit to send out a Morse code signal (in this example, the letters E and F) when the connector is dragged across the board. Provided the connector is always dragged in the same direction, the message sent will always be the same, just like running a computer program over and over.

THINGS TO CONSIDER

1   The Internet is filled with electronics project ideas. Most components are quite cheap to buy but there is no need to make complex circuits – many children find great satisfaction in planning and building their own simple circuits, like the ones illustrated here.

2   The project ideas in this chapter are designed to run from 1.5V AA cells; they should never be plugged into the mains!

Motorising models

Once children have an understanding of electrical circuits and the functions of the various components, they will want to start adding lights, sound and motion to their models. Adding bulbs or buzzers is fairly straightforward as the circuits can be built separately and then incorporated into the model at the end. However, adding a motor to a moving model requires some advance planning and also knowledge of gears and other mechanisms. The small motors used in model-making run very fast but are not very powerful. This means that although the motor turns rapidly on its own, when linked to a wheel or an axle it does not have enough power (or torque) to turn it. There are two ways to solve this problem. Either use gears or use a pulley system. In both cases, the small wheel should be attached to the motor and the larger one to the axle of the rotating part. This ensures that the motor produces enough power to spin the axle (see Chapter 6, Mechanisms).

HEALTH AND SAFETY

School electronics should be safe, but precautions should be in place regardless.

1   It is vital that children understand that the models they make run from batteries, not the mains. They should under no circumstance attach anything to an electric socket.
2   Wires can get hot enough to burn, so discourage children from holding connections together with their fingers. Where possible buy connectors, battery holders and components which can be clipped together. Otherwise, tape each connection firmly using electrical tape.
3   The components are very small, so be careful about how they are handled. Bulbs can break, producing small splinters of glass. Motors with fan blades made from hard plastic can cause a nasty bruise.
4   Connecting wire may scratch. Have rules in place about handling them and make sure the children are spread out so that they can't accidently whip a wire across another child's face. Limit the length of wire to be used.
5   It is sensible to make sure that the work space remains dry and that water is kept well away, so remove children's water bottles to a safe place.

IDEAS FOR PROJECTS

BULBS	• model lighthouse • pocket torch • lighting for a dolls' house
BUZZERS	• burglar alarms • electronic games • door bells
MOTORS	• fairground rides • motorised vehicles and cranes
SWITCHES	• burglar alarms • games

© 2016, *The Really Useful Primary Design and Technology Book*, E. Flinn and S. Patel, Routledge

CROSS-CURRICULAR LINKS

LITERACY	• models to illustrate stories for younger children (e.g. *The Lighthouse-keeper's Lunch*)
NUMERACY	• simple decimal addition to work out the voltage of a battery • right angles are required for accurate circuit diagrams
SCIENCE	• links directly to NC for Science in Y4 and Y6
GEOGRAPHY	• investigate the alternative energy sources used in many countries
HISTORY	• research the inventors of the light bulb, motor and battery – all vital to modern life
RS/RE	• illuminated displays about festivals associated with light
MUSIC	• buzzers aren't very musical, but with a Morse code switch, a repeating rhythmic buzz can be programmed
PSHEC	• design a torch or lamp for use in an emergency • alarms to protect vulnerable people, e.g. an alarm to tell a blind person when the bath is full
COMPUTING	• simple on/off programming of a switch • introduction to binary code
MFL	• make a vocabulary tester using the simple quiz board

© 2016, *The Really Useful Primary Design and Technology Book*, E. Flinn and S. Patel, Routledge

HOW TO MAKE SOME OF THE MODELS ILLUSTRATED IN THIS CHAPTER

HOW TO MAKE CONDUCTIVE DOUGH

- 250 ml water
- 240 g plain flour (gluten-free flour works too)
- 68 g salt
- 135 ml lemon juice (or 45 ml cream of tartar)
- 15 ml vegetable oil
- Food colouring (optional)

1 Mix 160 g flour with the rest of the ingredients and cook over a medium heat. The mixture should rapidly start to get chunky.

2 Stir well until the mixture forms a ball in the pan.

3 Let the dough cool and knead to a smooth consistency, mixing in the rest (80 g) of the flour.

© 2016, *The Really Useful Primary Design and Technology Book*, E. Flinn and S. Patel, Routledge

Quiz board

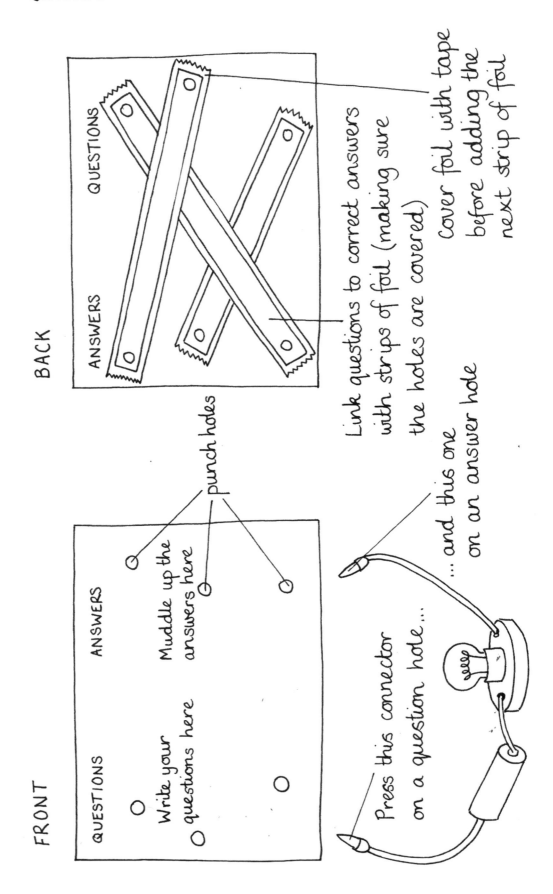

BACK

Link questions to correct answers with strips of foil (making sure the holes are covered)

Cover foil with tape before adding the next strip of foil

FRONT

QUESTIONS   ANSWERS

Write your questions here

Muddle up the answers here

punch holes

Press this connector on a question hole...

...and this one on an answer hole

© 2016, *The Really Useful Primary Design and Technology Book*, E. Flinn and S. Patel, Routledge

Pressure switch

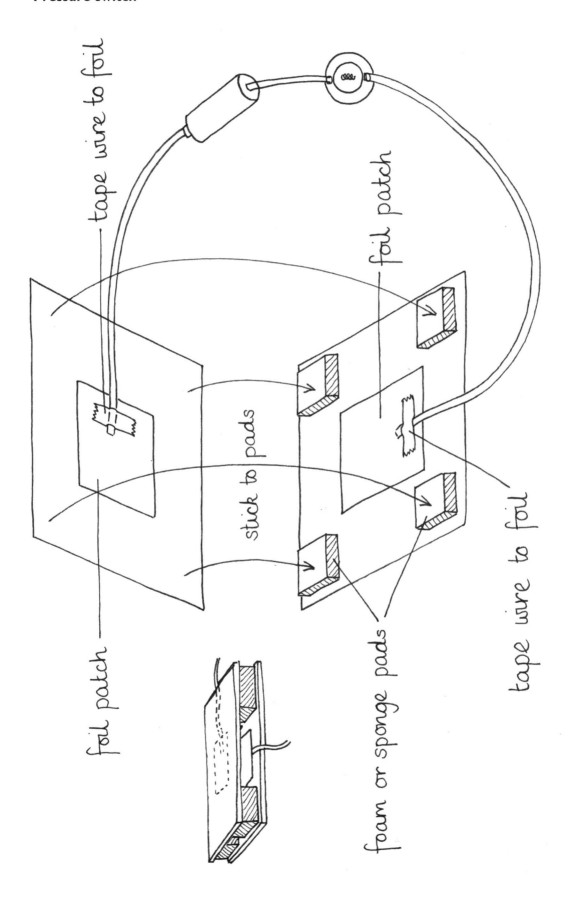

tape wire to foil

foil patch

stick to pads

foil patch

foam or sponge pads

tape wire to foil

© 2016, *The Really Useful Primary Design and Technology Book*, E. Flinn and S. Patel, Routledge

Tilt switch

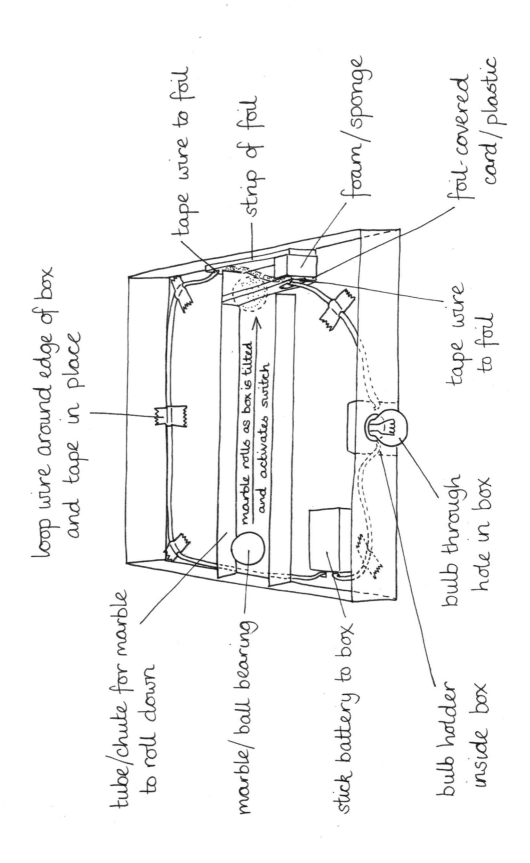

tape wire to foil

strip of foil

foam/sponge

foil-covered card/plastic

loop wire around edge of box and tape in place

tape wire to foil

marble rolls as box is tilted and activates switch

tube/chute for marble to roll down

marble/ball bearing

stick battery to box

bulb holder inside box

bulb through hole in box

© 2016, *The Really Useful Primary Design and Technology Book*, E. Flinn and S. Patel, Routledge

Golf game

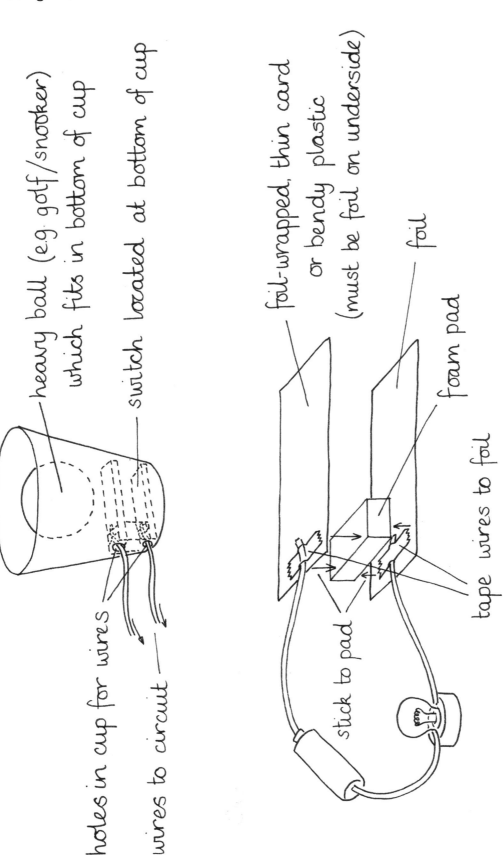

heavy ball (e.g. golf/snooker) which fits in bottom of cup

switch located at bottom of cup

holes in cup for wires

wires to circuit

foil-wrapped, thin card or bendy plastic (must be foil on underside)

foil

foam pad

tape wires to foil

stick to pad

© 2016, *The Really Useful Primary Design and Technology Book*, E. Flinn and S. Patel, Routledge

Steady-hand games

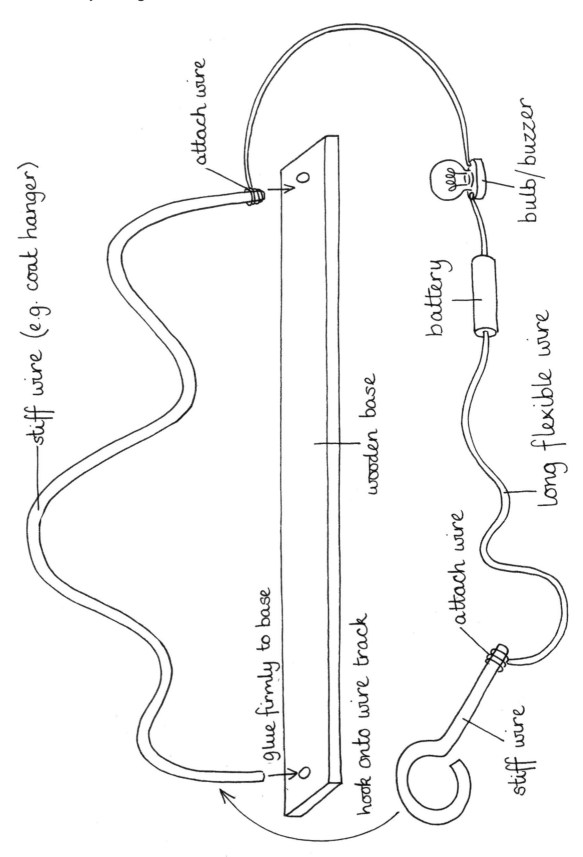

attach wire

stiff wire (e.g. coat hanger)

bulb/buzzer

battery

long flexible wire

wooden base

glue firmly to base

hook onto wire track

attach wire

stiff wire

© 2016, *The Really Useful Primary Design and Technology Book*, E. Flinn and S. Patel, Routledge

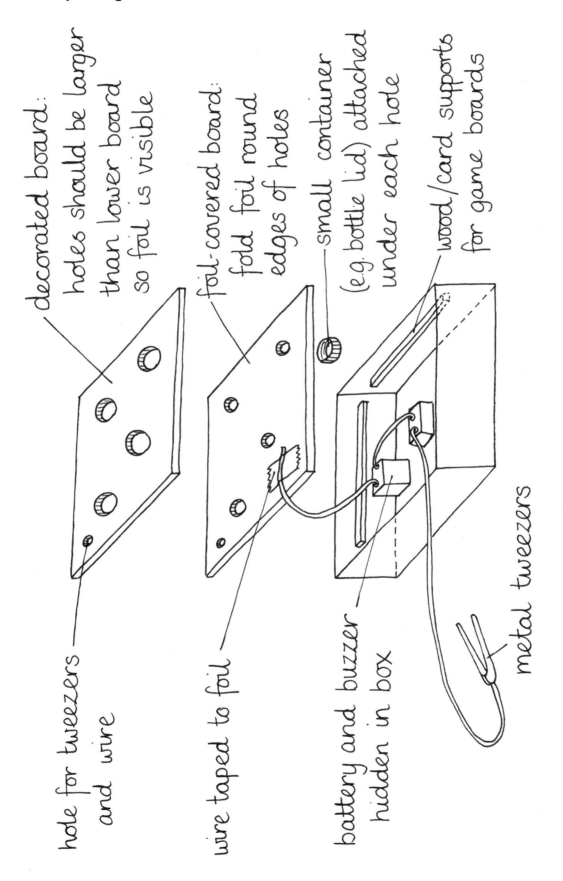

decorated board:
holes should be larger
than lower board
so foil is visible

foil-covered board:
fold foil round
edges of holes

small container
(e.g. bottle lid) attached
under each hole

wood/card supports
for game boards

hole for tweezers
and wire

wire taped to foil

battery and buzzer
hidden in box

metal tweezers

© 2016, *The Really Useful Primary Design and Technology Book*, E. Flinn and S. Patel, Routledge

Morse switch

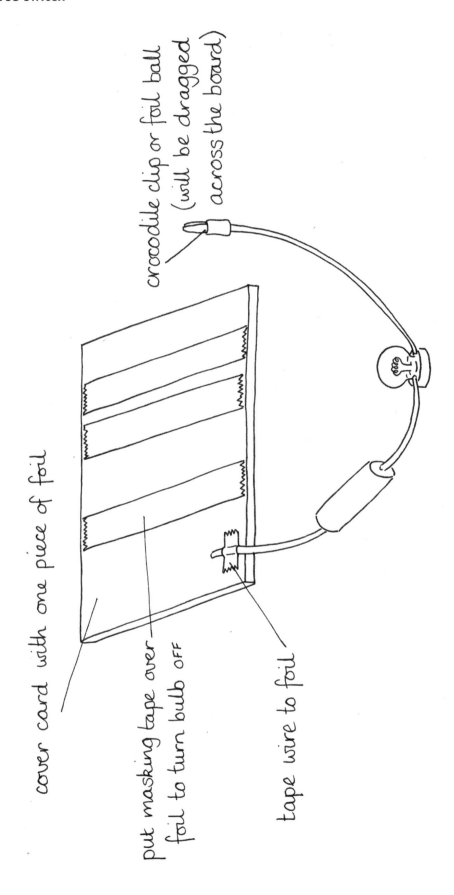

crocodile clip or foil ball (will be dragged across the board)

cover card with one piece of foil

put masking tape over foil to turn bulb off

tape wire to foil

© 2016, *The Really Useful Primary Design and Technology Book*, E. Flinn and S. Patel, Routledge

Loop and rod game

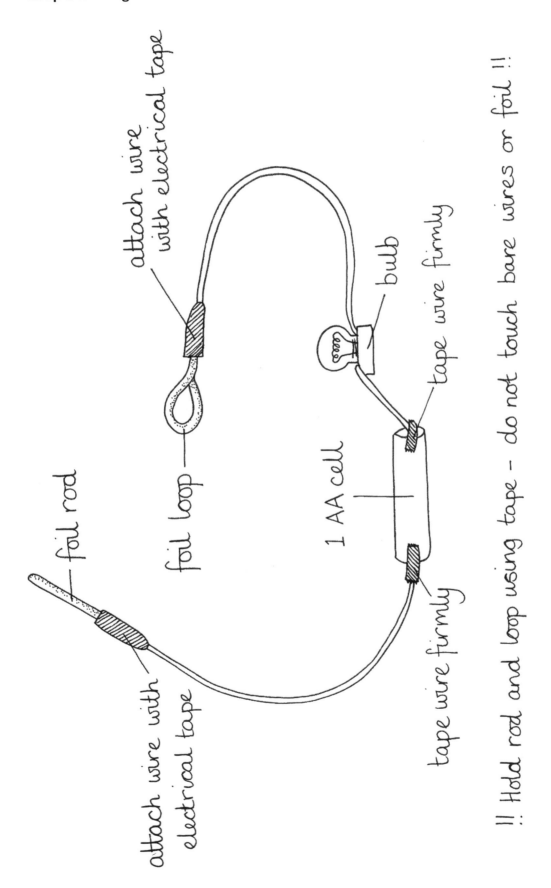

attach wire with electrical tape

foil loop

foil rod

attach wire with electrical tape

1 AA cell

bulb

tape wire firmly

tape wire firmly

!! Hold rod and loop using tape – do not touch bare wires or foil !!

© 2016, *The Really Useful Primary Design and Technology Book*, E. Flinn and S. Patel, Routledge

LESSON PLANS

LOWER KS2

Investigate switches and then design and make a steady-hand game to use at the school fete.

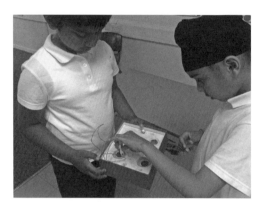 

UPPER KS2

Design and make a gadget which might help make an everyday task easier.

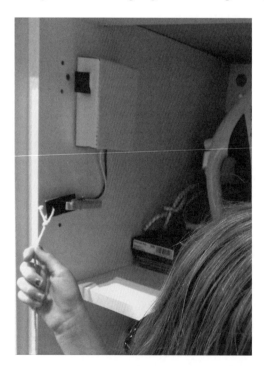 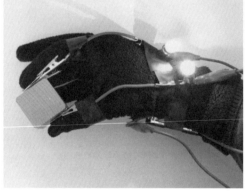

ELECTRONIC SYSTEMS: LOWER KS2 LESSON PLAN

Session	D&T skills	Lesson outline	Resources	Differentiation
1	Research	**Introduction** Introduce the project by discussing with the children the experiences they have had of games at fairs. They may not have come across steady-hand games as they are quite old-fashioned. Look at photos of previous school fairs and fetes in order to see what sort of games have been on offer in the past. **Main session** Once a list of games has been compiled, the children can discuss which ones they think might need an electrical circuit to work. The children should think about how the game works and whether they have noticed lights or sounds connected with the game. Ask the children to explain how they think the games work. Introduce ideas of conductors and insulators or switches that may be turned on or off in certain situations. Compile a class fact-file of all the ideas. **Plenary** Explain to the children that they are going to design and make an electronic game to be used at the school fete. Discuss the properties of a successful game: colourful, not too hard or too easy, quick to set up and to explain, simple but reliable equipment. If time, children can start thinking about a theme for their game.	• Photos from school or church fetes in former years • Pictures of the various games often seen at fairs (hook a duck, bash the rat, steady hand, skittles, coconut shy, hoopla) – an excellent non-Internet resource will be old reading scheme books	Be aware of children who, for religious or cultural reasons, may not have experienced a fair. The names of games will be hard for EAL children to grasp as many use old-fashioned words, however, the pictures should be accessible to all.
2	Design and make a prototype	**Introduction** Recap the design brief – an electronic game which will be fun for all. **Main session** Show children actual, working steady-hand games. Let the children see how they work, take the games to pieces to show what is going on inside. In groups, children should try to draw a diagram to show how the games work. Before they start to design and make their games, give the children an opportunity to make a small circuit with the resources available. Provide each group with a bulb (in a holder), an AA cell, two connecting wires and some foil. Using the wires to link the components, they should try to get the bulb to light. Once they have done that, they can use the foil to make a loop and rod game (see Figure 7.33, p. 183) – the idea being to try to pass the rod through the loop without lighting the bulb. The children can discuss what is happening and why.	• 'Operation' or similar and a wiggly wire steady-hand game (these are often sold as make-it-yourself kits) • Each group will need a battery, bulb, two connecting wires and foil • Buzzers • Word cards for EAL children showing a picture and the name of the component • Circuit sets, if available	Children who struggle with fine motor skills may find building a circuit very frustrating. Provide them, if possible, with components from a circuit kit which link together more easily. A circuit diagram may help children to understand how the electricity gets round the circuit.

© 2016, *The Really Useful Primary Design and Technology Book*, E. Flinn and S. Patel, Routledge

ELECTRONIC SYSTEMS: LOWER KS2 LESSON PLAN *continued*

Session	D&T skills	Lesson outline	Resources	Differentiation
		Plenary Discuss circuit building. Was it hard to get the bulb to light? Were there any technical problems? If so, ask the children to explain how they sorted them out. Ask children to explain how the loop and rod game works. Listen for children using the terms 'conductor' and 'completed circuit'.		This is an opportunity for EAL children to learn some scientific vocabulary. Extend HA by asking them to make a circuit containing a bulb and buzzer.
3	Design	**Introduction** Remind children about the design brief. **Main session** In groups, the children should come up with a design for their own game. They need to think about how to make the circuit as well deciding what the players will have to do. An 'Operation'-type game will need a theme – *what* is to be removed from/placed *where*? A wiggly wire game is also more attractive with a theme. Both games can be built in a box and so a suitable background design can be produced to make things look more attractive. The design should include information about how the game is played and how players will know whether they have won. **Plenary** Children share their ideas.	• Examples of steady-hand games, photos or idea cards for groups struggling to find a theme • Examples of the materials available for construction: cardboard boxes, foil, electrical components, stiff wire (from coat hangers), small pots and bottle lids, modelling clay or plastic toys (for picking out with tweezers)	Provide some help with the design by giving children an example of a similar game which they can take to pieces and examine. For children who are finding the process difficult, provide a template of a suitable game board with holes already cut in it. Offer a selection of plastic toys which can help to stimulate ideas for a theme.

© 2016, *The Really Useful Primary Design and Technology Book*, E. Flinn and S. Patel, Routledge

Session	D&T skills	Lesson outline	Resources	Differentiation
4	Make	<u>Introduction</u> Recap circuit building. Discuss the importance of making secure connections. <u>Main session</u> The children should start to make their games. The wiring of the circuit should be the last thing they do, but as they build their game, they should be aware of the necessity for a place to put batteries and buzzers and think about how to incorporate a bulb into the design.	• Cardboard boxes, foil, glue, scissors • Electrical components: battery, bulb, wire, tape or clips • Stiff wire (coat hangers), corks (to push over ends of wire), pliers • Metal tweezers or hooks, small pots, bottle tops • Colouring pencils/pens/paint	Pre-cut templates will help children who have poor fine motor skills. Most children will need help making holes in card. Provide pictures of a correctly connected circuit.
5	Make	Children continue to make and finish their games and test them to check that the circuits are working correctly before final assembly. Remind the children that the games must be strong enough to be used over and over. Check that all electrical connections are secure and that gluing is sufficient to hold things in place.	As above	As above
6	Evaluate	<u>Introduction</u> Explain the importance of evaluation. Discuss and compile a set of criteria to be evaluated. <u>Main session</u> Using the criteria they have discussed, the children evaluate their games. Some things they might think about are: *Did people come back to have another go? Were people fed up because it was too hard? Was it too easy so all the prizes got used up rapidly? Did anyone ask how it worked? Did anyone say it was a great game?* They should provide information on how well the games coped with continued use and should also consider how they could improve their design for next year. <u>Plenary</u> Ask the children to share their evaluations and, if appropriate, ask the rest of the class to comment, if they tried the game.	• The games • Photos/video of the fete showing customers playing the games • Records (from the children) about the number of winners or number of players, and any compliments or suggestions they got	LA could look at photos from the day and talk about whether it was easy or hard to show customers how to play. HA could consider the cost effectiveness of the game (if money was charged per go); provide them with the approximate cost of the various components.

© 2016, *The Really Useful Primary Design and Technology Book*, E. Flinn and S. Patel, Routledge

UPPER KS2

In this project, the children are asked to think of the needs of others and to consider how they could design and make a gadget that would provide useful assistance to someone with a specific need; for example:

- an alarm to signal when a door is opened
- a signal to alert someone that another person has entered the room
- a water level monitor for the bath
- a visible doorbell
- a buzzer that sounds when a light is switched on
- a vibrating (silent) alarm clock for a deaf person
- an alarm to warn if a drawer or a cupboard is left open
- a gadget to attract the attention of someone who can't see/hear you

While this is an opportunity for children to consider the needs of others who may be less fortunate than themselves, you might have children in the class who are already living with similar disabilities. If necessary, ask the children to solve the same problems for a different reason. For example: a doorbell which won't make a sound so that it doesn't wake a baby, a monitor to measure the level of water in an underground reservoir or a sensor to measure grip pressure for astronauts who wear thick gloves.

ELECTRONIC SYSTEMS: UPPER KS2 LESSON PLAN

Session	D&T skills	Lesson outline	Resources	Differentiation
1	Research	<u>Introduction</u> In discussion with the children, talk about the problems people may have if they are unable to see or hear, or if their sense of touch has been lost. Ask the children to think about everyday living and consider how many times we use sight, hearing or touch to help us. <u>Main session</u> Groups of children brainstorm problems of a sense loss and report back to the class. Give groups the names of people and organisations so that they can get more in-depth information online. <u>Plenary</u> Explain to the children that electrical circuits could be used to help solve some of the problems they have suggested. Ask them how they could alter a doorbell circuit (battery, switch and buzzer) to make it visual rather than aural.	• The RNIB and Action on Hearing Loss (formerly RNID) websites have information about gadgets that are available to help people with visual or hearing impairments. • Look for suitable information about Evelyn Glennie (the deaf percussionist), David Blunkett (the blind MP) or soldiers who have lost a limb in conflict.	Senses are something most children use all the time without realising. Ask children to close their eyes, or wear headphones and then think about what they are missing. Wearing a pair of ski gloves will help children to consider what lack of feeling in fingers is like. HA children could consider multiple sensory loss (Helen Kellar was deaf and blind).
2	Design	<u>Introduction</u> In groups, children will focus on one aspect of sensory loss and think about how to solve the problems they highlighted. As an example, ask the children to design a doorbell for a household containing hearing and non-hearing people. They will need to incorporate a bell and a buzzer which are both controlled by the same switch. A parallel circuit will probably be needed if the buzzer is to be loud enough (see Figure 7.11). Provide some examples of the different switches illustrated in this chapter. <u>Main session</u> Children use their own ideas and the examples provided to design a sensor gadget to solve a particular problem. They should show how the circuit will be constructed and draw a circuit diagram if possible. The main component of many of the gadgets will be a switch, which is designed to switch a bulb/buzzer on or off, to notify the user that something has happened. <u>Plenary</u> Ask the groups to explain their ideas and designs. Feedback from others at this stage may help to refine the designs and to highlight any possible problems.	• Examples of different types of switch, including a pressure switch and a tilt switch • Instruction sheets showing how to make these switches • Battery, five wires, bulb, buzzer and switch for circuit	Extend the HA children by asking them to design a circuit where the buzzer or the bulb could be turned off independently, so that on pressing the doorbell it either rings or lights up or does both. Parallel circuits are complex to assemble, so LA children may only manage a series circuit.

© 2016, *The Really Useful Primary Design and Technology Book*, E. Flinn and S. Patel, Routledge

ELECTRONIC SYSTEMS: UPPER KS2 LESSON PLAN *continued*

Session	D&T skills	Lesson outline	Resources	Differentiation
3	Design and build a prototype	<u>Introduction</u> Explain the importance of making a prototype. Explain that the prototype gadget may not be perfectly constructed and that it can be changed, but that it should activated by the correct stimulus. <u>Main session</u> Children continue to design their gadget. They should assemble a simple test circuit (using a bulb) and make sure their prototype functions and can be activated correctly. If they have to make a change to their product, the children should record this on the design. Ask children to consider other members of the household. Will they want to use the gadget? If not, how can they switch it off, or remove it, or know to walk around it? Ask the children to consider the packaging of their gadget, in order to hide the wires and battery. Ask them to design a suitable box to put the electronics in. <u>Plenary</u> In order to reinforce the idea that making a prototype is worthwhile, ask the children to explain whether they had to make changes to their design after making the prototype.	• Provide examples of materials that the children might need, e.g. card, foil, foam, sponge, pegs, wire, string, straws, dowels	LA may need help drawing a circuit diagram before they have assembled the circuit. They could draw a picture of their ideas and convert it to a circuit diagram, with help, after they know that the circuit works. Ask HA children to produce a list of materials or to provide them themselves if they can.
4	Make	Using the resources they have asked for or provided, the children make their gadget. They should make secure connections between each component in the circuit. The gadget should be rugged and reusable, so it will function repeatedly without complex resetting procedures.	• Circuit components, foil, wire, wire cutters and strippers, tape for joining • Card, string, straws, paper clips, dowels, etc. as required • Scissors, glue, pens or colouring pencils	Check the designs so that ideas which won't work or aren't practical can be weeded out early. Provide some photos of circuits to help LA children wire them up successfully. HA: see below.

© 2016, *The Really Useful Primary Design and Technology Book*, E. Flinn and S. Patel, Routledge

Session	D&T skills	Lesson outline	Resources	Differentiation
5	Make	Continue to make and finish the gadget. Test the gadget and ensure that the circuit is working correctly. Set up a situation with one child wearing a blindfold or headphones etc. and see whether they are able to use the gadget successfully.	As above	Children who produce a successful gadget could be asked how they could adapt it to work for someone who can neither see nor hear (vibrations might be the answer – how could they make something vibrate?). LA: see above.
6	Evaluate	<u>Introduction</u> Discuss the importance of testing and making changes to a design. Ask the children to consider the design process and to note down any changes they made to their original design after testing or during the manufacturing process. They should provide a reason for the change. <u>Main session</u> Children should test their gadget on someone who hasn't been involved in its manufacture. Was the tester able to use the gadget successfully? Did they understand what the buzzer/bulb was telling them and did they respond accordingly? Children should use this information to complete their evaluation. <u>Plenary</u> If possible, look up online to see whether a similar gadget is commercially available. If so, can the children spot any similarities between their gadget and the commercial one? If it isn't available, the children might like to consider why and could even write to the appropriate charity and give them details of their gadget. If nothing else, they should get a response from the experts.	• Evaluation sheet with prompts if necessary • A suitable area for testing of gadgets • Internet access to the websites detailed above	Provide LA children with a prompt list to help them to evaluate fully. Record answers or annotate on their plans, if appropriate. Take photos/film of the gadget in action to help the children to evaluate. HA children can consider the no-sight-no-hearing problem detailed above and think about how to adapt their design.

© 2016, *The Really Useful Primary Design and Technology Book*, E. Flinn and S. Patel, Routledge

8 IT control and monitoring

Control and monitoring is the remote control of mechanisms/machines by using environment sensors (e.g. light, motion) to initiate the control program. Control mechanisms are used in robotics, in manufacturing and in situations where it is too dangerous for a human to work.

WHY TEACH CONTROL AND MONITORING?

- The UK has a growing shortage of engineers, with four out of five manufacturers experiencing recruitment difficulties. Two-thirds of them say that this is because candidates lack technical skills (Groom, 2014).
- Modern manufacturing is highly computer controlled, so understanding how to control machines with computers is what many employers are asking for.
- Many children see these kinds of jobs as ' boring'. With the introduction of the use of computing to program, monitor and control products in the National Curriculum (2014), it is hoped that more children will enjoy using equipment such as 3D printers and Lego, which will (we hope) in turn enhance their technical skills.
- Control technology offers the opportunity for an investigative approach to solving problems and development in the complexity of giving and modifying instructions (Loveless, 2003).

INNOVATORS AND KEY EVENTS

Children in Key Stage 2 should be taught about how key events and individuals in D&T have helped shape the world (Department for Education, 2013).

Some key events

The creation of the microchip

The creation of the integrated circuit, known as the microchip in 1958 meant that more power could be compressed into less space. There was a real need for this, as early computers such as the ENIAC and Colossus were enormous; on average they were the same length and weight as three to four double-decker buses and contained thousands of buzzing electronic switches known as vacuum tubes. Despite their size, they were thousands of times less powerful than a modern laptop!

Figure 8.1 Microchip

The Internet

As you might expect for such an expansive and constantly evolving technology, it is impossible to credit one person with the invention of the Internet. The Internet was created by and continues to be shaped by the work of dozens of pioneering scientists, programmers and engineers who each developed new features and technologies that eventually merged to become the Internet.

Figure 8.2

Work on the Internet began in the 1960s when the potential of computers being able to share information was realised. The first workable prototype of the Internet was known as ARPANET (Advanced Research Projects Agency Network). It used packet switching to allow multiple computers to communicate on a single network. In the 1970s and 1980s the technology continued to grow to incorporate a communications model that set standards for how data could be transmitted between multiple networks. Then in 1990, Tim Berners-Lee, a computer scientist, invented the World Wide Web – the most common way of accessing data online in the form of websites and hyperlinks. The web enabled the Internet to become more user friendly, making it easy for people all over the world to access vast amounts of data on a daily basis.

The mobile phone

The technology behind mobile phones was developed in the late 1940s when it was first used in two-way radios for communication within the emergency services. Early mobile phones involved one very powerful base station covering a wide area, often referred to as 0G or zero generation mobile phones. Their mobility was limited, the service was poor and devices were heavy and also extremely expensive. Hence the development of 1G mobile phones which were introduced in the 1980s. These were smaller in size and utilised fully automatic cellular networks. A decade later 2G mobile phones were introduced. These had improved voice quality as well as offering additional services, such as paging, faxes, text messages and voicemail; however, the network offered limited data service. This was to be rectified with the development of 3G mobile phones which presented the opportunity for consumers to use audio, graphics and video applications, although such activities were severely constrained by network overload. More advanced 4G mobile phones offered a solution to this by providing transmission rates of up to 20 Mbps while simultaneously accommodating Quality of Service features. No doubt mobile phones, as all technology, will continue to improve and expand the services that they provide.

Figure 8.3

Key individuals

Charles Babbage – The first mechanical computer

Charles Babbage is considered to be 'the father of the computer', as he created the first mechanical computing engine in 1822 which eventually led to more complex designs. The computing engine, known as the 'difference engine,' was capable of computing several sets of numbers and making hard copies of the results. Although it looked nothing like the computers we know today (see Figure 8.5) it is considered by many around the world to be the birth of the modern-day computer.

Figure 8.4
Charles Babbage

Ada Lovelace – The computer algorithm

Ada Lovelace is recognised as leading the way in computer programming and is regarded as a mathematical genius. Lovelace developed the first computer algorithm during her employment with Charles Babbage. The algorithm was able to compute Bernoulli numbers (a sequence of rational numbers). Furthermore, Lovelace's work with Babbage resulted in her prediction of future computers to not only perform mathematical calculations, but also manipulate symbols, mathematical or not.

Figure 8.5 The difference engine at the London Science Museum

Figure 8.6 Ada Lovelace

Alan Turing – First concepts of what we consider a modern computer

Alan Turing is widely considered to be the 'father of modern computer science and artificial intelligence'. He developed the first theoretical concept of a modern computer that could turn thought processes into numbers. In 1936 Turing proposed the 'Turing Machine' – the first digital computer program which would enable a machine to read a series of ones and zeros which described the steps needed to solve a problem or task. Based on this, the first electric programmable computer, known as 'the Colossus', was created. The Colossus assisted Britain in winning World War II by deciphering encrypted German communications produced by the German computer Enigma.

Figure 8.7 Alan Turing memorial in Sackville Park in Manchester

Bill Gates

Bill Gates had an early interest in computing and began programming at the age of 13. Two years later he went into business with his friend Paul Allen and they developed the 'Traf-o-Data', a computer program which monitored traffic patterns in Seattle and earned them $20,000. In 1975, before finishing his law degree, Gates left Harvard to develop software with Allen for the newly emerging personal computer market. This software became known as Microsoft, the world's largest software business. Through technological innovation, keen business strategy and aggressive business tactics, Gates became one of the richest men in the world.

Figure 8.8 Bill Gates

SUBJECT KNOWLEDGE

According to the D&T National Curriculum (2014) the following aims should be introduced in KS2.

Design

- generate, develop, model and communicate their ideas through discussion, annotated sketches, cross-sectional and exploded diagrams, prototypes, pattern pieces and CAD

Technical knowledge

- apply their understanding of computing to program, monitor and control their products

Applying computing in KS2 to program, monitor and control products

Computing has strong links with mathematics, science, and D&T and provides insights into both natural and artificial systems. The core of computing is computer science, in which children are taught the principles of information and computation, how digital systems work, and how to put this knowledge to use through programming. Building on this knowledge and understanding, children are able to use information technology to create programs, systems and a range of content. In addition, the use of computing ensures that children become digitally literate.

What is computer programming?

The process of developing an algorithm, which is a set of instructions, written to perform a specified task on a computer.

What is computer control?

A set of instructions programmed into a machine which cause it to operate in a predetermined manner. Equipment and devices are controlled by pressing buttons on either a control panel or a remote control. For example if you press the button for a delicate wash on a washing machine the machine will run the program for this particular wash, e.g. cool water, light spin, etc.

What is computer monitoring?

Computer monitoring involves the use of sensors for two main purposes:

1   as a scientific measuring tool to record information about environmental changes over a period of time
2   as data logging to record the resulting information in a table or as a graph so that it can be examined

The role of a sensor

A sensor is a device that measures and responds to some type of input from the physical environment. The specific input could be light, heat, motion, moisture, pressure or any one of a great number of other environmental phenomena. The output is commonly a signal that is converted for observers to be able to read at the sensor location. For example the temperature shown on a thermostat for heating is transmitted electronically to the boiler which turns on the heating.

Sensors that you are most likely to use in Primary D&T are ones which detect temperature, sound, touch and light. Data loggers are often found in the depths of Science cupboards and would be ideal for monitoring the environment.

Table 8.1 Examples of equipment and devices which use computer control

Inside the home	Outside the home
washing machine	traffic lights systems
cooker	CCTV cameras
microwave	parts of car engines
TV	barcode scanners
burglar alarm	aircraft
telephone	lifts

Table 8.2 Advantages and disadvantages of using computer control

Advantages	Disadvantages
• more consistent results	• requires skilled operators
• reduces labour costs	• expensive to set up
• faster for high-volume production	• can be slower for one-off or low-volume production
• improves accuracy by automating tedious, repetitive tasks	• if there is a power cut the system will not work
• improved safety and hygiene	• if the computer malfunctions the system will not work
• easier monitoring	

Table 8.3 Sensors and their roles

Type of sensor	Measures	Function
heat sensors	temperature (degrees Celsius)	may detect the presence of a person or control the heating
magnetic sensors	magnetic field	used to detect metal and can be placed in roads to monitor traffic flow
infra-red sensor	infra-red radiation	security alarm systems
water sensor	amount of water	swimming pool or windscreen wipers
touch sensor	detects if one object bumps into another	computer controlled robots
pH sensor	acidic/alkaline levels	environmental experiments, e.g. water pollution
sound sensor	levels of sound (decibels)	security alarm systems
light sensor	light (lux)	security lights

UNDERSTANDING AND USING THE CONCEPT OF A 'SYSTEM'

A control system is a device, or set of devices, that manages the behaviour of other devices or systems. Digital control systems use a program or series of commands to control the system's functioning. All systems have the following elements: input(s), process(es) and output(s).

There are two common classes of control systems: open-loop control systems and closed-loop control systems. The most basic type of system is called an open-loop system (Figure 8.9). In open-loop control systems, output is generated based on inputs. An example is a light switch – lamps glow (output) whenever the light switch (input) is on irrespective of whether light is required or not.

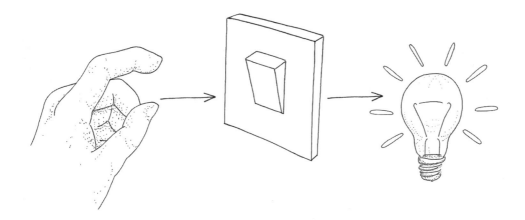

Figure 8.9

In closed-loop control systems current output is taken into consideration and corrections are made based on feedback. A closed-loop system is also called a feedback control system. An example is climate control:

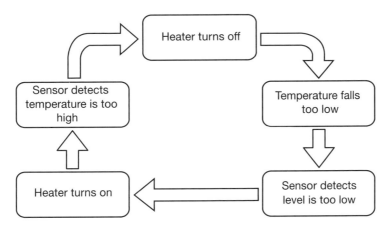

Figure 8.10 Feedback cycle for climate control

Computer Aided Manufacturing (CAM) efficiently controls and monitors production using computers. It is used for planning the different manufacturing operations, e.g. drilling, cutting, additive manufacturing such as 3D printing (currently being introduced into primary schools), to create a product.

Table 8.4 Advantages and disadvantages of using CAD/CAM

Advantages of using CAD/CAM	Disadvantages of using CAD/CAM
• Generally more accurate as it reduces human error	• Staff should to be trained
• There are some software packages which are free	• Software can be expensive
• It is easy to modify designs and you can save and edit as you go along	• Hardware and upkeep costs are high
• 3D visualisation	
• Understanding the need for quality and precision in making	

Computer Aided Design (CAD) is when computers are used to design products. Solid modelling is used to show how finished products will look. Different colours and textures can be added to the model and the product can be rotated to show different views. CAM uses data from CAD software to control machinery to ensure that the product is the same as the model.

Using CAD is a good way to enthuse children about designing, as well as giving them first-hand experience of seeing the benefits and challenges of using software that modern-day architects, designers and engineers use. Engaging with CAD programs enables children to strengthen their computer skills.

RESOURCES: SOFTWARE AND HARDWARE

Key Stage 1

2Design & Make is an easy-to-use CAD program produced by 2Simple. It contains a range of projects, which can be designed and made, such as a house, a car and a face mask. The software allows users to:

- change the thickness of the paint brush to add fine marks
- drag words onto the picture to label different parts
- use the 'undo' and 'redo' buttons to correct mistakes/modify the picture
- type simple captions into the text box at the bottom
- export designs into a format that can be printed on a 3D printer

A significant positive of the program is that while children design their model they can see a 360 degree view of it, as well as the net of their model. This aids their understanding of the relationship between 2D shapes, 3D shapes and nets. The nets can then be printed out, supporting the process of making them. The projects use set templates, which can be manipulated to a certain extent, by adding and removing points. The house project is a

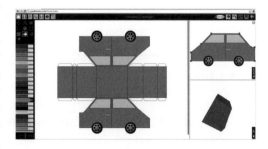

Figure 8.11 2Simple CAD software to design and make

good option for children wishing to be more creative, as the template, can be manipulated into any model.

Floor robots

Bee-Bots and Roamers are programmable floor robots and most schools have these for use in computing. However, they also make a great resource for control and monitoring in D&T. They are easy to operate and are a useful tool for teaching sequencing, estimation, problem-solving and programming.

Figure 8.12 Ute (made from a 3D net) being towed by a Bee-Bot

Bee-Bots and Roamers can be made to move forwards and backwards and turn left and right by pressing the arrow keys. The Bee-Bot can remember up to 40 commands, enabling increasingly sophisticated plans and programs. The Roamer comes in different styles, from the basic (forwards, backwards, left and right) to the more complex (degrees need to be inputted for turns and it also has sensors). The Probot is the 'big brother' of the Bee-Bot and is for teaching more advanced control techniques, such as drawing routes with a simple pen mechanism and using sensors. All these floor robots have corresponding software so

Figure 8.13 Bee-Bot mouse cover

that children can operate them independently or alongside the PC with the software. The Bee-Bot software allows children to design mats for the Bee-Bot, as well as jackets so that the Bee-Bot can be turned into a mouse, car or whatever the children desire. Children could also design and make vehicles (using 2Design & Make) so that the Bee-Bot can tow particular items or cargo depending on the design brief. Wheels can also be added (see Chapter 6 Mechanism).

THINGS TO CONSIDER

You can now buy Bee-Bots which can be charged via your computer with a USB lead. Unfortunately the rest of the floor robots are yet to follow suit, so have spare batteries at the ready!

Figure 8.14
Bee-Bots and charger

Figure 8.15
Probot

Figure 8.16
Roamer

Key Stage 2

Google SketchUp Make is a CAD software which can be used with children from Year Three and upwards, for 3D modelling. The software is free to download for students and educators (there is a pro version which you can purchase). It can be used to create pretty much anything from simple 3D shapes to complex models. You can create a room, a house, or entire neighbourhood, as well as everyday objects like furniture and vehicles. The software has a relatively smaller tool set compared to other CAD software such as AutoCAD and SolidWorks.

The software offers a range of videos that give in-depth advice on how to use each individual aspect of SketchUp, from concepts and shapes in the 'New to Google SketchUp' section to advanced Photoshop techniques in 'Creating models for Google Earth'.

Using Google Earth with SketchUp

SketchUp integrates with Google Earth, allowing children to import either a particular house, car, tree or a whole area into their design. This tool enables children to get thinking about the design brief, which may include ensuring that their building fits into a particular context. For example children could create a new design for their school on a real image of their old one.

Top tips

- Buildings with no curves on them are the easiest and most effective models for the children to build while they are still learning about the full capabilities of the program.
- Check the design from all angles before printing, as if you have joined shapes together you often find gaps which will need closing before it can be printed.

A common mistake is to believe that CAD can only be used to draw products, when in fact CAD can be used to design circuits, for example. The software can use system blocks to help identify which components are needed as well as helping to generate the design required for the layout of the circuit diagram, supporting the design process. The major benefits to using CAD software are that design ideas can be changed promptly and without difficulty and the circuit can be built and tested virtually before making it.

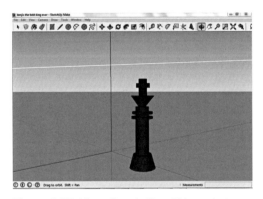

Figure 8.17 Using Google SketchUp to design a chess piece

THINGS TO CONSIDER

- If you add many images from Google Earth it will start to slow down your model.
- It is very fiddly – getting objects onto the correct plane can take a bit of time and is often achieved through trial and error.

Lego Education

Lego Education have produced a WeDo construction set which enables children to build Lego models that attach to the computer via USB, enabling models to be controlled by a computer program. The set contains a range of sensors such as a motor, tilt and a motion sensor which add movement and intelligence to the

Figure 8.18 WeDo Lego software

model. The WeDo software (which comes with the set) is used to create programs by dragging and dropping blocks into a sequence on the computer screen or canvas. Blocks control the sensors as well as the computer keyboard, display, microphone and speakers. Children can build many structures, such as a drumming monkey, a dancing birds, a hungry alligator and many more, from the one kit and the WeDo software provides easy to follow step-by-step instructions combined with clear pictures to construct each of these models.

Figure 8.19 WeDo Lego crocodile

Once children have mastered making the models suggested by the kit, they can start to think about what they could design and make using the kit that would meet a design brief, such as a device which provides treats for pets when they walk up to the box, a burglar deterrent or a rain cover activated by a sensor.

THINGS TO CONSIDER

- They are expensive, currently retailing at £100.79 (at the time of publishing) for one set, and obviously more than one will be needed for a class of 30 children.

- Each sets contain many tiny pieces which can easily get lost. Each set comes with a handy contents list with pictures, but as there are so many pieces it would be impractical to get children to check that each piece is back in the box at the end of every lesson. However, organising the pieces into the tray provided makes it easier to locate the correct pieces.

Figure 8.20 Organising WeDo Lego

- The problem with following precise instructions is that the children may not know why they are being asked to do certain actions. Ensure that you provide children with creative activities, such as making structures, which are not listed in the WeDo construction set, so that they have to use and apply what they have learned.

3D printing

3D printing is the creation of 3D solid objects from a digital file. This is achieved by laying down successive layers of materials above each other until the entire object is created. It can be achieved by using a CAD file that is converted by a 3D modelling program into a digital file that is uploaded to the 3D printer. The design is then outputted in numerous layers. The 3D printer binds all layers together, resulting in a final 3D printed object with no visible joints.

Figure 8.21
Ultimaker 3D printer is a popular printer for primary schools

3D printers certainly have the 'wow' factor but they also demonstrate to children how 2D sketches can be translated into 3D models, developing their ability to visualise items in three dimensions. In addition it provides children with knowledge of the 3D printing process and enables them to produce items with a much higher degree of accuracy than they could have achieved using normal primary school D&T processes.

THINGS TO CONSIDER

- Storing: thankfully a 3D printer is small, about the size of a microwave.

- Expense: 3D printers are very expensive. An alternative is to send the designs to be machined remotely, just as industry does. See www.3dhubs.com to find 3D printers in your area.

- The upkeep, e.g. ink cartridges and materials, is also costly, so think wisely about the project you choose; smaller products will mean cheaper overhead costs.

- Items take a long time to print (on medium quality it will take an hour to print a chess piece).

- Training for staff to use the printer and CAD software is required.

Raspberry Pi

Raspberry Pi was developed by the charity. The Raspberry Pi Foundation with the intention of providing low-cost computers and free software to students. It is a credit-card sized computer that plugs into a computer monitor or TV and uses a standard keyboard and mouse. It enables children to learn how to program in languages such as Python and Scratch. The device is able to do everything you would expect a desktop computer to do, from surfing the Internet, to making spreadsheets and playing games.

The following Raspberry Pi projects were designed and created by primary school children:

- *A door answering system for elderly or disabled people*: a wireless keyboard allows the person to unlock the door or send a message to the person outside the house from anywhere in the house.
- *Raspberry running*: at the end of each lap, the runner taps the Raspberry Pi with their tag, which logs and uploads their time to a special website for everyone to view. This enables runners to view their time and have a little bit of friendly competition with each other.
- *Pen Pi*: the device is a modern version of a pen friend. Schools are linked up in a more cost effective way, using discarded keyboards, monitors, Raspberry Pi and SKYPE.

For further details see: www.techradar.com/news/computing/8-great-raspberry-pi-projects-created-by-kids-1143243.

THINGS TO CONSIDER

- *Additional accessories* such as power cables, SD cards and speakers are required. You can also buy a Raspberry Pi camera if you want to program surveillance, for example. As they don't run off batteries they need to be plugged in all the time, so you may want to consider purchasing a *PiHub* which is capable of powering four Raspberry Pis at a time. The Raspberry Pis can be connected to a DVI monitor fairly cheaply (via an HDMI-to-DVI adapter); to connect to a VGA monitor you will need a digital-to-analogue conversion.

Figure 8.22 Raspberry Pi

- *Set-up time*: you will need time to insert the SD card and power lead, disconnect the keyboards, mice and monitors from the school computers and connect them to Raspberry Pis and then ensure you have time to restore the computers back to their original state. If you are restricted by time you may want to buy the ready-to-assemble project kits.

Makey Makey

Makey Makey is an invention kit which allows you to create computer controllers from everyday items. It utilises any material that will conduct even a slight electrical current, for example Play Doh, pencils, grapes, etc., and turns these into input devices such as touch-pads. It can also connect to the Internet.

Figure 8.23 Makey Makey

The kit includes everything you will need: crocodile clips, connection cables and a USB cable. It is easy to use; you simply load up a program, whether it be games, instruments, word processors, and plug in the Makey Makey board. Then it's just a case of deciding what does what.

Below is a list of ideas for projects using Makey Makey, you can find these and many more on Makey Makey's website.

Operation game

The game uses Makey Makey, Scratch and some recycled materials. Children can create their own Operation game, which involves removing the patient's bones and organs without touching the sides (see: http://makeymakey.com/guides/pdfs/Makey Makey ScratchOperationGame.pdf). This could be adapted to make other board games that relate to other subjects the children are learning such as memory games, factors games, interactive displays, etc.

Make a musical instrument

There are many different types of musical instruments children could make, such as a water piano, a cardboard guitar and wind chimes. The website also shows a miniature working drum kit using Makey Makey, Scratch and a 3D printer.

Security deterrent

The anti-theft alarm goes off when anyone tries to take the object in question. The device uses Makey Makey and Scratch.

Rain gauge

The rain gauge is made using a 3D printer and works using Makey Makey, and Scratch.

THINGS TO CONSIDER

It can seem like a gimmick unless you use Scratch to program the device.

Stop motion animation

Stop motion (also known as stop frame) is an animation technique to make static objects appear as if they are moving on their own. The object is moved in small increments between individually photographed frames, creating the illusion of movement when the series of frames is played as a continuous sequence. The technique is often used in puppet-based animation so could be linked to puppet projects (see Chapter 5 Textiles).

Before children consider filming they need to have had time to plan a short story, which they will need to practice with the puppets/Play Doh models/dolls (anything which can make small movements), so they can see what potential movements they can perform. This can then be planned using a story board so that children think about what will happen in each frame. They will also need to consider the scenery and whether this will change.

Children will need to understand that the point of a stop motion piece is **not** individual photos but a multiple image series, capturing motion. Rather than editing each individual shot, they will be editing the series by means of gathering and placing the images into a timeline.

Adding audio

Audio may not be the main point of a stop motion film; however, it can bring a film to life and add to a multi-sensory experience. Audio can be as simple as adding background music or sounds, such as the rustling of leaves as a character walks, or it can be narration/characters conversing. It may even be all three depending on the children's abilities and time available for the project.

Editing

Once the images are uploaded, titles and credits can be added as well as special effects or transitions.

Who is your audience?

Consider how you want to share the piece: do you want to post it to the school's website, share with other schools, post to a blog or burn it to a DVD? Decide this before choosing your software as some are more suitable for certain outputs.

What you will need will depend on whether you are using an App or a website. Possible equipment required for each group includes:

- a digital camera (or web camera which allows you to take individual pictures)
- a set of computers (laptop/desktop)
- or just an iPad or smartphone with an inbuilt camera (the only difficulty here is keeping the iPad/phone in the same position each time, but this can be overcome by using an iPad/phone stand)

Animation techniques

- *Onion skinning*: lets you see two or more images at once, some are of the previous frames and the others represent the pictures you are about to take. This allows each new frame of animation to be placed directly on top of images of previous frames (the images are dimmed, more so for the earlier ones, to make it possible to draw over them without getting confused about what's new and what's old). This helps create a smooth motion.

Figure 8.24 Onion skinning

- *Morphing*: changes (or morphs) one image or shape into another through a seamless transition. Most often it is used to depict one person turning into another through technological means or as part of a fantasy or surreal sequence.
- *Chroma key*: is a technique for mixing two images or frames together, in which usually a single colour from one image is removed (or made transparent), revealing another image behind it. The technique is also known by other names such as greenscreen, blue screen, colour keying and colour-separation overlay.
- *Time lapse animation*: simply click on that tab and you are presented with options for how often each picture is taken and for how long you want it to continue to snap the shots.

Software

There are many programs available to schools, some of which you can download for free. Table 8.5 shows a few recommendations depending on your needs.

Table 8.5 Potential websites and apps to make stop motion animation (all under £4.00 at time of publication)

Name of app	Review	
	Pros	**Cons**
iMovie	• easy-to-use interface • fun trailer feature • effective help tool • plenty of sharing options • speedy performance features such as onion skinning, zoom, speed changes, picture-in-picture and split-screen	• some operations are not so intuitive • you can't share to desktop iMovie through iCloud • limited text formatting
ABCya Animate	• child-centred interface • appropriate for KS1 • short video tutorial shows how to use controls and create animations • it allows users to adjust playback frame rate (slow, medium, fast) • onion skinning • use in app or website	• provides no option to add narration
Smoovie	• easy to use • visual effects: chroma key (for green and blue screen) and colour splash • you can customise each effect • effects can be chained together • you can vary the pace and mood of your animation • onion skinning	• only works on Mac or iPad • compatible only with the built-in cameras • you can only fine-tune your animation within the app
SAM Animation	• free to download (demo version) • SAM Animation site has online help-guides • snap images from a live web-cam feed or import pictures • onion skinning • add text and shape overlays to each frame • import movie files • export your project into a variety of movie formats	• you can't use it on a Mac

THINGS TO CONSIDER

- You and your children will need a lot of patience and time!

- Try to complete the filming over the course of a morning or, if you are going to need to come back to it, get children to create a map of where the camera and props need to be positioned.

- Shoot at 12 frames a second (the standard for most of the applications listed in the table).

- Shoot 12 shots at the start of the movie without anything moving. This allows the viewer to settle into the movie.

- Think carefully about group sizes, if using puppets you will need one person per puppet and you will need one person to film each scene, and you may want someone to be in charge of the scenery.

General things to consider for control and monitoring units:

- Have a small number of children who are pre-trained in using the software/equipment and who can then be tasked to help others. This can drastically improve a class's progression, as it reduces the waiting time for children during the early learning of the software/equipment and can direct more advanced help to those most in need.

- Don't be afraid to relinquish control! This will encourage children to learn new techniques and skills which they can demonstrate to you and the class.

- All of the suggested software are ideal vehicles to stimulate and engage EAL and SEN learners as they are not language based.

- Children can generally pick up the basics of the suggested software/equipment in a couple of lessons. Once children are confident using the basic tools they can be given a brief which includes specific design criteria.

IDEAS FOR PROJECTS

3D PRINTING	• jewellery • memory stick holders • board game pieces, e.g. chess, Monopoly • dolls' house furniture • miniature drum kit
CAD	• buildings • vehicles • chess piece • circuits • robots
MAKEY MAKEY	• musical instrument • interactive displays • anti-theft alarm • entertainment devices
WeDo Lego	• fairground rides (see lesson plan) • robots • treat box for pets (opens using motion detection) • moving vehicle
RASPBERRY PI	• door answering system • weather surveillance • burglar deterrent
FLOOR ROBOTS	• design and make a floor robot trailer which can carry cargo (see lesson plan)

© 2016, *The Really Useful Primary Design and Technology Book*, E. Flinn and S. Patel, Routledge

CROSS-CURRICULAR LINKS

LITERACY	• following complex instructions
NUMERACY	• creating and following algorithms • problem-solving, e.g. debugging • measuring accurately, e.g. when creating nets and designs to meet a specified size • scale drawing of design
SCIENCE	• design light covers, links to light and shadows
GEOGRAPHY	• use CAD to design game pieces from different cultures • design Aztec/Egyptian pyramid using CAD
HISTORY	• use CAD to design WW2 Anderson shelters • discover when computers were invented and how they have impacted on technology today
RS/RE	• design religious buildings using CAD
MUSIC	• create music for animation • fairground ride theme music • create music using Makey Makey
PSHEC	• group work, problem-solving • PSHEC theme for animations
MFL	• program Lego structure to speak your chosen language

© 2016, *The Really Useful Primary Design and Technology Book*, E. Flinn and S. Patel, Routledge

HOW TO MAKE SOME OF THE MODELS ILLUSTRATED IN THIS CHAPTER

How to make a fairground ride using WeDo Lego

Using WeDo software create a program which spins the Lego people around

© 2016, *The Really Useful Primary Design and Technology Book*, E. Flinn and S. Patel, Routledge

To program and control a box to open and close using WeDo Lego

Make a box, see structures chapter for nets

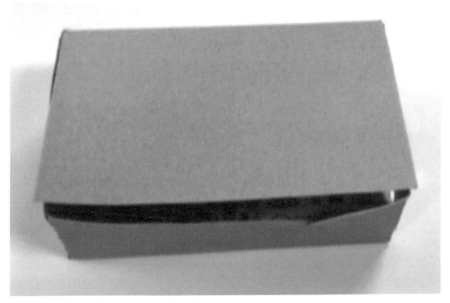

Using WeDo Lego make a motorised lever

Using the WeDo software create a program which opens and closes a box when the sensor detects movement

© 2016, *The Really Useful Primary Design and Technology Book*, E. Flinn and S. Patel, Routledge

Make a camera trap

Jewelled Box

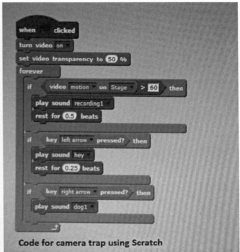

Code for camera trap using Scratch

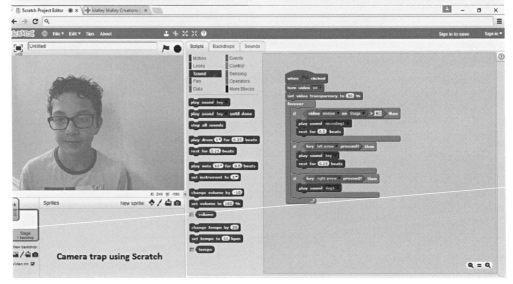

Camera trap using Scratch

© 2016, *The Really Useful Primary Design and Technology Book*, E. Flinn and S. Patel, Routledge

Net for Bee-Bot

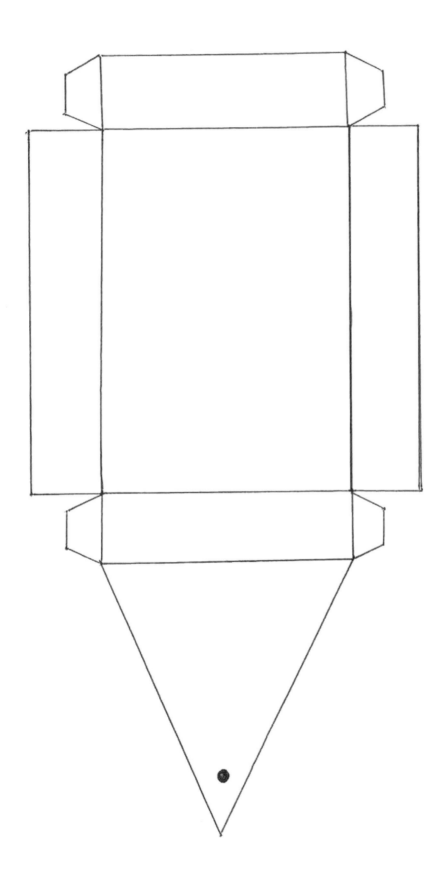

© 2016, *The Really Useful Primary Design and Technology Book*, E. Flinn and S. Patel, Routledge

Net for Bee-Bot

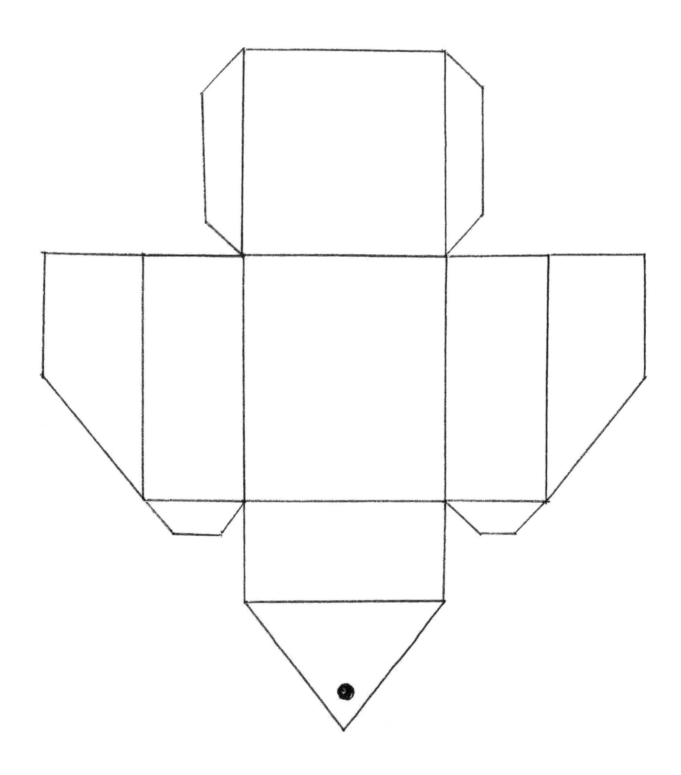

© 2016, *The Really Useful Primary Design and Technology Book*, E. Flinn and S. Patel, Routledge

Net for Bee-Bot

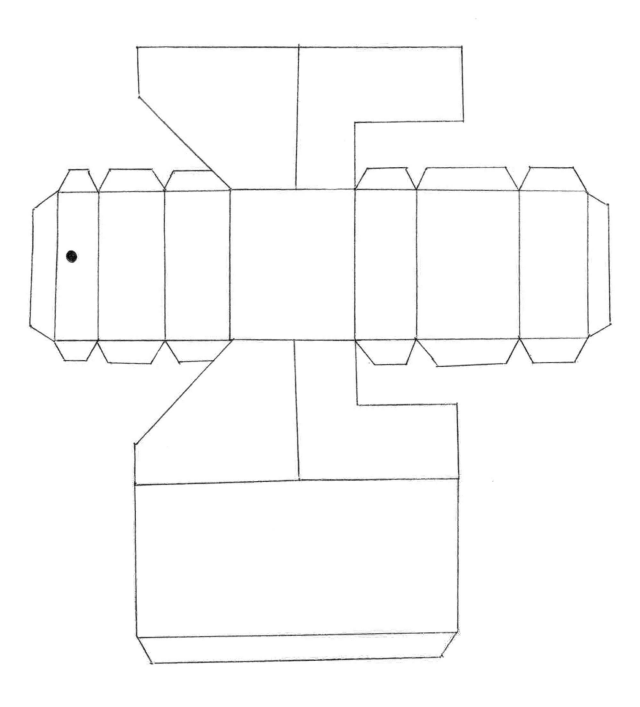

© 2016, *The Really Useful Primary Design and Technology Book*, E. Flinn and S. Patel, Routledge

LESSON PLANS

KS1

Although control and monitoring is not a requirement for D&T in KS1, this lesson plan links D&T with computing objectives from KS1.

Controlling Bee-Bots for a particular purpose

KS2

Using Makey Makey and WeDo Lego© to control and stimulate environments

IT CONTROL AND MONITORING: KS1 LESSON PLAN

Session	D&T skills	Lesson outline	Resources	Differentiation
1	Research	**Introduction** Introduce the Bee-Bot, explain and demonstrate how to move it using the arrow buttons and go. This could be done with the class sitting in a circle around the Bee-Bot. Show a Bee-Bot map and choose children to program the Bee-Bot to move to certain position, e.g. to the 'school.' **Focused practical task** The children can work in pairs or in groups of three or four to investigate how the Bee-Bot moves. Make sure each group knows how to use the basic tools of the Bee-Bot: switch on and off; clear the memory; move forwards, backwards, turn right and left. You may want to check their understanding by setting some basic tasks such as getting the Bee-Bot to move: • around a book • to the end of the table and back • forward 5, backwards 5: where did you end up? • forward 5, turn right, forward 5, turn right, forward 5, turn right, forward 5: what have you drawn? **Plenary** Bring children to sit back in a circle and ask children to demonstrate some of the activities above. Introduce the design brief for the project: To design and make a maze for you to navigate your Bee-Bot through. Introduce mazes, show the class a range of mazes such as Longleat Safari Park hedge maze, York maze cut out from a maize field, Peace maze made from Yew trees, Water maze in Kent and the Minotaur maze made from basalt and recycled glass. You could link this to the Tudors and take the children to Hampton Court, which has a fantastic hedge maze that children can go through. Explain that next lesson they will design their maze.	• Website for images of mazes: www.telegraph.co.uk/gardening/gardeningpicturegalleries/9956772/Amazing-British-mazes.html!frame=2520954 • Bee-Bots for each group • Bee-Bot map	<u>Support</u>: could be supported by adults or more able children. <u>Extend</u>: children could be asked to make the Bee-Bot: • turn in a full circle • make a rectangle • make a square

© 2016, *The Really Useful Primary Design and Technology Book*, E. Flinn and S. Patel, Routledge

IT CONTROL AND MONITORING: KS1 LESSON PLAN *continued*

Session	D&T skills	Lesson outline	Resources	Differentiation
2	Design	**Introduction** Remind children of the design brief. Check children's understanding of mazes and go through the key features that a maze needs to have: an entrance, an exit, pathways with no exit and a pathway to the exit. Write these up so that children can refer back to them. Introduce children to your chosen CAD* program (you could use 2DIY 3D). Model how to design a maze on the IWB using CAD. Show children how to build pathways and remove blocks if they make a mistake. Create a simple maze together, then demonstrate how to check if the maze works by 'playing the game'. Leave the class maze on the IWB so children can use it for support. **Focused practical task** Children to work in pairs or small groups to use the CAD program to design their maze. **Plenary** Children could try each other's mazes or you could show some on the IWB. Refer to the list of features of a maze so that children can self assess the mazes. *If you don't have an appropriate CAD there a lots of free online maze generators which you could use.	• CAD program, such as 2DIY 3D • laptops/computers This lesson could be done in an IT suite	<u>Support</u>: children could make a maze with only 2 pathways. <u>Extend</u>: children could design a more complex maze which has two paths to the exit, plus other pathways with no exits.
3	Design	**Introduction** Explain to the class that in this lesson they will be designing their maze. Refer back to the last lesson and ask children what they need to remember when designing their maze. Ask children if they can remember the features of a maze. Model how to design a maze on the IWB with squared paper background. Demonstrate, using a ruler, how to make sure that the pathways keep an equal width (you could use the width of a ruler). Check that there is a clear path to the exit. Model labelling the entrance, exit and any dead ends.	• Squared paper • Bee-Bots for each group	<u>Support</u>: children could make a maze with only 2 pathways. <u>Extend</u>: children could design a more complex maze which has two paths to the exit, plus other pathways with no exits.

© 2016, *The Really Useful Primary Design and Technology Book*, E. Flinn and S. Patel, Routledge

Session	D&T skills	Lesson outline	Resources	Differentiation
		Task In groups, children to design their mazes on squared paper. **Plenary** Groups to swap their designs. Can they find the exit wing 1 of the pathways? Children to use the list of features of a maze to peer assess the mazes.		
4	Make mock-up	**Introduction** Explain to the class that in this lesson they will be using their designs to make a mock-up. Explain what a mock-up is and the importance of this stage in the making process. Model how to design a maze on large squared paper using the design from last lesson to inform the mock-up. Also show children that they must make sure that the pathways are wide enough so that the Bee-Bot can fit. Use the features of a maze to check that all the features have been included. Get children to sit in a circle. Ask children to program the Bee-Bot through the correct pathway to the exit. Discuss whether any aspects of the design need changing. **Task** In groups, children to use their design to create their mock-up. **Mini-plenary** Share any changes children have made. Encourage children to keep checking that the Bee-Bot can move along the pathways. **Plenary** Groups to swap their mock-ups and test out if they work using the Bee-Bots. Groups to feed back to each other.	• Metre ruler • Large squared paper • Bee-Bots for each group	<u>Support</u>: children could be supported by adults to add an alternative 'dead end' pathway. <u>Extend</u>: children can be challenged to make more complex pathways.

© 2016, *The Really Useful Primary Design and Technology Book*, E. Flinn and S. Patel, Routledge

IT CONTROL AND MONITORING: KS1 LESSON PLAN *continued*

Session	D&T skills	Lesson outline	Resources	Differentiation
5	Make	Decide on what materials they will use to make their maze. You may want everyone to use the same material or you might want to give a selection of options such as Play Doh, Duplo, Multi-link, etc. If children use materials which cannot be stuck down such as Multi-link you will need to have an area large enough and preferably off the ground to store/display these. Introduction Using the mock-up from last lesson, model how to use this to build your maze. It is easiest if children use the mock-ups as a template and sit materials on top of the pathway walls. Task Provide children with their mock-up maze and any materials they need to build their maze. Plenary Children to show their mazes so far and to say what they need to do next lesson.	• Children's mock-ups • Bee-Bots for each group • Materials to make the maze	<u>Support</u>: children use larger blocks such as giant Lego blocks to make their maze. <u>Extend</u>: children can be extended by asking them to think about the aesthetics of their maze. For example, if their maze is made from Play Doh they could shape it in a particular way or if they used Lego they could incorporate patterns using the colours of the Lego pieces.
6	Make	Introduction Children to say what they need to do in this lesson to finish their maze. Explain the task to the class. Task Finish their mazes and program their Bee-Bot to travel to the exit. If there is time they could decorate the pathway and surrounding areas. Take pictures of the mazes which can be used for assessment purposes and to create a display. Plenary Children to feedback on whether they were able to complete their maze. Discuss: *Did the Bee-Bot fit on the pathway? Does their maze have an exit? Entrance? Is it easy to complete?*	• Bee-Bots for each group • Materials to make the maze	<u>Support</u>: children supported by adults. <u>Extend</u>: children could be extended by asking them to think about how their maze could be made more challenging.

© 2016, *The Really Useful Primary Design and Technology Book*, E. Flinn and S. Patel, Routledge

Session	D&T skills	Lesson outline	Resources	Differentiation
7	Evaluate	**Introduction** Sit in a circle with one group's maze in the middle. Ask children to program the Bee-Bot to travel to the exit. Discuss: *What was good about the maze? What could be improved?* Examples could be that the pathways were too wide/narrow; the route was too easy/difficult; there was a clear entrance and exit. **Task** Organise children so that they have another group's maze in front of them. Give them time to program the Bee-Bot to reach the exit. **Plenary** Children to provide feedback on whether they were able to complete the maze. Refer children back to the features of a maze and get children to use this to peer evaluate the maze. *Do they have any suggestions for how the maze could be improved?* This could be recorded on sheet with a star (one thing they liked about the design) and a wish (one thing they would change).	• Bee-Bots for each group	Support: children to evaluate using one star and a wish. Extend: children could be extended by thinking of two stars and a wish.

© 2016, *The Really Useful Primary Design and Technology Book*, E. Flinn and S. Patel, Routledge

IT CONTROL AND MONITORING: KS2 LESSON PLAN

Session	D&T skills	Lesson outline	Resources	Differentiation
1	Research You may require an additional lesson	WeDo Lego fairground ride and use of CAD Tell the children that they will be designing and making fairground rides using WeDo Lego. Show a range of different fairground rides on the IWB or better still take the class on a trip to a fairground. Evaluate the fairground rides, asking questions such as: *Does it look fun to ride? Is it safe? How many people can ride at a time? Discuss how the ride works. Which components make it move?* Show children the WeDo Lego and demonstrate how to make one of the models. Emphasise the importance of following each step and using the exact piece the program tells you to use, otherwise the model will not work. Allow children to work in groups and create one of the models. If possible, try to have an adult to support one-two groups. It would be good to teach this unit alongside teaching programming in computing. If not, you may want to spend another lesson getting children to make different models so that they become familiar with the software. Plenary Groups to show their models. Did they have any problems? How did they overcome them? How does their model move?	• Pictures, clips of fairground rides • WeDo Lego sets • Computers/laptops	Mixed ability groups or: Support: make simplest models Extend: make a more complex model.
2	Design	Show children the Design Cycle. Discuss why research is important. How has it helped children with their task? What will come next? Which part of the design cycle is most important? (all) Why? Ask children: *What are they going to be making in their D&T lessons? What is its purpose? Who is the user? What is the function? Ask children what they did in the last lesson: so what will they be doing today?* Discuss why children need to design their fairground ride before they make it. Ask children what features a design needs to include and write up the success criteria. Model how to design a fairground ride including all the essential features. Remind children that the design should fill the page. Discuss how light and sound could be used.	• WeDo Lego sets • WeDo Lego software • Extra Lego people • Computers/laptops	You could give different ability groups different criteria that their fairground ride must include, e.g: sound, motor, sensors, lights and/or it must be able to hold X number of Lego people. Challenge and extend more able to draw an exploded diagram.

© 2016, *The Really Useful Primary Design and Technology Book*, E. Flinn and S. Patel, Routledge

Session	D&T skills	Lesson outline	Resources	Differentiation
		Plenary Choose a child's design and, as a class, assess it using the success criteria. Give children time to use the success criteria to peer assess each other's design. What have children done well? What could they improve on?		
3	Research	Ask children what skills they are going to need to make their fairground ride (make a program to use a sensor/motor/sound/light depending on their ability and build a ride with Lego which can hold Lego people). Explain that this lesson will focus on practising these skills. Model how to: • build a fairground ride out of Lego • create a program which can make a sound • create a program which can turn a light on • create a program which uses a motor to create a rotating movement **Focused practical task** Children to have a go at the tasks modelled. **Plenary** Children to self assess: did they complete all the tasks they were set? Which were the hardest? Easiest? Are their rides safe/secure? Are their rides fun?	• Extra Lego people • WeDo Lego set • WeDo Lego software • Computers/laptops	Mixed ability groups or differentiate by design criteria given to ability groups, e.g.: <u>Support</u>: complete sound and motor task with adult support. <u>Extend</u>: complete all tasks modelled.

© 2016, *The Really Useful Primary Design and Technology Book*, E. Flinn and S. Patel, Routledge

IT CONTROL AND MONITORING: KS2 LESSON PLAN *continued*

Session	D&T skills	Lesson outline	Resources	Differentiation
4	Make a Prototype	Tell the class that they will be making a prototype based on their initial design. Discuss what a prototype is and why designers use them. Either choose a child's design or use yours from the previous lesson and demonstrate how to make this. Mini-plenary It is likely that lots of children will have difficulty getting their program to control the sensors and motors the first time round, so ask those who have been successful to share how they solved bugs within their programs. Plenary Children to show their prototypes and describe what has worked well and any changes they need to make. Ask children to talk through any problems they had and how they overcame them. Check that there is somewhere for the Lego people to sit.	• Extra Lego people • WeDo Lego set • WeDo Lego software • Computers or laptops	Mixed ability groups or differentiate by design criteria given to ability groups, e.g.: Support: create a fairground ride which holds four Lego people and uses a motor and produces sound. Extend: create a fairground ride which holds 10 Lego people, can rotate, uses lights and produces sound.
5	Make	Tell the children that they will be making their fairground ride in this lesson. What will they need to help them? (design, computers/laptops, WeDo Lego construction set and software, and Lego people). If possible have an adult on each table (you could invite parents in for these lessons). Remind children of the importance of being systematic and to check that each part of their program works before adding additional blocks. Plenary Children to share any problems that they had during the making and how they have or will overcome them. *Have their original designs changed? If so, why? Do they think a famous D&T designer such as Bill Gates made changes to his original plans?*	• Children's designs • Extra Lego people • WeDo Lego set • WeDo Lego software • Computers/laptops	Mixed ability groups or differentiate by design criteria given to ability groups, e.g.: Support: create a fairground ride which holds four Lego people and uses a motor and produces sound. Extend: create a fairground ride which holds 10 Lego people, can rotate, uses lights and produces sound.

© 2016, *The Really Useful Primary Design and Technology Book*, E. Flinn and S. Patel, Routledge

Session	D&T skills	Lesson outline	Resources	Differentiation
6	Evaluate	Refer children back to the Design Cycle. *What will they be doing in this lesson? What was their design brief? Do you they think the product meets the design brief? How do they know?* Allow children to test out their fairground rides and the fairground rides of others in the class. *Can it carry the specified number of Lego people? Which do they like the most? Why?* As a class, produce the success criteria for their fairground rides. Use the success criteria to self assess their ride. Tell children that they are going to write a review of another child's fairground ride. This could be done as a blog so that a video of the fairground ride can be included. Discuss what should be included in the review and write this up in a list so that children can refer back to it. Provide a list of technical vocabulary to use, such as sensors, structure, sound sensor, light sensor, motor, etc. Plenary Choose a few reviews to read out. Are they accurate? Do they use technical vocabulary? Are they useful to a potential buyer? Discuss how computers have changed over the years. If there is time, get children to use the computers to do some research about this. Discuss how computers have had an impact on our lives today and in particular how technology has impacted the types of rides that are made today.	• Children's designs • Extra Lego people • WeDo Lego set • WeDo Lego software • Computers/laptops	Mixed ability groups or: Support: provide a writing scaffold and a word bank. Extend: create a blog which includes a video of their fairground ride and pictures of their original designs.

© 2016, *The Really Useful Primary Design and Technology Book*, E. Flinn and S. Patel, Routledge

REFERENCES

Groom, B. (2014). 'Lack of engineers threatens UK recovery, say industrialists', *The Financial Times* 16 March. Available from www.ft.com [Accessed 28 July 2014].

Loveless, A. (2003). *The Role of ICT*, London: Continuum.

9 Assessment of children's progress in D&T

ASSESSING PRACTICAL SKILLS AND KNOWLEDGE

A busy teacher will not have time to sit with each child in turn to analyse their progress in D&T every lesson. However, a brief survey of a group of children can provide an overview of their progress. Try using the six pointers below.

Are the children:

- showing understanding by explaining how things work?
- naming tools and materials correctly?
- able to discuss of the properties of materials?
- using tools and materials safely and accurately?
- following their plans?
- identifying and trying to solve problems?

TRACKING PRACTICAL SKILLS AND KNOWLEDGE

The following tables give an outline of the practical skills and knowledge that children should be developing during their D&T lessons.

Table 9.1 KS1: practical skills and knowledge

STRUCTURES	• use construction kits to make working models • choose and use a selection of materials for model-making (e.g. card, wood, tubes, cotton reels, straws) • join components using glue or tape; know which is appropriate for the material • cut wood with a hacksaw and bench hook • use sandpaper to smooth cut ends of wood • join wooden components with glue • watch an adult using a glue gun • use Jinks' corners to strengthen structures
MECHANISMS	• use a hole punch • use paper fasteners • assemble a lever to make a moving picture • use levers and linkages to make a picture move • put wheels on axles to make a moving vehicle • make a sliding picture • cut card with scissors following straight and curved lines • make a simple mechanism using an axle and pulley
TEXTILES	• draw round a template and cut out fabric shapes • join fabrics with staples or glue • sew using running stitch • decorate fabrics with paints, pens and haberdashery (ribbons, buttons, sequins, etc.)
FOOD	• name familiar foods • know where food comes from • group familiar foods, e.g. as fruit or vegetables, and understand the need for a mixture of foods in a healthy diet • work hygienically and safely • cut, grate and peel foods using tools and hands • mix ingredients with hands or a spoon • use simple measuring aids (spoons, cups, scoops) • prepare foods for cooking in an oven
CONTROL	N/A
ELECTRONICS	N/A

Table 9.2 Lower KS2: practical skills and knowledge

STRUCTURES	• use pre-drawn nets to make 3D card structures • cut, score and fold card accurately • make stable frameworks using strengthening struts, Jinks' corners, etc. • cut wood with a hacksaw and bench hook to 10 mm accuracy • sand wood evenly to produce a smooth finish • use a glue gun with one-to-one supervision
MECHANISMS	• use scissors and hole punch with some accuracy • cut out slots and windows in card • assemble complex linkages using card or string to make a figure move • use pulleys to form a transport system • use a balloon on a syringe to make a pneumatic model
TEXTILES	• create a pattern (template), taking seam allowances into account • understand how a prototype improves a clothing design • join fabrics with running stitch, back stitch or over-sewing • decorate fabric with haberdashery and appliqué • use simple fastenings, e.g. buttons and loops, Velcro
FOOD	• know and understand the components of a balanced diet • make healthy choices for snacks • follow a simple recipe • cut, chop, peel and slice food safely and hygienically • mix ingredients with a spoon or whisk • combine food to make a tasty snack, taking flavour and texture into account • use an oven under close supervision
CONTROL	• control a model or circuit using an appropriate program or switch
ELECTRONICS	• build a circuit with a bulb, battery and switch • make a simple switch with foil

Table 9.3 Upper KS2: practical skills and knowledge

STRUCTURES	• create nets for 3D shapes • measure and cut wood neatly to 1mm accuracy • sand wood to shape it for a purpose • use a hand drill to drill holes in wood • join materials with glue, nails or screws, as appropriate • use a glue gun under supervision • design and make strong frameworks to hold mechanisms
MECHANISMS	• cut accurate slots in card (using a craft knife and cutting mat under supervision) • use gears or pulleys to transfer movement from a motor to a model • explain why small and large gears/pulleys are needed in a motorised model • use cams to make an up/down mechanism • describe the motions produced by various shaped cams • use linkages and cams together to make a more complex movement • use linked syringes to make a model move
TEXTILES	• name and know the properties of some common fabrics • understand how fabric properties can affect the structure and appearance of a product • cut fabrics accurately using pattern pieces • pin and tack pieces before sewing • use a seam allowance • join fabrics using a variety of stitches or machine sewing (under supervision) • assemble 3D products from patterns or templates • decorate products appropriately at a suitable point in the construction of the product
FOOD	• taste a range of foods and develop a food vocabulary • know how some foods are grown, reared, caught or processed • prepare foods safely and hygienically • choose foods for a purpose (e.g. a snack, a cool drink, soup), showing awareness of the need for a balanced diet • choose foods which are in season and know where the food has come from or how it is grown • weigh ingredients using kitchen scales • cut, slice, peel and grate foods as appropriate • combine ingredients by kneading, beating and whisking • cook foods on a stove or in an oven as appropriate
CONTROL	• control a model using an appropriate program • use sensors (motion/light) to operate a model
ELECTRONICS	• use bulbs, buzzers, motors and switches effectively in models • understand how to draw a circuit diagram • build a switch for a particular purpose • trouble-shoot a circuit which isn't working (dead battery, blown bulb, poor connections)

ASSESSING DESIGN AND EVALUATION SKILLS

There are opportunities to assess children's written work in D&T through their design ideas and their evaluations.

Assessing design skills

The following points should be covered when assessing a design:

- Has the design been drawn using appropriate techniques such as cross-sectional or exploded diagrams?
- Is there a realistic order/sequence to the assembly?
- Have correct materials and tools been selected?
- Has the appropriate technical vocabulary been used?
- Is there evidence of research?
- Was a mock-up or prototype made? If so, has it informed the design process?
- Does the finished product match the final design?

Assessing evaluation skills

When assessing an evaluation, look or listen for comments from the children covering the following points:

- Does the product do what it should? If not, have the children been able to explain why and have they mentioned modifications to their design?
- Have the needs of users been identified and met? If not, is there a comment about how to rectify the problems?
- Have all changes which were made during the manufacturing process been noted down and explained?
- Is there a comment about the look of the finished product?
- Have the children been able to point out where their design was too ambitious or complex?
- Have the children thought about how to improve their product?

TRACKING DESIGN AND EVALUATION SKILLS

The following table summarises the skills a child should be showing in their designs and evaluations as they move through the primary years.

Tracking design and evaluation skills

	KS1	Lower KS2	Upper KS2
DESIGN	• use pictures and words to describe what they want to do • explain what they are making and which tools they are using • select materials and tools from a limited range • make a plan based on previous experience • use construction kits to make a mock-up	• use existing products to help with design • draw labelled diagrams • choose appropriate equipment, components and techniques • plan order of work • understand the usefulness of making a prototype • recognise that design must meet a need	• use knowledge of existing products to help with design • produce annotated diagrams and drawings • use correct technical vocabulary • produce step-by-step plans • think of several ideas and select the most appropriate • make a prototype first and use it to evaluate design • use various sources of information and market research
EVALUATION	• explain how a product works • recognise what has been done well • suggest things they could do better in future • compare to original design • show an awareness of the need for modification of original ideas	• recognise what isn't working and suggest a modification • show where they have changed the design for the better • evaluate in relation to design criteria and user's needs	• evaluate different designs and select which one to use • modify during manufacture and explain why • critically evaluate appearance and function • justify choice of materials and construction methods • develop own criteria for evaluation

© 2016, *The Really Useful Primary Design and Technology Book*, E. Flinn and S. Patel, Routledge

ASSESSING A FINISHED PRODUCT (TEACHER AND/OR SELF-ASSESSMENT)

In summary, a finished product should be assessed for:

- quality of manufacture – is it well constructed or poorly made?
- type of construction – from a kit or from scratch?
- function – does it work?
- appearance – how attractive is it?
- meeting design criteria – does it do what it should and have the needs of the user been met?
- purpose – does it have a clear purpose?
- innovation – is this a new idea?

TRACKING THE SKILLS REQUIRED TO PRODUCE A GOOD FINISHED PRODUCT

The following table gives some examples of what to expect from a finished product. Some expectations such as presentation and finish are the same regardless of the topic, but there are also some topic-specific requirements.

Tracking the skills required to produce a good finished product

	KS1	Lower KS2	Upper KS2
STRUCTURAL, MECHANICAL AND ELECTRICAL PROJECTS	• models may be built from reclaimed materials or from one type of kit • some type of simple movement incorporated • product assembled with increasing care and accuracy • product generally matches the design intention • appropriate details and features added to make product attractive	• models made from construction kit components combined with other materials • structures show some signs of strengthening • moving parts incorporated made from construction kits or from scratch • a prototype is made before assembling with some accuracy • product resembles design intention • product finished and presented to a reasonable standard	• models made without use of components from construction kits • structures are stable and strong • moving models incorporate a mechanism or motor • evidence of trialling ideas and making a prototype to produce a functional product • product shows evidence of ideas drawn from evaluations of existing products • well finished and presented
TEXTILE PROJECTS	• fabrics joined in correct orientation • product assembled with care and some accuracy (e.g. following a seam line) • product generally matches the design intention • appropriate details and features added to make product attractive or lifelike	• fabrics joined using a suitable stitch • use of pre-produced pattern to cut out components • a prototype made before measuring, marking and cutting • product assembled with some accuracy using stitching rather than glue • product resembles design intention • product finished to a reasonable standard with raw edges folded under or neatened	• fabrics joined and details added using neat stitching, using seam allowances where appropriate • evidence of creating own pattern after producing prototypes. • product shows evidence of ideas drawn from evaluations of existing products • neatly finished with no raw edges visible and strong seams
FOOD PROJECTS	• ingredients chosen appropriately (i.e. fruit is chosen for a fruit salad) • choice of ingredients reflects a knowledge of taste • food is cut, peeled or grated reasonably well • the final product is assembled as neatly as possible and some thought is given to the look of the dish	• choice of ingredients reflect the idea of a healthy diet • choice of ingredients shows some understanding of taste and appearance • choice of ingredients reflects the season • ingredients are prepared carefully and there is some consistency in the size of chopped items • the final product is presented attractively	• choice of ingredients shows an understanding of healthy eating and a balanced diet • choice of ingredients shows an emerging understanding of taste, texture and smell • choice of ingredients reflects the season and the locality • food is prepared carefully, chopped to an appropriate and consistent size, peeled neatly and cooked correctly • ingredients are cut, weighed and combined accurately and mixed thoroughly • dishes are decorated and presented attractively

© 2016, *The Really Useful Primary Design and Technology Book*, E. Flinn and S. Patel, Routledge

10 D&T subject leader: roles and responsibilities

ROLE OF THE SUBJECT LEADER

The role of a subject leader is to provide professional leadership and management for a subject in order ensure that high quality teaching is secure, resources are used effectively and standards of learning and achievement for all children are high. In order to do this they are required to:

- keep up to date, examining recent documentation and literature, reporting changes back to colleagues, and collecting and disseminating information around the school;
- support, guide and motivate teachers and support staff in D&T;
- evaluate the effectiveness of teaching and learning in D&T;
- secure high standards of teaching and learning in D&T;
- assist in providing guidance on assessment and recording of work, progress of children in developing knowledge, personal capability in the subject, safety awareness and attainment targets;
- provide a policy outlining the schemes of work that match the programmes of study and attainment targets for each age group and draw up guidelines giving continuity, progression, breadth and balance within the subject at each key stage;
- take responsibility for estimating, ordering, maintaining and managing equipment and material resources across the school;
- report back to the head teacher and governors on progress within the school;
- establish links with other primary and secondary schools;
- communicate with parents, local industry, possibly making requests for contributions in the form of material resources;
- identify the needs of D&T in the school and use this to produce an annual action plan which will be part of a school Foundation Subject Development Plan.

EVALUATING YOUR SCHOOL'S NEEDS

One of the first tasks you will have as subject leader will be to evaluate your school's needs. To find out what is already happening in the school you may want to consider the following questions.

Documentation:
- Is there a policy?
- Is there an action plan?
- Is there long, medium and short term planning for D&T? Is it up to date?

Evidence:
- What evidence is there around school that your subject is being taught? (Displays, theme days, etc., photos of work, samples of work.)

Children's attitudes towards D&T:

- What do children think of D&T? Which aspects do they most/least enjoy and why?

Teachers' attitudes towards D&T:

- How do teachers feel about teaching D&T? Is there any training they would like? Note down any suggestions they have for improving the running of D&T in school.

Headteacher's vision for D&T:

- How does the headteacher see the subject developing?
- What did Ofsted say last time and what has been done since?
- What are standards like?

Resources:

- What resources are there? Is there a budget for resources? What is the need? How are they organised/accessed/accounted for?

Extra curricular:

- Are D&T clubs being run? Are children being taken on D&T trips? Are visitors for D&T being invited? Are these successful?

Next steps

Draw up an action plan for:

a) anything that needs doing before next academic year;
b) what can be achieved next year. Keep it manageable!

Follow your action plan, keep any evidence in your subject file and demonstrate good practice in your subject in your own class. Review your plan regularly (each half term/each term)!

CURRICULUM PLANNING

The essential, core knowledge, understanding and skills that all children should learn from KS1 to KS3 are set out in the D&T programmes of study. Wider aspects of D&T which are not considered by the National Curriculum will need to be considered by schools. As a result, all schools will develop their own individually tailored and continually evolving curriculum.

Long-term plan

A long-term plan shows how the teaching units are distributed across all the years in Foundation Stage and Key Stage 1 and 2 in a sequence that promotes curriculum continuity and progress in children's learning.

Table 10.1 Example Early Years Foundation Stage (EYFS) long-term plan based on the curriculum guidance for D&T for Foundation Stage (2014)

EYFS	Autumn 1	Autumn 2	Spring 1	Spring 2	Summer 1	Summer 2
Understanding the world	**Using technology**	**Nutrition and cooking**	**Construction/ joining**	**Using technology**	**Nutrition and cooking**	**Construction/ joining**
	Use programs/apps on the class desktop, laptop, iPad	Sandwiches Fruit salad Smoothies	Materials and their properties Paper weaving Learn to use a range of media and materials	Use a digital camera to take pictures Program Bee-Bots	Salads Soups Biscuits	Use junk modelling equipment and construction kits to build 3D constructions Learn to use tools

Table 10.2 Example KS1 and KS2 long-term plan based on the National Curriculum programme of study for D&T (2014)

Year group	Autumn	Spring	Summer
One	Food and nutrition Preparing fruit and vegetables	Construction structures Free-standing structures	Textiles Templates and joining structures
Two	Mechanisms Sliders and levers	Control and monitoring using CAD to generate, develop and model	Electrical and mechanical components
Three	Construction Structures Shell structures	Electrical and mechanical components	Food and nutrition Healthy and varied diet
Four	Textiles 2D shape to 3D product	Mechanisms Wheels and axles	Control and monitoring Program, monitor and control products
Five	Food and celebrating seasonality	Textiles Combining different fabric	Mechanical systems Cams and pneumatics
Six	Electrical and mechanical components	Control and monitoring program, monitor and control products using a 'system'	Construction Structures Frame structures

If resources are limited, try to make sure that, as much as possible, year groups are not studying the same unit at the same time. As you will see, this is impossible to achieve for all units.

Early Years Foundation Stage medium- and short-term planning

D&T forms part of the learning children acquire under the 'Knowledge and Understanding of the World' and the 'Expressive Arts and Design' branch of the Foundation Stage Curriculum.

Based on the Curriculum guidance for the Foundation Stage, here are some of the typical D&T learning experiences children will be encouraged to do in EYFS:

- learn how to use simple tools such as scissors and hammers
- use a range of techniques such as sticking and folding, to shape, assemble and join materials
- build with a wide range of objects, selecting appropriate resources and adapting their work where necessary
- think about uses and purposes of materials
- have experience of simple cooking techniques
- experiment with colour, design, texture, form and function
- discuss reasons that make activities safe or unsafe, for example: hygiene, electrical awareness, and appropriate use of senses when tasting different flavourings
- they will also learn to record their experiences by, for example, drawing, and making a tape or model

KS1 and KS2 medium-term planning

Using the objectives from the National Curriculum, learning objectives for each unit of work are identified. Potential teaching activities are matched with learning outcomes and essential key objectives are planned for, at least once throughout the year. Basic skills and cross-curricular links are made in planning where applicable.

KS1 and KS2 short-term plans

Short-term planning is prepared weekly and relates to the medium-term plans. The following activities have been removed from the National Curriculum (2014), but they are recommended by the Design and Technology Association (DATA) and should still be considered when planning:

- IDEAs: investigating, disassembly and evaluation activities (how familiar products work and what they are supposed to do)
- FPTs: focussed, planned tasks (developing a range of techniques, skills, and knowledge)
- DMAs: design and make assignments using a range of materials (KS1 – including food textiles and items that can be put together; KS2 – including electrical and mechanical components, food, textiles and stiff and flexible sheet material)
- Children to plan the sequence in which they make their products

Progression

The D&T programmes of study for KS1, KS2 and KS3 have been published together, ensuring that there is clear progression from primary through to and including secondary Key Stage 3. As a result, when planning units of work it is vital that teachers look at what has been taught before and what will be taught in the future. It is essential that age related expectations (see Chapter 9 Assessment) are utilised so that planning includes learning from previous Key Stages which is developed upon, ensuring that learning is developed cumulatively.

Assessment

As the D&T leader you will need to have an overview of the standards children from each class are meeting in D&T. Below are some suggestions for how you could do this:

- keep a portfolio of children's work (from the whole process, i.e. research, design, finished piece and evaluations)
- 'interview' children from different classes about their D&T experiences
- collect summative assessments at key points throughout the year

For information on how and what to assess in D&T see Chapter 9 Assessment.

Professional development

As Primary D&T is a developing subject which rapidly changes, it is crucial to keep abreast of these changes. The following strategies should help you in doing so:

- attend courses and local meetings
- establish a link with the D&T department at your local secondary school
- build a collection of D&T books
- have a collection of catalogues for ordering resources
- join professional associations like the Design and Technology Association (DATA)

The area of CPD you choose for teaching staff will depend on your school's needs. However there are increased technical demands and significant CPD needs for KS2 which you will need to consider. In particular, these include applying computing to program, monitor and control products and using CAD to develop and communicate ideas. CPD on gears, pulleys and levers (could be combined with Science CPD) would also be beneficial as these are highly technical.

You may also want to consider general CPD, such as how to address the Design Cycle, assessing D&T, different ways to evaluate in D&T lessons as well as planning D&T, including how trips/visitors can be incorporated.

The following organisations provide up-to-date CPD for Primary D&T:

- The Design and Technology Association (DATA):
  www.data.org.uk/for-education/primary/
- The National Stem Centre:
  www.nationalstemcentre.org.uk/news/affordable-cpd-for-design-and-technology-teachers
- Many universities, including Middlesex University:
  www.mdx.ac.uk/courses/short-courses/cpd-courses/cpd-short-courses-for-primary-schools-and-early-years-settings
- Food – a fact of life provides CPD on cooking and nutrition:
  www.foodafactoflife.org.uk/Sheet.aspx?siteId=20&sectionId=118&contentId=718

Although young people value technology, few study it beyond GCSE, which has left this country with a shortage of employees in these areas. Consequently primary education's role is vital in developing children's understanding of and interest in technology. National Foundation for Education Research (NFER) recommends that stimulating interest in this subject before GCSE choices (or equivalent) can increase engagement and encourage children to make subject choices that will help in pursuing a career in this area. Therefore one of the most important roles of the subject leader is to make a case to ensure that the profile of D&T within the school remains high. So, how can you do this?

Planning and going on school trips

Experiencing the real world is an essential part of education and school trips are the perfect way to do this. A school trip provides a learning venue that matches children's natural inclination to know more about things and engages even those with short attention spans. Trips put D&T in context and are therefore likely to have an impact on children's career choices. They are also one of the things children most look forward to and the experiences and memories from them are long lasting.

D&T trips can vary from cooking classes in restaurants, to workshops at the Apple Store, to visiting the orbit at the Olympic park and visiting museums such as The Comic Museum, The Museum of Brands and The Design Museum.

Organising school visitors

Inviting visitors to host workshops or speak to children is a fantastic way to increase the profile of any subject. For D&T there is a wide variety of skills you could invite parents/guests to provide; for example, you could ask parents to teach children how to make a dish, you may have parents who work in IT, who could provide support for an animation workshop, or you may have parents who are able to help with teaching children different sewing skills.

A great way to inspire children is to invite guests who have jobs which involve design and technology to come and speak to children about how they got into their field of work, and what they enjoy about their job. This is crucial as the UK needs many more engineers and equipping young people with aspirations is key to their future employability. Email and video conferencing can also be used to communicate with experts from other localities.

Organise a D&T themed week

Organise a D&T week where you plan some hands-on classroom activities that allow children to explore their creative side. Here are some ideas:

Cook off

Children to design and cook a meal for staff/another class/parents/governors. Each class could have a different country from which they have to prepare a celebration meal.

Survival

Each class is given a variety of different materials which they have to use to build a shelter. Classes could be given different design briefs, such as it must hold X amount of people, people need to be able to sit down/lie down comfortably, it needs to withstand wind/rain, etc.

Games

Each class designs their own game for other classes to play. These could be online games, outdoor games (e.g. giant versions of popular games) and board games which could involve electronics, etc.

Puppet show

Each class could make their own puppets; for example Reception could make wooden spoon puppets and Year Six could make rod puppets. The shows could be filmed and put on the school website, classes could perform to each other and/or some could be shown in assembly.

Book week

Each class to design and make a pop-up book about their class's topic.

Racing vehicles

Each class or each team in a class builds 'vehicles' that they can 'drive' in a race. This event could be similar to the Red Bull soapbox race, minus the jump! The children could also be responsible for designing the race course. Alternatively each class could be given a different design brief to design and make a vehicle and a race could be held for each class. For example, Reception could use floor robots (e.g. Bee-Bots) and design covers whereas Year Six could design and make cars which move using motors or pedal power.

Displays

Displays should inspire and motivate children as well as celebrate their successes in D&T. Ideally, D&T displays should show the whole design process, i.e. examples of the children's research, their designs, products (final as well as mock-ups/prototypes) and evaluations. They should also support children in their learning by displaying key vocabulary, key questions and, where viable, an interactive aspect that engages children and gets them thinking.

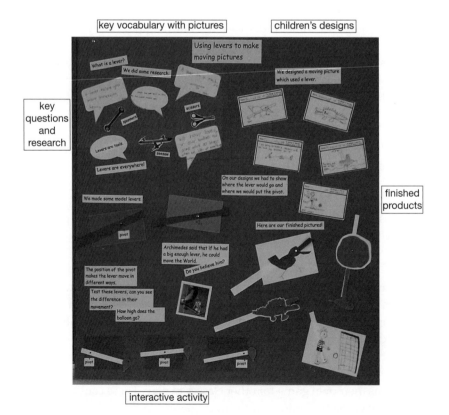

Figure 10.1 Levers display

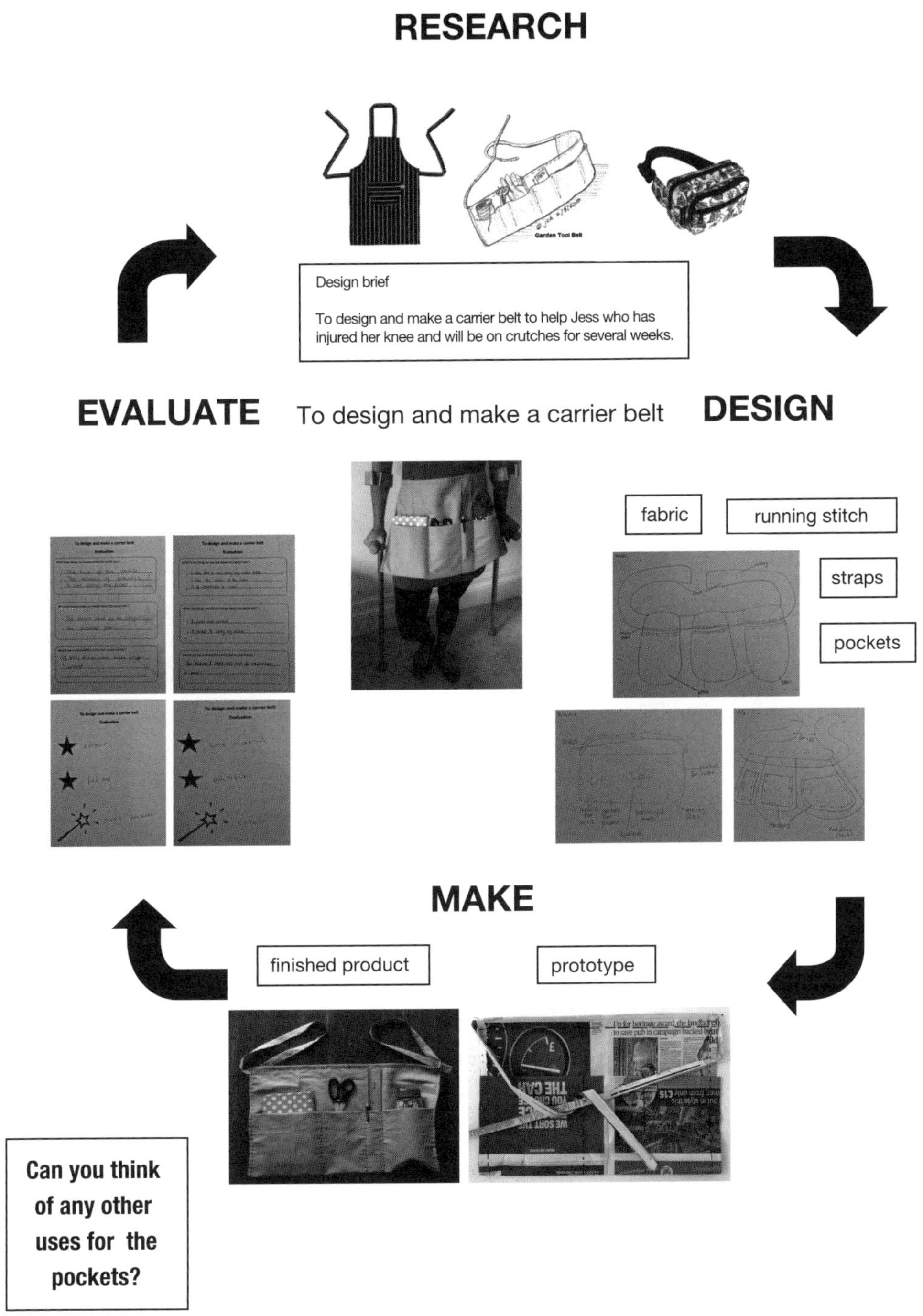

Figure 10.2 Display plan for a carrier belt

Figure 10.3 Showcasing final D&T products is a good way to highlight children's achievements

GOING FOR THE DESIGN MARK

The Design Mark is a quality standards framework developed jointly by the Design Canal and the D&T Association. It is awarded to schools that are able to demonstrate excellence in their teaching of design.

The Design Mark framework provides a quality 'standard' against which schools can evaluate their practice. You may wish to use the Design Mark framework for self evaluation purposes only and not apply for the quality mark.

To find out more, visit www.thedesignmark.org.

D&T POLICY

Many schools upload their subject policies onto their websites so you might want to start by looking at a few to get some ideas on what you want to include.

Generally, subject policies will include the following sub-headings:

- key aims (this can come from the National Curriculum or you may want to include your own, or a mix of the two)
- roles and responsibilities (head teacher and governors)
- role of the subject leader
- role of the class teacher (planning and assessment)
- implementing D&T (time allocation, timetabling, D&T week)
- curriculum planning (the long-term plan for D&T for the whole school and the process for medium-term and short-term planning – are these written by the teachers or is a particular scheme used?)

- monitoring and assessment (How and when will D&T assessment occur? Who will collect the data and how will it be used?)
- equal opportunities (How will all children be catered for in D&T lessons?)
- staff development (What is the process for staff being trained? Is CPD offered in-house or externally?)
- resources (What is available? Where are they kept? What is the process for ordering resources?)
- health and safety (should be linked to the school's health and safety policy and should refer to your local authority's guidelines for D&T)

D&T action plan

It is important that a subject leader has an understanding of how their subject contributes to school priorities and to the overall education and achievement of all children. The action plan outlines what you intend to do and how this will impact teaching and learning (see example on the next page).

TOP TIPS

You can't do everything at once, particularly if you find your subject has been rather neglected in the past. Therefore it is best to prioritise tasks and aim to do just one onerous task per term (e.g. reviewing the D&T curriculum) so that it doesn't become too time-consuming. Tasks such as organising and purchasing resources will be ongoing and you will need to plan ahead for this.

Table 10.3 Example of D&T action plan

Action/focus	Lead person	Impact on learning	Monitoring	Resources	Cost	Deadline	Evaluation
Update health and safety guidelines for use of tools	D&T leader	Ensure that teachers and children know how to keep safe in D&T lessons	Give revised safety guidelines to all staff	Set of guidelines for each classroom	N/A	September	
Staff INSETs to review D&T scheme of work; teachers to go through D&T scheme of work and match it with NC (2014) and the school's curriculum topics – update and change where necessary	D&T leader	Ensure children are being taught an up-to-date D&T curriculum which complements their class topics	Planning scrutiny	NC (2014) school curriculum map	N/A	Autumn term	
Provide CPD for teaching staff on control and monitoring and mechanisms	D&T leader	Improve the standards of teaching and learning	Lesson observations Planning scrutiny Book/work sample scrutiny Discussions with children	Need to purchase Makey Makey X 5	£40 × 5 = £200	Spring term	

Checklist for D&T subject leader

- You will need a subject leader's file. Your school may have an agreed format for how to divide this into sections. If not, you can use the headings from the Design Mark framework.
- Develop and maintain a scheme of work.
- Keep informed of current developments in D&T – carry out INSETs when required.
- Provide assessment materials for teachers and collect assessment data in each term.
- Provide a school policy for D&T – make sure staff are familiar with this and that it is being successfully implemented.
- Provide a school action plan for D&T – review this annually.
- Make connections with the D&T department at your local secondary school.
- Purchase and organise resources – ensure they are readily available and maintained.

RESOURCES

In order to cover the curriculum requirements for D&T effectively, appropriate resources for all units will need to be provided. It may be helpful to provide each class, year group or Key Stage with a box of resources for each unit. See Table 10.4 for suggested resources.

FUNDING

D&T resources and CPD for staff can add up and your subject budget may not cover this. If this is the case you might want to consider applying for funding from one of the following organisations:

- *Big Lottery Fund*: worth applying to if you are planning to run an after-school D&T club. www.biglotteryfund.org.uk/funding
- *National Lottery*: offers lots of funding opportunities for good causes such as educating children in technology. www.lotterygoodcauses.org.uk/funding-finder
- *Ford Britain Trust*: offers small and large grants for projects focusing on education. www.ford.co.uk/experience-ford/AboutFord/CorporateSocialResponsibility/Ford BritainTrust
- *Tesco Charity Fund*: offers funding for providing equipment and resources for projects that provide opportunities for young people in the local communities around their stores in the UK. www.ourtesco.com/our-community/tesco-charity-trust/

HEALTH AND SAFETY

Children should understand that having a safe classroom is a shared responsibility between teachers and themselves. Classrooms should be arranged so that there is enough space for each child to work comfortably and safely. Before undertaking practical tasks, children should be taught to use tools correctly in order to ensure safety. Teachers should be aware of any physical limitations which a child may have, and make suitable arrangements to enable the child to use the equipment safely. It is important that all teaching staff know how to use equipment safely and that children using equipment are supervised.

Staff need to consider the school policy on health and safety and know about any incident procedures and what to do in any emergency. They also need to be aware of any local education authority directives about: toilet roll tubes, safety knives, saws, hot melt glue guns, low melt glue guns, solvent glues and other fixings, etc., food allergies and the storage and disposal of food.

Table 10.4 A list of suggested resources you may want to consider when organising and/or buying
D&T resources

Cooking and nutrition	Textiles
• use of school kitchen or mobile cooker • measuring spoons, jugs, scales • chopping boards • palette and vegetable knives • garlic press • kitchen scissors • grater • peeler • kebab sticks • saucepan • whisk • blender • mixing bowl • wooden spoon • cake tins • pastry brush • cookie cutters • icing bag/pipe	• collection of scrap material • needles • pins • embroidery thread • embroidery silk • wool • felt • Binca • buttons • sequins • beads • snap fasteners knitting needles/crochet hooks • chalk pencil • sewing machine • fabric scissors
Control and monitoring	**Mechanisms**
• computers/laptops/ipads • digital cameras • floor robots (e.g. Bee-Bots, Probots, Roamers) • Raspberry Pi • Makey Makey • Scratch (free online program) • Google SketchUp • 2Design (2Simple software) • 2DIY (2Simple software) • data logger • WeDo Lego	• thin card in various colours • scrap card (from packaging) • felt pens/colouring pencils/paints • drinking straws • scissors • hole punch • paper fasteners • glue sticks or glue guns • tape • card cams (eccentric, snail, pear-shaped) • dowel • syringes (20 ml and 5 ml) • thin plastic tubing to fit syringes • balloons • card wheels, pre-punched axle holes • gear wheels (large and small) • pulleys or cotton reels • clothes pegs • string
Structures	**Electronics**
• clean junk plastic and card boxes, rolls, etc. • thin card • PVA glue or glue guns • scissors • craft knives and cutting boards • paper fasteners • pegs • pine stripwood • dowel • junior hacksaws with pistol grip • bench hooks or cam bench hooks (one for each saw) • sandpaper (various grades) • Jinks' corners • bamboo canes • plastic cable ties • string	• AA batteries • battery holders • small MES bulbs (size: 1.5 V 200 mA) • bulb holders • insulated wire • wire cutters • electrical tape • push or toggle switches • buzzers • motors (6 V) • Blu Tack • foil • paper clips • paper fasteners • scrap card • foam

Below is general guidance on some of the key issues for health and safety when teaching D&T:

Food hygiene

- long hair tied back
- all jewellery and nail varnish to be removed
- cooking surfaces wiped with antibacterial spray and covered with clean plastic cloths
- equipment is clean and ready to use (count knives and sharp tools out and in)
- children and staff to wear aprons
- hands are clean – have been washed with antibacterial soap or a sterilising rub has been used
- all food allergies to be taken into consideration when preparing and cooking food

Glue guns

- In KS2, children may use low temperature glue guns under supervision, wearing safety goggles.

Craft knives

- In KS2, children may use cutting equipment under supervision, using a cutting mat and wearing safety goggles.

Sawing

- Bench hooks and clamps must be used when sawing any material.
- Safety goggles must be worn and any loose items of clothing/hair must be tucked in.

For examples of D&T risk assessments, visit:

- https://schoolleaders.thekeysupport.com/administration-and-management/risk/curriculum-risk-assessments/art-design-and-technology-risk-assessment-primary
- www.foodafactoflife.org.uk/Sheet.aspx?siteId=20&sectionId=118&contentId=718

Glossary

Absorbent
Able to soak up liquid easily.

Aesthetic
Relates to the appearance, i.e. beauty.

Algorithm
A set of rules used for calculations or problem-solving, especially by computers.

Antioxidant
A substance that reduces damage due to oxygen. Well-known antioxidants include enzymes and other substances, such as vitamin C, vitamin E and beta carotene.

Appearance
The way something looks.

Appliqué
A technique in which pieces of fabric are sewn or glued decoratively on to a base fabric.

Arable farming
The growing of crops and cereals.

Aroma
Smell or scent.

Authentic
A product with a clear purpose.

Axle
A rod on which wheels are mounted, allowing them to spin freely.

Bacteria
Single-celled microscopic organisms, some of which can cause disease (also known as germs).

Battery
Several electrical cells linked together to provide electrical energy.

Bench hook
A tool that enables a piece of wood to be held firmly in position on a workbench or table while it is cut.

Binary code
A computer coding language consisting of the digits 0 and 1.

Blend
To mix so that substances combine together.

Bradawl
A small tool with a pointed end for making holes.

Bulb
A component which converts electrical energy into light.

Butcher
To cut up an animal for food.

Buzzer
A component which converts electrical energy into sound.

Calcium
A mineral found in many foods. The body needs calcium to maintain strong bones. It is also required by muscles, the nervous system and the circulatory system.

Cam
A simple machine consisting of a shaped wheel on an axle which converts circular motion into up and down motion.

Cancer
A disease caused by uncontrolled division of abnormal cells in part of the body.

Canning
The process of preserving cooked food by sealing in cans or jars.

Carbohydrates
Provide energy to the body. Carbohydrates come in simple forms such as sugars and in complex forms such as starches and fibre.

Cell
A component that provides a source of electrical energy, such as an AA battery.

Chaff
What is left when the grain has been separated from the ear.

Chassis
The base framework of a motor vehicle.

Chroma key
A technique for mixing two images or frames together, in which a single colour from one image is removed (or made transparent), revealing another image behind it. The technique is also known as green screen, blue screen, colour keying or colour-separation overlay.

Circuit diagram
A representation of an electrical circuit, drawn using standard symbols and straight lines.

Climate
The weather conditions in a particular region.

Closed-loop control system
A system where information from external sensors control and adjust the output from the system. Also called a feedback control system, e.g. an air conditioner functions only when the temperature of the room reaches a certain level.

Cloth
Woven or felted material used for a purpose such as tea towels and dishcloths.

Component
Part of a circuit or model, e.g. a bulb.

Compressed air
Air which has been squashed into a small container and is therefore at a pressure greater than normal.

Computer Aided Design (CAD)
When computer software is used to design products.

Computer Aided Manufacture (CAM)
Control and monitoring of production using computers.

Computer control
Set of instructions programmed into a machine which cause it to operate in a pre-determined manner.

Computer monitoring
The use of sensors for two main purposes, as a scientific measuring tool or as data logger.

Computer programming
The process of developing an algorithm to perform a specified task on a computer.

Conductor/conductive
A material which allows electricity to pass through it.

Control system
A device or set of devices that manages the behaviour of other devices or systems.

Crochet
A method which uses a special needle called a crochet hook to draw thread or yarn through intertwined loops. This process creates stitches which look similar to knots.

Cross-sectional drawing
A drawing showing the internal structure of an object.

Current
A measure of the rate of the flow of the electric charge (electrons) carrying the energy around a circuit. It is measured in Amps.

Découpage
The art of covering a surface with varnished layers of scraps of paper.

Design Cycle
A representation of the iterative process of designing and making a product.

Diabetes
A disorder of the metabolism causing excessive thirst and the production of large amounts of urine.

Drill bit
The part of the drill which makes the hole. Comes in a range of sizes.

Durable
Able to exist for a long time without significant deterioration, i.e. it can withstand wear, pressure or damage; hard-wearing.

Embroidery
The use of stitches such as back stitch, knotting and satin stitch to create patterns on fabrics.

Essential fatty acids
Nutrients which are required for good health but which the body cannot make itself, e.g. Omega-3.

Evaluate
Assess or appraise a piece of work.

Exploded view
Shows the components of a mechanism or structure as if separated by an explosion but in the normal relative positions.

Fabric
Any material made by weaving, knitting or felting, etc., that may be used in the production of further goods such as garments.

Felting
The process of making felt by shrinking or matting fibres together using moisture, heat and pressure to form a dense fabric that can be cut without fraying the edges.

Fertiliser
A chemical or natural substance added to soil or land to increase its productivity.

Fibre (food)
Helps food move through the digestive system and contributes to disease protection. Also known as roughage.

Focused practical task
An activity to enable children to gain an understanding of how a product works.

Framework
A supporting structure.

Fray
To unravel, become worn or tattered at the edge.

Freshwater
Rivers or lakes.

Functional
Capable of serving the purpose for which it was designed, i.e. it is useful.

Garter stitch
Created by knitting every row.

Gear
A simple machine consisting of a toothed wheel which meshes with another to transmit rotation movement.

Gimmick
A product with no real purpose apart from to make money for the seller.

Hacksaw
Saw with a narrow blade set in a frame.

Heart disease
A term covering various heart conditions, including heart attack and heart failure.

Herbicide
A substance or preparation for killing plants, especially weeds.

Horticulture
The production of flowers, fruit, vegetables or ornamental plants.

Hydrate
To drink water to restore or maintain a balance of fluids.

Hydraulic

A system which uses the energy stored in fluids under pressure to do work. By controlling the release of the fluid the energy can be turned into movement.

Innovation/Innovative

A new or original product rather than a copy or update of something already available.

Insulator

A material that prevents electricity from passing through it.

Isometric paper

Paper printed with dots or guide lines, allowing 3D shapes to be drawn with the planes and axes correctly aligned.

Iterative process

Something that is done repeatedly.

Jinks' corner

A right-angled triangle cut from card and used to give strength to joints in frameworks.

Kilocalories

A measure of the amount of energy in food; commonly referred to as calories.

Kilojoules

A measure of the amount of energy in food.

Knead

To mix and work into a uniform mass, by folding, pressing and stretching with the hands.

Knitting

A method which involves manipulating thread or yarn to create consecutive rows of loops, called stitches. As each row progresses, a new loop is pulled through an existing loop. The active stitches are held on a knitting needle until another loop can be passed through them.

Lap joint

Two pieces of wood joined at right angles by sticking the end of one piece to the side of the other.

LED

A diode with a high resistance which produces light instead of heat. A diode is a device which allows the electricity to pass through it in one direction only.

Lever

A simple machine consisting of a rigid bar or rod pivoted at one point along its length. A force on one end of the lever produces a movement at the other end.

Linkage

A series of connecting rods which allow a motion to be directed elsewhere.

Load

Something which is to be carried, often heavy.

Loom

A tool used for weaving. It holds the warp threads in place while filling threads are woven through them.

Machine

A device for doing work.

Macramé
A method which involves using knots such as the square knot to form a fabric or cloth.

Market gardening
The relatively small-scale production of fruits, vegetables and flowers.

Market research
Study of consumers' or users' needs and preferences.

Material
The matter from which something is made.

Mechanism
A device which takes one type motion or force, and produces a different one, to make a job easier to do.

Mesh (gears)
The teeth of two separate gear wheels engaged correctly with each other.

Minerals
Materials found in foods that are essential for growth and health.

Mitre joint
Two pieces of wood joined at right angles. The ends of both pieces are cut at 45°.

Mixed farming
The combination of arable and pastoral farming.

Mock-up
A model which looks like the real thing, but which doesn't show the functionality. It can be made of any suitable material.

Morph
To change one image or shape into another through a seamless transition. Most often used to depict one person turning into another as part of a fantasy or surreal sequence.

Motor
A component which converts electrical energy into movement.

Net
A pattern that can be cut out and folded to make a solid 3D shape, e.g. a cube.

Non-woven fabric
Made from long fibres, bonded together by chemical, mechanical, heat or solvent treatment.

Obese
Grossly fat or overweight.

Onion skinning
A 2D computer graphics technique which allows the animator to see several frames of a cartoon at once. The images are superimposed and the earlier images are dimmed to show the order in which they appear. This helps the animator to create a smooth motion.

Open-loop control systems
When the output is generated based on inputs. An example is a light switch – lamps glow (output) whenever the light switch (input) is on, irrespective of whether light is required or not.

Organic farming
Farming without artificial chemicals which can harm the environment and human health.

Osteoporosis
A medical condition in which the bones become brittle and fragile, normally as a result of hormonal changes, or deficiency of calcium or vitamin D.

Parallel circuit
A circuit in which the components are arranged so that there is more than one path for the current to take.

Pasteurisation
Partial sterilisation of foods at a temperature that destroys harmful micro-organisms without big changes in the chemistry of the food.

Pastoral farming
Rearing and production of animals, including pigs, chickens, sheep, beef and dairy cattle.

Pathogenic microbes
Small organisms able to cause an infection in the body.

Pin hammer
A lightweight hammer which is used for knocking in small very small nails, panel pins and tacks.

Pivot
A short shaft or pin on which something turns.

Pneumatic
A system which uses the energy stored in compressed air to do work. By controlling the release of the air the energy can be turned into movement.

Preserving
The process of treating and handling food to stop or slow down food spoilage, or loss of quality, edibility or nutritional value, and thus allow for longer food storage.

Property
Characteristic of a material, e.g. strength, water resistance or elasticity.

Protein (food)
Used by the body to repair and build muscles, skin, hair and bones. Proteins are also used by the body to manufacture hormones and enzymes.

Prototype
A working model of a design, not necessarily full size.

Pulley
A simple machine for raising loads consisting of one or more wheels with a grooved rim to take a belt.

Pulley belt
An elastic band which is used to connect two pulley wheels.

Purl stitch
Created by knitting stitches backwards every row.

Push switch
A switch which has to be pushed down in order to turn a circuit on.

Reed switch
A switch operated by a magnet.

Relief (geography)
The highest and lowest elevation points in an area.

Research
Discovering and collating facts using books, Internet, market research and products.

Resistance
Something which causes the flow of electricity in a circuit to slow down.

Resistor
A component which limits the current passing through the circuit.

Roughage
Helps food move through the digestive system and contributes to disease protection. Also known as fibre.

Sandpaper
Paper with sand stuck on it, used for smoothing and polishing.

Saturated fats
These can raise cholesterol, increasing the risk of heart disease and strokes.

Score
To make a deep line in, or to cut partly through, a material in order to be able to fold it accurately.

Seam
A line of stitching joining two or more pieces of fabric.

Seam allowance
The distance between the stitching and the cut edge of the fabric.

Sensor
A device that measures and responds to an input from the physical environment.

Series circuit
A circuit in which all the components are arranged so that there is a single path for the current to take.

Silage
Hay and grass which have been preserved under pressure in airtight conditions. Used for animal feed in the winter.

Slaughter
To kill an animal.

Stop motion (also known as Stop frame)
An animation technique to make static objects appear as if they were moving on their own.

Story board
A sequence of pictures outlining the plan of a project from start to finish.

Switch
A component which controls whether an electric current flows or not.

Template
Something to draw around to mark a shape onto material, so that it can be cut or shaped.

Textile

A flexible material made from woven threads or yarn.

Textile printing

The process of applying colour to fabric in definite patterns or designs.

Texture

The properties of a material that are sensed by touch.

Time lapse animation

When many shots are taken over a long period of time and then shown quickly in sequence so that a slow process is speeded up.

Toggle switch

A switch with a lever that has to be moved in order to turn a circuit on. The switch will remain on until the lever is moved back.

Torque

The turning power of a motor.

Type 2 diabetes

The most common form of diabetes which occurs when the body does not produce enough insulin to function properly, or the body's cells do not react to insulin. This is known as insulin resistance.

Unsaturated fats

Help to lower cholesterol and provide the body with essential fatty acids.

Variable resistor (rheostat)

A component which can be used to control the speed of the flow of electricity in a circuit.

Viticulture

Cultivation of grapes.

Voltage

A measure of the energy available for the components in the circuit. It is measured in volts.

Waterproof

Able to prevent the penetration of water.

Water resistant

Able to resist but not entirely prevent the penetration of water.

Weave

A method which involves interlacing two distinct sets of yarns or threads at right angles to form a fabric or cloth.

Worm gear

A gear which can convert a large movement into a tiny movement.

Woven fabric

A textile formed by weaving.

Yarn

A continuous strand of twisted threads of natural or synthetic material, such as wool or nylon.

Index